HISTORY OF THE
JEWS
IN
AMERICA
LINDA GUTSTEIN

HISTORY OF THE JEWS IN AMERICA

LINDA GUTSTEIN

A QUANTUM BOOK

Published by Chartwell Books
A Division of Book Sales Inc
114 Northfield Avenue
Edison, New Jersey 08837
USA

This edition printed 1996

ISBN 0-7858-0732-2

This book was produced by
Quantum Books Ltd
6 Blundell Street
London N7 9BH

Art Director Peter Bridgewater
Designer Ian Hunt

Typeset by Central Southern Typesetters, Eastbourne
Manufactured in Hong Kong by
Regent Publishing Services Limited

Printed in Singapore by Star Standard Industries Pte. Ltd.

Contents

ABOVE

Isaac Aboab de Fonseca was the first rabbi in the Western Hemisphere. Born a Marrano in Portugal, he went to Amsterdam with his family when he was a child. In 1624, he went to Recife in Brazil (then a Dutch colony) as rabbi of the Jewish community there. When the Portuguese recaptured the city in 1654, Aboab fled back to Amsterdam, where he continued a distinguished career until his death in 1693.

CHAPTER ONE

THE NEW WORLD

In 1524, when Giovanni da Verrazano set eyes upon this new world, he saw a group of sleepy islands: a long sandy one that jutted into the ocean, and a small one set between two rivers, where huts lined the high ground on which natives hunted, planted, and walked down to the river to fish.

For over a hundred years European eyes alighted on these bits of land – and left. In 1609 Henry Hudson explored these waters. Adrian Block and crew were forced to spend the winter of 1613 on the island between the two rivers, Manahatin, where they rebuilt their ship.

It wasn't until 1625, under the auspices of the Dutch West India Company, that the first group – four ships of Dutch settlers – arrived.

Manahatin became their "Niew Amsterdam," and with Peter Minuit's famous $26 purchase of the island from the Indians, in 1626, their settlement was secured.

And so it was that in 1654, when a ship carrying 23 Jewish men, women and children, sailed into New Amsterdam's harbor they saw a fort, windmill, houses, and a timber wall built against attack. These weary travelers were Portuguese, Spanish, and Ashkenazi Jews.

A new ship in the harbor was always an event. It could be bringing sorely needed goods and longed-for luxuries from Holland. But it couldn't have taken long for the Dutch who gathered at the port to see that this shop bore impoverished passengers. With nothing to trade in a trading port, what could they offer? They had fled from Recife in Brazil, where the Portuguese had retaken the territory from the Dutch, and in a group of 16 ships started back to Holland. With what was at the time considered merciful providence, every other ship made it back to the mother country.

As recounted by the Amsterdam rabbi, Saul Levi Morteira, in 1660, "By divine grace and providence, all of them saved themselves, and escaped many tortures and other misfortunes. One of these ships was captured by the Spaniards, who wanted to surrender the poor Jews to the Inquisition. However before they were able to carry out their evil intentions, the Lord caused a French ship to appear on the scene, which freed the Jews from the Spaniards and took them to safety in Florida, or the New Netherlands, whence they arrived peacefully in Holland."

Rabbi Morteira's notion of "divine grace and providence" did indeed extend to the lone ship that had been attacked by Spanish pirates if for no other reason than that its passengers resolutely refused to leave New Amsterdam.

They arrived in the small port with no goods, no cachet, and with the French sea captain dogging them for the passage they had agreed to pay him. What these needy new arrivals could offer was not readily apparent – especially to the short-sighted governor, Peter Stuyvesant, who was at his choleric worst when confronted with untoward events.

The newcomers understood the rigors of the colonial experience. Spanish Jews had begun to settle South America in the 1500s. After the Dutch victory over Recife in Brazil, with freedom from the Spanish Inquisition beckoning, whole groups of Jews arrived. By 1645 one-half of the white population of almost 3,000 was Jewish.

Born in Holland, Portugal, Brazil, Germany and Poland, the Jews of Recife were representatives of both the painful uprootedness of the times and its new energy. In their bones they carried a tumultuous history. Some were born in Portugal and left the gruesome life of that country's Inquisition under one of the escape clauses that allowed Crypto Jews, or New Christians, with knowledge of trade and commerce to settle and enrich Portuguese territory.

Some were born in Holland of forebears who had fled Spanish or Portuguese inquisitions. Others sought the relative freedom of the newly independent, Protestant Holland – which after its long war with its Spanish Catholic rulers was imbued with the spirit of seeking and defining liberties of religion and conscience – to escape from the dead-end ghetto life of middle Europe. These Ashkenazi Jews became part of the adventure of the newly emerging Holland, and along with New Christians and Sephardic Jews were pioneers in the Dutch West India Company's South American ventures. The com-

CHAPTER ONE

RIGHT
New Amsterdam in the 1650s. The 23 Jews who arrived there from Brazil in 1654 – the first Jews in America – found a thriving colony with plenty of opportunity.

pany was founded in 1621 just as the 12-year truce between Spain and the Netherlands expired. The Dutch were eager to replenish an economy that had been weakened by the costly struggle against Spain.

The turns of history that brought the Jews of the sixteenth century to South America could not have converged without Jewish mastery of sea navigation and trade. It was in large part the efforts of Sephardic astronomers, scientists, and mariners that made the age of exploration possible. The Sephardic Jews had been refining their civilization for almost two thousand years, longer than the Visigoths who would later claim it. The Iberian peninsula was their homeland, their identity; they were integrally woven into its fabirc. They suffered the Catholic Visigoth's campaign (612–711) to convert them forcibly to Christianity (and stave off increasing conversions to Judaism), enduring until the more harmonious rule of the Moslems a hundred years later enabled them to express their religion.

The Jews of Spain were well-educated, knowledgeable about trade and commerce, and in a pivotal position to transmit the cultural legacies of the Eastern world to the West – Mohammedan Spain's greatest gift to Western history. They spoke Arabic, Greek, Latin, and Hebrew, as well as other languages, and could thus translate Greek and Hebrew philosophy and literature for the Arabs, and Hebrew, Greek, and Arabic literature and philosophy into Latin for the European royal courts. They also translated books on the art of medicine from Arabic into Hebrew and Latin. Along with Moslems, they practiced a medicine far superior to that mixture of superstition and heavy knife-wielding foisted upon patients by the unscientific Western Europeans. It wasn't long before every royal house in Europe had its Jewish doctor – and even in the midst of the harshest persecutions against their people, and despite edicts forbidding Christians to seek them, these doctors were called upon to minister to the Christian ill.

The Jewish philosopher and translator Ibn Daud introduced the Arabic numeral system and the concept of zero to Europe. Jews served in the highest posts in the Mohammedan administration.

From the days when they sailed with the Phoenicians to distant lands such as Carthage, where they traded and established colonies, the Jews evolved a system among themselves based on trust and a common language. This enabled them to work on international credit and to share information about markets and news of events with Jews in other lands.

This network, as flimsy or enduring as the people in it, was to be the strongest house they built. Theirs was a self-contained system based on letters of credit – a most important business invention – and the accruing of capital – all conducted from an ocean-going world where common business procedures included acts of piracy. This Jewish mastery of sea and trade routes, maintained through an exclusive trust with their coreligionists around the world, yielded such high profits for their respective kingdoms that later even the more fanatic Christian monarchs would seek to protect them as a group. Monarchs were desirous of the wealth that Jewish enterprise brought to their coffers.

Since the days of their exile in Babylonia, Jews had traded in India and China. The silk, perfumes, and spices they brought back were in the greatest demand in a Western Europe that had been cut off from the East by the Islamic conquests of the eighth century. The fur markets of Asia Minor were also inaccessible to the West except for the Jewish traders who could get to Rhaga, the large commercial center near Teheran that served Armenia, Chazaria, and Chorosan. Trade with the Chazarians, a tribe of warriors and herdsmen from the area around Kiev, yielded ties that encouraged their leaders to convert to Judaism.

The Crusades of the eleventh and twelfth centuries encouraged attacks, garbed in missionary zeal, on Jewish vessels with the aim of ending Jewish sea trade. This was accomplished, but the Jews continued their overland trading to remote parts of a world more mythic than real to the majority of Western Europeans.

In times of persecution, the trade routes and networks Jews had built would become a support system in the dispersions.

STUDIES OF STAR & SEA

THE WAY TO A NEW WORLD

Was it chance, or the sense of things to come, that made the learned Jews the best map-makers of the Age of Exploration? Next to their maps, most others were considered inaccurate. Everyone was looking for another world, but only some would require one for their survival.

Jewish mathematicians worked hard to assure the accuracy of their charts and maps. Leon de Bagnols (1288–1344), also known as Jacob Ben Makhir, and Levy Ben Gerson invented the Jacob's staff, a navigational instrument that measured the position of the stars.

Among the most famous of map-makers was the Cresques family. Abraham Cresques, known as the "Master of Maps and Compasses" to the House of Aragon, completed the greatest work of cartography of that era in 1377. His son, Judah, called the "Map Jew," was director of the nautical observatory at Sagres, where Prince Henry of Portugal had assembled a school of scientists. Prince Henry's academy transformed the theoretical study of astronomy and geography into a practical tool for mariners; future leaders of expeditions studied with its scientists.

Abraham Zacuto, mathematician and astronomer, published his famous astronomical tables in Spain in 1473, tables that Columbus and others used in their voyages of discovery. Zacuto invented a metal astrolabe, an instrument that measures the angle between a heavenly body and earth so as to determine latitude. His astrolabe was used by Vasco da Gama on his trip around the Cape of Good Hope to India.

The most important New Christians and Jewish advisers and administrators at court rallied around Christopher Columbus and managed to secure the financing for his voyage. Luis Santangel, Chancellor of the Royal Household, who came from a family of powerful financiers and investors, contributed the largest sum of money to the undertaking. Abraham Senior, tax collector of the realm and Isabella's favorite adviser (later to be appointed Chief Rabbi of Spain), exerted his influence along with Isaac Abrabanel, head of finance.

But as the Inquisition tightened its grip on Spain, the lives of these men and all Spanish Jews were to be brutally disrupted.

In 1492 Isabella signed the order expelling the Jews from Spain. Ironically, the success of the last campaign against the Mohammedans was in no small part due to the skill of Don Abraham Senior, chief administrator of all state revenues, who had pleaded with Queen Isabella to rescind the order. Isabella would not hear of her long-trusted adviser, who had helped to bring about her marriage to Ferdinand, leaving her court. She wanted him there and she wanted him baptized. It is rumored that she threatened harm to the departing Jews if he didn't comply. Don Senior, a man in his eighties, was converted, along with his sons, in a ceremony at which the jubilant Isabella and Ferdinand stood as godparents. The Senior family was renamed Coronel, and they continued to hold a position of eminence in Spain.

The dynamic Don Isaac Abrabanel, head of finance for the crown, offered the royal couple huge sums of money to stop the expulsion. The grandees supported

him, but to no avail. Abrabanel had frequently paid ransoms to rescue fellow Jews who had been taken captive in military campaigns in other countries. He once supported a dispersed group for a year. In his own life he had experienced much upheaval. He had been finance minister for the king of Portugal and was forced to flee, after the king's death, due to court intrigue. In Spain he was befriended by Don Senior and called upon by the royal couple to take charge of the country's finances. Now he chose to leave their court rather than convert. He went to serve the king of Naples until that throne came into jeopardy and he had to flee to Apulia. In his old age he had lost his wealth, and lived uprooted, separated from his wife and children. His older son, Judah, became an honored scientist in Genoa. Judah's younger son had been forcibly taken from him by the Church in Portugal – as it had taken hundreds of other Jewish children – and reared a Christian.

Noted astronomer Abraham Zacuto first emigrated to Portugal, where he became court historian to King Manoel, only to be uprooted a few years later by Manoel's expulsion order – a condition for Manoel's marriage to the daughter of Ferdinand and Isabella. Zacuto fled to Tunis, where he summoned the peace of mind to complete another work. When the Spanish troops got too close to that territory, he went to Turkey. This man, who had once headed a famous school of mathematics and astronomy teaching Christians, Mohammedans and Jews, and whose works were widely read and respected, lived his last years in exile.

What must it have been like for the newly baptized Don Abraham Senior to watch his friends, Abrabanel and Zacuto, leave, with hundreds of thousands who had held steadfast to Judaism? Forbidden to take gold or silver with them, they had to sell their possessions for a pittance (a mansion for a mule, as the saying went), and in this unhappy state endure yet another purposely timed appeal from Grand Inquisitor Torquemada to convert.

Jews spent their last days at the graves of their relatives. Of all their tribulations, leaving these consecrated grounds was the hardest. In Toledo, they copied the tombstone inscriptions. In other regions, they gave all of their communal property to the local authorities with the condition that the cemeteries be preserved. The Jews of Spain dispersed to Portugal, Holland, North Africa, Turkey, to points north – and within 15 years, to South America. Many were robbed and killed by ship captains, or held for ransom.

The timing has often been remarked upon: As the thousands and thousands of expelled Spaniards made their way to the port, musicians among them playing songs to distract them from their grief, Christopher Columbus began his journey to the New World. It was August 3, 1492, the ninth day of Ab – the day that commemorates the destruction of the First and Second Temples. He watched their brave and sorrowful trek, and noted in his diary: "After the Spanish monarchs had expelled the Jews from all their kingdoms and lands in January, in that same month they commissioned me to undertake the voyage to India with a properly equipped fleet."

The debate about Columbus's background still rages. There is strong evidence to suggest he may have been a Marrano – outwardly a Christian, secretly a Jew. But whatever his origin, he was sympathetic to the plight of Marranos and Jews, and he, too, seemed to dread the tenor of the times with its Catholic persecutors. At the courts of Portugal and Spain he formed friendships with influential Jews. They took up his cause, as did many of his Jewish friends who were scientists and scholars.

In fact, much of the considerable Jewish contribution to the discovery and charting of the New World has only slowly come to light. The Iberian Jews and Marranos frequently used a string of different names in order to travel, conduct business, and stay out of reach of the Inquisition. The need was for camouflage, not praise.

At least five out of the 120 passengers on Columbus's ships were Jews; two ship's surgeons, two seamen, and one Luis de Torres, a Marrano, a linguist, a great adventurer who had, likely as a condition of his participation in the voyage, been baptized just before he sailed.

On October 12, the ships landed off the coast of an island – until recently thought to be San Salvador. But newly published studies place the land fall at Samana Cay, in the Bahamas, 65 miles southeast of San Salvador.

Hopeful that with his several languages, de Torres could converse with the natives, Columbus sent him to scout the territory. Six days later, when he returned to the ship, he described the natives – whose language was new to him – as living a simple, peaceable life. They had the enjoyable and strange custom of rolling up leaves, lighting them, and drawing the smoke into their lungs.

The ships continued on to Cuba, where de Torres and a companion, Rodrigo de Jerez, decided to spend the rest of their lives. An island in the new world free from the terrors of the Inquisition – clearly he was not bound to the closely monitored society of his new religion.

Thus this Jewish man became the first New World settler. It was de Torres, and not Sir Walter Raleigh, who first introduced tobacco to Europe. He became the first white man to cultivate maize and introduce this nutritious food into the European diet.

Soon Spanish and Portuguese Jews and New Christians, avid to find opportunities away from the shaky life of the Iberian peninsula, were well represented among the earliest settlers of Iberia's New World territories. In 1502 Fernando de Loronha, a Marrano, signed a contract with King Manoel of Portugal that allowed him to settle Brazilian territory in return for exploring 300

CHAPTER ONE

LEFT
These scenes from the life of Christopher Columbus form a door of the United States Capitol. At least five members of Columbus' crew were Jews: two physicians, two seamen, and one translator.

leagues of Brazilian coastline every year, and building forts where he and his people – five shiploads of passengers – landed.

AN ENTREPRENEURIAL HABITAT

It was established practice that European monarchs should meet their living expenses through revenues from their own properties, with exceptions in emergencies for wider levies. But by the sixteenth century even these wider levies could not meet the expenses of the larger undertakings of the royal governments. Therefore, in the race for new territories, the Crown frequently entered into contracts with explorers who raised much of the money for their own expeditions. This gave the explorers property rights, while the Crown had ultimate authority over the territories.

The rewards for the individual were immense, and go a long way to explain why the captains of Western Europe, with ragged fleets and limited trade experience, acquired the land and harnessed the riches of the American continents.

But all too soon the Iberian rulers became fearful of losing their feudal control. The Inquisition was allowed to put down roots in the new Spanish lands; those Marranos in the colonies who had accumulated wealth were ripe for the picking.

An important example of these arrangements gone afoul was the charter issued by the Spanish Crown in 1579 to Don Luis de Carvajal for a land grant of 280,000 square miles, including territory that would eventually become part of Texas.

It is estimated that at his own expense Carvajal took up to 200 families with him to settle his vast kingdom, called Leon. Carvajal was a religious Catholic who had been educated in a monastery, apparently unaware of his Jewish ancestry until he was in his twenties. But many in his immediate family were secret and fervent practitioners of Judaism. Their beliefs made him vulnerable. When political squabbles arose with the governors in adjoining provinces over his governing of the Indians, his enemies attacked his New Christian ancestry and he was arrested. He was convicted in 1590 of harboring heretics, and his property was confiscated. He died in prison, but the travails of his family continued. His nephew and namesake, Luis, was so devoted to Judaism, at least what he could glean of it from the books available to him, that he performed a circumcision on himself with blunt scissors. In his *Autobiography of Luis de Carvajal the Younger* he would write that having "received the seal of the holy sacrament upon his flesh, it served as a bulwark against lust and an aid to chastity." Luis was a poet and mystic who renamed himself Joseph Lumbroso (the enlightened) for the day when he saw the light of Judaism.

How Marrano families were divided in their beliefs between Judaism and Catholicism is seen in the saga of the Carvajals. Despite a previous arrest and imprisonment, Luis preached Judaism openly among New Christians, as did his mother and three of his sisters. All were sentenced to burn. Luis's older brother Gaspar was a rigorously religious monk, but two other brothers who escaped to Europe took the name of Lumbroso.

As the Inquisition spread in the Spanish territories of the New World, Marranos fled north to what is now New Mexico. In the 1520s Bernardo Lopez de Mendizabel, a Marrano, was governor of the New Mexico territory. Like Governor Carvajal he, too, was vulnerable to the Inquisition. He was charged with changing his linen and washing his feet on the eve of the (Jewish) Sabbath. His agreements were canceled and his property confiscated. He, too, died in prison, the first such Inquisitorial case to happen on territory that is now part of the United States.

To keep a jump away from the Inquisition, Marranos fled to the West Indies; some went to southwest Texas. It is estimated that thousands of present-day Texans are the descendants of those Marranos.

IN SEARCH OF NEW JERUSALEM

The expulsion of the Jews from Spain and Portugal to a Christian Europe that was for the most part closed to them should have ended any hope they nurtured of thriving there as they once had on the Iberian peninsula.

But in an ironic turn of events the Jews would gain true equality on the sovereign territory of the merciless and unrelenting King Philip II of Spain. Philip inherited the Low Countries in 1555, and, true to the legacy of his great-grandparents Ferdinand and Isabella, he was determined to stamp out self-government and install an effective Inquisition in these territories so infused with the Protestant spirit. The Netherlands rebelled. An 80-year war followed, one that would see Holland emerge as a first-class power and Spain shrink into its past. The Jews and the Dutch had a common enemy. The struggles of The Netherlands left it poor, but Sephardic and Marrano money and know-how helped make it into a first-class power. The Sephardim helped form the Dutch West and East India companies. With their experience in international trade and sea commerce, they helped to break the trading monopoly of Portugal (then under Spanish rule). Some of that Marrano money had been amassed in Spain from venture capital in the newly discovered America.

Amsterdam was becoming an international center of culture, and in this atmosphere – where many a dissent-

CHAPTER ONE

ing Protestant sect, along with the Jews, was finding respite from persecution – the Marranos openly repossessed their Judaism. Suddenly individuals living under cover of Christianity found their way to Amsterdam and openly professed Judaism. Fra Vincente de Rocamora, a Dominican priest who had been the father confessor to the Infanta Maria of Spain, arrived in Amsterdam and studied medicine under the name of Isaac. A famous playwright, knighted for his valor in the Spanish army, showed up as a professing Jew. And, in 1599, Pablo de Pina, a young man from a prominent Lisbon Marrano family, was on his way to Rome to join a monastic order when he visited a family friend, the famous Jewish doctor Elijah Montaldo, in Leghorn, and came away a confirmed Jew. He eventually went to Amsterdam, where he took the name Reuel Jessurum, became a noted author, and sired a family that played a part in both English and American colonial history. His grandson Rowland Gideon was an entrepreneur whose business activities had him living in the Barbados, then Boston, and finally settling in London where he received the honor of the Freedom of the City of London – only the second Jew to have that distinction, the first being his brother. Rowland's son Samson Gideon worked to bring about the passage in England of the Jews' Naturalization Act of 1753, which helped the Jews gain more political equality there.

Soon the children of the Sephardic and Ashkenazic Jews nurtured in Holland would be making their way to the Dutch colonies such as Recife, in Brazil, and after 1654 to New Amsterdam. When they settled Recife they had told the Dutch they hoped to make it into a 'New Jerusalem'. When Recife fell to Portugal and they fled to other colonies, they took their spiritual craving with them. In this they were not unlike the English Pilgrims, who had set out from Holland in 1620 on their *Mayflower* journey and also landed off course, on the shores of Massachusetts, where they hoped to build their own New Jerusalem.

HOPE BECOMES REALITY IN NEW AMSTERDAM

Their destination may well have been Holland, but chance enters into the story of the 23 – four married men and their wives, two widows and 13 children – the first group of Jews to land in North America. Given three months by the Portuguese to convert or get out of Recife they left, along with Dutch Protestants, on the ship *Valck.* After a stopover in Martinique it is believed their ship was attacked and burned by Spanish pirates as they neared the waters of Jamaica, leaving them stranded in dangerous Spanish territory. There the Marranos among them were seized by the Inquisition – and all of that was just the beginning of their voyage to North America. With the release of the Marranos the group managed to get to Cuba, where they made arrangements with Jacques de la Motthe, the captain of a French man-of-war, the *St. Charles* (called *St. Catherine* in some accounts), for passage to New Amsterdam. De la Motthe charged them an exorbitant 2,500 guilders. Confident that they would somehow raise the money, they agreed.

Individual Jews had been on the North American continent since the other European adventurers who waded into what must have seemed to them like a new dimension. Two Jews had immediately preceded the 23: Solomon Peterson, who was already becoming a successful businessman, and Jacob Barsimson, who was a settler sent by the Dutch West India Company. But no one had sent the 23. They had left Recife, with its beautiful white beaches, mild, tropical climate, lush plants, flowers, and sweet pomegranates. It was a place they themselves had a hand in building; as it grew and prospered, they had envisioned it as a New Jerusalem. Some of them had become very rich, but had to abandon their plantations, mills, and homes, and then endure the robbery at sea of what little capital they were able to take along. Here they were at a small provincial trading port with nothing to trade but some furniture and household items.

Of the 2,500 guilders promised to de la Motthe, the 23 could come up with only 933. De la Motthe's first order of business in New Amsterdam was to register the debt at the Stadt Huys, the courthouse, where it was ordered that the 23 auction off what goods they had to meet the debt. When they still could not meet it three of the men, Moses Ambrosius, David Israel, and Asser Levy van Swellem, were briefly interned against the remainder; the others tried to persuade the authorities that the money would be arriving from their coreligionists in Amsterdam.

Like Adrian Block's crew 41 years earlier, the 23 waited out the winter on Manhattan. But they were not like Block's sailors rebuilding their ship and anxious to be on their way. They were experienced settlers and in that briny, cold climate something had coalesced for them; they were determined to stay.

They were penniless, but they were educated, and had experienced both sides of a world shifting from Catholic to Protestant culture. If the Dutch of New Amsterdam had no confidence in this long-journeying lot, the Jews knew better.

Peter Stuyvesant, however, was determined to get them to leave.

Stuyvesant was at best unimaginative. In a world with more unmined resources and rugged terrain than any one of the European groups could then have envisioned, he was concerned about keeping competitiors out of his colony. Of these, the Jews ranked high on his list, as he was well aware of their economic success in the Caribbean.

CHAPTER ONE

In keeping with his unimaginative properties, he was a religious bigot who kept watch lest groups of Quakers, Baptists, or Presbyterians creep into his enclave. He brought the sores of Europe with him and most of all hated the Papists. Individual Jews here and there could be tolerated – just three weeks before he had assigned Jacob Barsimson a hut right beyond the wall – but if a group of such heretics settled in it could make others, like Catholics and Quakers, clamor for admission. He petitioned the governors of the Dutch West India Company for permission to expel "these blasphemers of the name of Christ." Allow the Jews to settle, he warned, and "we cannot refuse Lutherans and Papists."

The Jews asked their brethren in Amsterdam to intercede for them with the West India Company. In a petition that was both convincing and shrewd, the Amsterdam "merchants of the Portuguese Nation" did just that. They reminded the directors that the Jews of Recife had defended it against the Portuguese onslaught, losing life and immense amounts of money on behalf of the company. "The company consented that those who wish to populate the Colony shall enjoy certain districts and land grants. Why should certain subjects of this state not be allowed to travel thither and live there?"

They were shrewd enough to include in their suit facts that could help render a decision in their favor. They pointed out that France and England were permitting Portuguese Jews to settle their overseas territories. The Dutch were already feeling the pinch of competition from England for trade, and they did not want to lose their valuable Portuguese Jewish merchants to London.

They threw in some sops to soothe Stuyvesant in his defeat. As he had mentioned, they too did not want to see the colony "infected by people of the Jewish nation, for we foresee therefrom the same difficulties which you fear [that the Papists and Lutherans would soon follow]. "The company mentioned the losses the Jews had sustained in Brazil, and the many shares they had invested in the firm. They instructed the governor to allow the Jews to stay. But that did not stop Stuyvesant and his cronies from trying to constrict the lives of these "deceitful" heretics. The Jews would have to fight for their rights if they were to eke out a decent living.

Fight they did, more boldly and logically and with more tenacity than anyone could have foreseen. They were not allowed to travel, to trade, to sell at retail or to own real estate. In 1655 Abraham de Lucena was arrested for selling at retail and fined the enormous amount of 600 guilders. Jacob Cohen Henriques was ordered to stop baking bread for sale – this was allowed only to licensed bakers. The Jews wanted to get into the fur trade and to go to Fort Orange (today's Albany) and to the Delaware River, where the real action was. These rights were, for the most part, denied. Again the Jews appealed to Amsterdam. When the reply came it was to rebuke Stuyvesant. His worry over their "heretical" religion was not the issue; the company made it clear that the liberties extended to the Jews were political and civil. Only if they petitioned for a "free exercise of religion" would the company take action.

Asser Levy van Swellem, a native of Amsterdam and one of the men who had been held in prison against the debt of the 23, came out fighting. The remaining restrictions were still intolerable. Stuyvesant had excluded the Jews from the right to stand guard along the wall (built against Algonquin attacks) where Wall Street stands today. In place of serving the Jews paid an "exemption tax" reminiscent of the huge exemption taxes they were forced to pay in Europe. On November 5, 1655, van Swellem, along with Jacob Barsimson, petitioned the town council for the right to "keep guard with other burghers, or be free from the tax which others of their nation pay, as they must earn their living by manual labor."

By this time Stuyvesant was apoplectic at the gall of these people, especially van Swellem. But Asser's gumption was winning him a following in the Dutch community, and they had begun to enjoy this squaring off between their pious, rigid governor, and the man they called "Stuyvesant's Nemesis." The petition was refused and the two petitioners were told they were free to leave the colony at any time. Undaunted, Levy went to perform his military duty anyway. His services were accepted. Thus, after the Mexican Marranos, Levy was the first Jewish colonist officially to bear arms for the defense of a North American settlement.

In April of 1667 Levy demonstrated that progressive pursuit of his ends that made Stuyvesant rankle with indignation – and disbelief. He went to court and requested to be admitted as a burgher, since he already "keeps watch and ward like the other Burghers." He also stated that he had been a burgher in Holland. The New Amsterdam burgher law was designed to restrict the nonsettlers, the fortune-hunters and fast money men who would drift into the colony, make their money, and move on without paying taxes or taking on responsibilities in the settlement. Nothing could be further from the seriousness of purpose of the small, but growing, Jewish community.

That van Swellem was finally admitted as a burgher – the first Jewish citizen in North America – was due to the backing of four Sephardic merchants, most of whom had arrived in 1655, and whose families carried great weight in the commercial world of Amsterdam: the aforementioned Jacob Henriques, would-be baker; Salvador Dandrada, Abraham de Lucena, and Joseph D'Acosta. They were the most active in gaining the right to trade. But it would be some time before the right to worship in public, be in the retail business, or practice crafts would be formally allowed.

CHAPTER ONE

In securing their own rights the Jews secured rights for the others – the Lutherans, Baptists, Quakers, Catholics – every one of the religious denominations that was not Dutch Reformed. From the very first Jews in New Amsterdam set their stamp on the pursuit of such rights, a role they would continue to pursue – with a sense of obligation – on behalf of all Americans.

Once he had secured economic rights, van Swellem was able to give expression to his many skills. He went into the prized activity of fur trading and bought real estate in Albany and New Amsterdam. He had been a ritual slaughterer in Holland and now became one of six butchers selected to be licensed in New Amsterdam. Such a respectful plane had understanding reached that he was excused, in accordance with Jewish law, from slaughtering hogs. In 1678 he built a slaughterhouse at the eastern end of Wall Street on what is now the site of the New York Stock Exchange. He operated it with Garret Janson Roos, a gentile who became head of the hog-slaughtering operation. The two also opened a tavern next door.

Within ten years of coming to the New World. Levy was one of the richest men in New Amsterdam and so gained the honor of meeting with the other richest men and with the authorities on the defense needs of the city. His friends were numerous; he acted as custodian for the court of goods that were in litigation between two Christian friends; he was executor of wills for several others; and in 1671 he advanced funds that enabled the Lutherans to build their first church in New Amsterdam.

Asser was known far and wide. When he appeared in a Connecticut court on behalf of a Jewish man who had been heavily fined for breaking the Sabbath, the court reduced the fine "as a token of their respect to the said Asser Levy."

Asser Levy van Swellem was a self-made man. He embodied many of the traits that have come to be valued by Americans – indeed, seen as American: He was pragmatic, entrepreneurial, tenacious, and community-minded.

In a day and age when small settlements were founded in North America for the welfare of particular religious groups (excepting those few founded on new social ideals), van Swellem, with the backing of the small but vocal Jewish community, managed to secure rights for themselves and the other groups coming into the colony. Thus began the Jewish-American process of fighting against exclusionary laws and social and economic exclusions that have periodically arisen against various religious or national groups.

FOR TIME IMMEMORIAL

There was no stronger evidence of the resolve of the Jews to stay in New Amsterdam than their request, shortly after arriving, to purchase land for a cemetery. Though they were not yet allowed to worship in a synagogue, they had formed a congregation in the Sephardic rite, and held services in private homes. They called themselves Shearith Israel, or Remnant of Israel.

It is against Jewish tradition to bury the dead in a common burying ground. As Rabbi David de Sola Pool writes in his book *Portraits Etched in Stone* which offers biographies of the early members of Shearith Israel, "In Jewish life – to a greater degree than elsewhere – establishment of common consecrated burial ground is a significant sign of permanent settlement." The Jews, however, were told not to purchase burial ground until there was a death. And so, in 1656, they purchased their first cemetery, on a site near what is now Chatham Square in New York City's Chinatown. It was most likely small, since by 1682 they needed another. Records show land was purchased with the community's money in the name of Joseph Bueno de Mesquita, and again in 1728 and 1729, in the name of Lewis Gomez and others of his family, respectively.

In those years only the Dutch Reformed and Episcopalian churches had received patents of incorporation and could, therefore, own real estate directly. How the other denominations dealt with this problem reveals how adroit they had to be in forging their paths in the colony. The Presbyterians, Rabbi Pool points out, were more "farseeing" than the "prudent" Jews. They didn't want to put title to their real estate in the name of individual trustees. On March 3, 1720 they petitioned for a charter of incorporation; it was not granted. In 1730 they decided to vest the title to their church property in the General Assembly of the Church of Scotland. Later petitions for incorporation by the Presbyterians and Lutherans continued to be denied, but the Presbyterians had managed to avoid the legal complications that invariably arise in future generations when the title deed for a group is in the name of private individuals.

It is noteworthy that no member of Shearith Israel was accorded preference of burial plot. Like death's unwavering equality, equality of burial was insisted upon. When Daniel Gomez, the last survivor among the original trustees, asked for a family plot, his request was denied. Bodies were buried in rows in the order in which they died. The synagogue wrote the following answer to a member's request for a family plot: ". . . each person should be Buried in the Row, as it shall please God in his own good time to call us himself – for whatever distinction exists in Life, there is none in Death; and to give the opulent a preference over the pious and religious poor might tend to cause them feelings which in no manner could be compensated, and which we shall on all occasions avoid . . ."

Even where custom would have permitted, as at the death of the revered first American-born leader of the

CHAPTER ONE

RIGHT
The original burial ground of Congregation Shearith Israel, the oldest congregation in North America, still exists today in New York City's Chatham Square.

congregation, Gershom Mendes Seixas, no exception was made. In a town where family plots and vaults were becoming *de rigueur* among the other congregations, this custom of equality was quite a test.

Today what remains of Shearith Israel's burial ground, the Chatham Square Cemetery, nestles off the Bowery on St. James Place in lower Manhattan. It is believed to be the oldest Jewish cemetery in the United States. Burials were made there from 1683 to 1831; the stones bear such family names as Nathan, Abraham, Gomez, Seixas, Phillips, Hart, Pinto, Henriques, Hendricks, Hays, Burgos, Lopez, Rivera, Myers, Isaacs, Franks. Out of the 107 graves that are identifiable, 18 are still decorated every Memorial Day; five graves have bronze tablets that were dedicated in 1932 by the Daughters of the American Revolution. During the Revolution the cemetery, which was on high ground, was one of the defense sites used by the Patriots.

"How this curious old cemetery ever got wedged in between the buildings that surround it is a mystery . . . Passing down the Bowery on the elevated railroad, by looking on the left-hand side just after the train branches off toward Pearl Street, this queer nook may be discovered, and if the inmates only had the power of knowing the progress of the times, they would be considerably astonished to see their descendants whirled over their heads on a railroad in the air." So the actor Joseph Jefferson, famous for playing Rip Van Winkle (which opened at the Booth theater in 1870), recounted his years growing up with this cemetery at the back of his house.

The graves at Chatham Square tell the story of the early coming together of two cultures, the Sephardic and Ashkenazim, on new territory, where they helped to form yet a third, an American culture.

WHAT THEY LEFT, KEPT AND CHANGED

The small Jewish communities of New York, Newport, Philadelphia Savannah and Charleston were part of the American quilt for 120 years before Independence, when the shape of America was in the making. As they developed, these communities became a new entity in Jewish history. Much of Europe's population still lived under feudalism; some were but slowly divesting themselves of it. In America no feudal structure separated and controlled the population. In pioneer life improvisation is all. And so it was that life in the colonies allowed everyone to discard old baggage and keep what was felt to be essential.

Since there was no corporate or feudal structure, Jews no longer had to worry about maintaining separate courts to get justice. Those who came from the ghettos

of central Europe, where they had been compelled to pay taxes as a group, now paid as individuals.

In Europe, the constraints of religious life and ritual had ordered their lives (lapses were duly noted by the community). In America this existed to a much smaller degree; the kind of religious commitment made was more of an individual matter. In fact, the whole idea of individualism could begin to take root in a place where the pressures of involuntary religious group constraint were considerably lessened. Christians regularly flouted the blue laws. Jews making their way through the wilderness to new trading territories, or living far from the main congregations, decided for themselves what degree of religious ritual to follow. Some Jews did manage to keep kosher in the wilds; the German peddlers of the 1840s, for instance, were called egg-eaters by the Indians they traded with.

The Jews intermarried freely with Christians, although it is interesting to note that even without religious constraints, and even in intermarriage, most did not become baptized, and chose to keep their membership in the synagogue. Their children, however, were most often raised as Christians, especially in outlying areas where the synagogue was a journey away.

A major change in American Judaism was present from the start. The Americans emphasized the congregational aspects of Judaism. The authoritarian rabbinical tradition could not take root here. Rabbis were not needed to adjudicate, since Jews went to civil court along with everyone else. There were no ordained, practicing rabbis among the early settlers; in fact, until 1840 there were no ordained rabbis in permanent posts in the United States and it wasn't until the second half of the nineteenth century that American seminaries were established to teach and ordain rabbis.

It was their role as judge in civil and religious matters (often combined in Talmudic law) that gave rabbis great power in their European communities. As a way of keeping feudal control, monarchs reserved for themselves the right to appoint the chief rabbis. Although as historical circumstances dictated, rabbis had more or less power in the community, in Judaism itself they are allowed no greater spiritual powers than the laity. No one can come between the worshipper and God. Men and women are held solely responsible for their acts. Rabbis are primarily teachers of the Jewish religious tradition. Their learning is considered to be a sacred gift to be used for the benefit of the community, but there is no religious rite that only rabbis can perform; any knowledgeable layman can conduct a service. In colonial America, services were often led by cantors or by members of the congregation.

The very nature of Judaism allows for it to be practiced in the simplest of circumstances. Even on an uncharted continent, thousands of miles away from an overcrowded and religiously baroque Europe, the requirements for religious practice could be met. A *minyan* (ten men) is needed to form a congregation; we know that in 1654 there were at least ten Jewish males over age 13 in New Amsterdam. (Today in America, as part of a burgeoning movement to change their traditional roles in Judaism, women are accepted as part of the minyan in many non-Orthodox congregations.) The synagogue itself may be the plainest of structures, as long as there is a place to house the Torah in its Ark. No ceremonies are required to sanctify the building, for in Jewish teaching God is everywhere, and so may be invoked anywhere. In Jewish tradition the synagogue is the center of religious and community activity; it stands for a place of prayer, study (a Hebrew school is usually part of the synagogue), and congregation, the sharing of social concerns with members of the community.

Life in the five main early Jewish communities revolved around their congregations, and their patterns were similar. They were strictly organized, but democratic. There was a president, treasurer, and a board elected yearly to oversee community business. The early settlers worshipped discreetly in private homes; later they rented a house for worship. As their prosperity increased they bought a building. The last step, the fulfilment of their goal, was to build their own synagogue.

Synagogue life kept colonial Jewish communities cohesive. But the new democratic ideals inspired them to exercise greater individuality, especially in protection of their new freedoms. When major disputes arose within the congregation, as happened in 1825 at the Sephardic Synagogue Shearith Israel when it refused to allow Ashkenazic members to introduce the Sabbath scriptural reading, the latter seceded and formed their own congregation, B'nai Jeshurun. This congregational autonomy continues up to the present, an American phenomenon with roots in the earliest Jewish colonial experience in forging freedom. With every wave of immigration new congregations have formed – there were perhaps sixty in New York City alone by the middle of the nineteenth century. This pattern of breaking away and reforming became strongest among the Russian and Polish immigrants of the late nineteenth and early twentieth centuries.

SEDAKAH AND KASHRUTH

TWO JEWISH PRACTICES CONTRIBUTE TO SOCIAL WELL-BEING

Shearith Israel rented its first house in New York City, a simple red brick structure, in 1700 on Mill Street (today's South William Street). The congregation established a school in 1731. In keeping with the Jewish tradition of *sedakah* – social justice – it was tuition-free for the poorer children. The principle of sedakah is essential to the Jewish tradition and is followed as rigorously today as it was in colonial times.

When the first 23 Jews in America were granted permission to stay in New Amsterdam, the Dutch West India Company made it a point to include the condition that they care for their own poor. But sedakah is so important in the Jewish tradition that such a stipulation was most unnecessary. Sedakah is not charity as such. Rather, it is a way, often through anonymous giving, to insure that justice is operating in the community. If a person is without the means of making a living, or if his livelihood cannot sustain him, then he is being deprived of his share in the goods of this world. The fault must therefore lie with the society. Sedakah restores the balance and is given in the spirit of justice, not pity. Sedakah takes in the larger community as well; in Europe in times of famine Christians regularly went to the ghetto to be fed. "They give for God and alms to all the poor who wish to receive it, so to Jews as to Christians." This is one of the frequent recountings of Jewish charity given in testimony to the Inquisition in Spain by a Christian woman living outside of Madrid.

The responsibilities of sedakah were an impetus behind private social-welfare organizations and social services started by German Jews during the mass immigrations of the East European Jews. Later, federal legislation to aid the poor was a cause espoused by many Jewish voters in the spirit of sedakah.

The laws of *kashruth*, keeping kosher, induced an abiding concern that has reverberations in today's consumer movement. In March of 1798 Uriah Hendricks, a successful retailer and supplier for the Colonies during the French and Indian War, wrote to the members of Shearith Israel: "From my own observations I think it a duty incumbent on me to lay before you a most gross abuse of our holy religion, at this season the meat at market appears fresh even when ten or twelve days old and, by the seals remaining on, a number of our society are deceived . . . a remedy is very necessary and, in my humble opinion deserves your immediate consideration."

ABOVE

Jacob Franks (1688–1769) helped build the first synagogue in New York. He came from a prominent merchant family, and shrewdly married a daughter of Moses Levy. This brought together two of the great Jewish merchant families in America, and produced a number of distinguished descendents.

NEW AMSTERDAM BECOMES NEW YORK

CHAPTER TWO

The English took possession of New Amsterdam bloodlessly in 1664, gaining a clear Atlantic coast from New England to Georgia. Jews had been readmitted to England informally under Oliver Cromwell in 1657; England's attitude toward the Jews in the new colony amounted to a policy of live and let live. The Jews retained the civil liberties they had gained under the Dutch; unlike the Lutherans and Catholics, they were not restricted from worshipping in public. However, they lived with political restrictions – having to swear an oath as a Christian – that barred them from public office. But by 1727, New York's General Assembly voted against making the words "on the true faith of a Christian" a mandatory part of the oath of office. Political restrictions became of greater concern to them during the Revolution, when they began to register protest.

The colonial Jews comprised a broad-based middle class. The majority earned their living as small store owners, craftsmen, and petty traders. The rich Sephardic families, who were important in the world of shipping and commerce, intermarried and developed a network of interlocking families and businesses, with relatives in other American colonies as well as in European port cities.

Jews set up trading posts along the Delaware River, extending clear into southwestern Pennsylvania. Trading with the Indians could accommodate all manner of venturesome folk, including the undercapitalized. A precursor to the German-Jewish backpacker, or if richer, wagon peddler, was the early colonial Jewish trader with his horse and saddlebags full of trinkets. Jewish women, too, engaged in business.

Jacob Rivera, a member of one of the five major Sephardic shipping families, founded Newport's spermaceti industry. This waxy substance, found in sperm whales, became the main ingredient in candlemaking, replacing the more expensive tallow. In fact, candle manufacturing was a Jewish enterprise in the colonies.

In 1710, Lewis Gomez convinced the New York City Council to permit him to ship wheat to Madeira. He had arrived in the colonies from England, where his family had fled after his father, the financial advisor to Philip IV of Spain, was thrown into prison by the Inquisition.

Lewis, along with his young son Daniel, amassed a fortune in the wheat business. Daniel also managed to do quite well by trading in wheat, sugar, and a variety of commodities. His advertisement for his products in the New York *Gazette* of 1751 is a remarkable contrast to the push and scream of today's advertising: ". . . earthenware in casks and crates, Cheshire cheese, loaf sugar, cutlery ware, pewter, grindstones, coals and sundry other goods too tedious to mention."

Daniel Gomez found his real business passion in the fur trade; in which he was an innovator. He bought cheap land in Ulster County, wilderness land, 2,500 acres of it around Newburgh, New York. There, where several Indian trails met, he built a trading post. More than a post, it was a solidly and beautifully constructed home – with thick walls to fend off attack – and a spacious parlor with a large fireplace. The Indians sat by the fire, talked, and traded. Gomez employed them as skinners and fur trappers, something not done until then. Gomez was a patriot. Like many of the members of Shearith Israel, who left New York City to the Tories during the Revolution, he left the Tory territory of Newburgh for Philadelphia. His son, however, stayed at the trading post, and wrote that he had hired a young German immigrant, Jacob Ashdor (later known as Astor), as an apprentice. But the young, well-bred, third-generation American Gomez was put off by Ashdor's boorishness and fired him, remarking, "The fool has no head for this business, absolutely."

In 1729, Shearith Israel built its first synagogue. Bilhah Abigail Franks, wife of Jacob Franks, one of New York's richest merchants, helped raise the funds by getting contributions from the women in the congregation. The Jewish women contributed – if not money, then jewelry, trinkets, or anything that could be converted into cash.

Abigail, with her seven children, her good works and concerns, was a worrying Jewish mother. She fretted over whom her children would or should marry, and was heartbroken when her daughter Phila eloped with the

CHAPTER TWO

RIGHT
The house built in 1714 by Lewis Gomez (1654–1740) as a trading post near Newburgh, New York, still stands. The home is the oldest Jewish residence as well as one of the oldest residences of any sort in America. Benjamin G. Gomez (1769–1828), great-grandson of Lewis, was the first Jewish bookseller in North America.

CENTER
Located at Pearl and Broad Streets in the heart of New York City's financial district, Fraunces Tavern is now a landmark building best known as the site of George Washington's farewell to his officers in 1783. However, long before that (in 1719) it was the home of Phila Franks and her husband.

boy next door, Oliver Delancey. When she lived in Philadelphia she had watched as many of the Sephardic Jews married into the city's elite Christian families, and she was bent on keeping her own in the fold. Oliver retired with his bride to the family house, built in 1719. (This house became Fraunces Tavern, a New York City landmark that stands today.) The couple lived there through the years. Oliver joined the Tory army as brigadier general of the Delancey Battalions. The property was eventually confiscated and the Delanceys went to live in England. Two other of Abigail's children, David, Abigail, and one grandchild, Rebecca, would end up not just in England, (David returned to America in later years), and married to gentiles, but with grandchildren who became royal governors, generals, an Episcopal clergyman, members of Parliament, and whose descendents include members of the nobility.

Like many rich Colonials of their day, the Franks and their children had their portraits painted by one or another of the fraternity of portraitists who sought subjects in New England and New York – artists such as Charles Wilson Peale, Thomas Sully, and Gilbert Stuart. They were among the earliest patrons of art in America.

Abigail's granddaughter Rebecca was the belle of Philadelphia. Her letters are a fascinating record of the social behavior and vanities of the day. She was famous – some would say infamous – for attending, in the midst of the Revolutionary war, the lavish gala given by the British in 1779 for their retiring general, Sir William Howe. Nearly a thousand guests were served a sumptuous buffet feast. Knights in medieval costume pretended to joust. The two teams of jousters each chose a Queen of Beauty. Rebecca Franks was one of them.

The ball may have been the highlight of Rebecca's debutante career, but her well-publicized presence there has been linked to her father's subsequent business troubles. David Franks was a top Philadelphia merchant and as such had been chosen by the Continental Congress to supply goods and food for the British prisoners held in Philadelphia. But after Rebecca's election as a Queen of Beauty at a ball given while Continental troops suffered the hunger and cold of an exposed winter in Valley Forge, Frank's purveying began to be viewed as unpatriotic. His business fell off; when he could no longer supply the prisoners with rations, he was arrested for treason. The case against him was unjust and it was dismissed for lack of evidence.

During a stay in New York with her father, Rebecca wrote home to Philadelphia about the social life in that rival city. Her view is not so far removed from the observations and complaints made about New York today. "To all appearances 'tis the ladies and not the gentlemen that show a preference nowadays. 'Tis here, I fancy, always leap year . . . And scandal says with respect to most who have been married, the advances have first come from the ladies' side . . . I fancy there would be more marriage was another mode adopted. But they've made the men so saucy that I sincerely believe the lowest ensign thinks 'tis but ask and have . . ."

At the onset of the Revolution the majority of colonial Jews were Patriots, but there were Tories, too, as in the Franks family. Since the leading Sephardic families had married among themselves, the Revolution caused interfamily dissent and splits. Among the Loyalists were

CHAPTER TWO

LEFT
Jacob Franks, one of the leading merchants in colonial times, was the father of David and Phila. When the Revolution came, David remained loyal to the king and ended up in jail. After the war he returned to mercantile life; he died in 1793.

Sephardic Jews whose families had found safety in England after leaving the Iberian peninsula. Ashkenazic and Spanish Jews who had fled to Holland had no such gratitude.

Generally, the families in commerce led aristocratic lives, with town houses and country homes where they rode to hounds. They were purveyors (Jacob Franks made much of his fortune purveying to the crown during the French and Indian War) and large land holders. The shipping magnates exported furs, dried fish, indigo, sugar, flax, rice, and rum. By the early eighteenth century they were bringing many luxury goods into the colonies, including a large array of textiles: Benjamin Gomez sold crepes, silk, scarlet cloth, damask, printed cotton, Irish linen, satin, calico, and raven duck.

LOPEZ OF NEWPORT

By the middle of the eighteenth century, Newport, Rhode Island, outranked New York as a major port; its leading Jewish merchants had helped make it so. The first Jewish families settled in Newport, in 1658, in the colony founded by Roger Williams on principles of religious equality and tolerance.

Williams was born in England into an Anglican family in 1603. He found himself in dissent against the Established Church and longed to see a separation of the religious and political spheres, whose unity he felt had deprived much of mankind of a true freedom of conscience. He was a serious Hebraicist who shared in the new dedication to Hebrew scripture of the Puritans and many of England's scholarly elite. Among his friends was the great poet John Milton, to whom he taught Dutch in return for instruction in Hebrew. He wrote, "I have longed for some trading with Jews themselves, for whose hard measure I fear the nations and England have yet a score to pay . . ."

In Massachusetts, Williams broke with the Puritans, who themselves had created a theocratic hierarchy to govern the colony; he was tossed out of that pious territory. He then purchased land from the Narragansett Indians and fashioned a colony of diverse groups that were held together by civil law, a precursor to modern civil society. He was a pioneer of what we call the American dream, the "first rebel against the divine church-order established in the wilderness," as Cotton Mather described him. Six years before the first Jewish settlers came to Rhode Island he wrote, "I humbly conceive it to be the duty of the civil magistrate to break down that superstitious wall of separation (as to civil things) between the Gentiles and the Jews, and freely, without their asking, to make way for their free and peaceable habitations amongst us."

The early Jewish settlers in Newport brought different levels of skills. There were metalworkers, snuff-

CHAPTER TWO

RIGHT
The cornerstone of the Newport synagogue was laid by Aaron Lopez in 1763. Born to a Marrano family in Portugal, Lopez (1731–1782) arrived in Newport in 1752 and went into business with his father-in-law, Jacob Rodriguez Rivera. They promoted the whaling industry and the town of Newport, but resettled in Massachusetts after the British captured Newport in 1777.

CENTER
Woodford, the home of David Franks in Philadelphia, was built in 1756. The house still stands today and is open to the public.

makers, bakers; the richest were shippers. Mordecai Campanel's home was the first place of worship for their new congregation, Kahal Kadosh; he was elected to be its leader. (The house was the site as well for the first meeting of the Masonic Order.)

Aaron Lopez, who would become one of Newport's leading ship owners, arrived there in 1752. He was born into a Marrano family in Portugal and baptized with the name Duarte. He is said to have witnessed the burning of a Marrano for heresy and to have then vowed to live in a country where he could openly practice Judaism. There were precedents for this in his large, successful family. Aaron Lopez had relatives in the West Indies, and a half-brother, Moses, in Newport. He was in his early twenties when he took his wife and baby daughter out of Portugal and arrived in Newport. There, in a first step into the sunlight, he took the Hebrew name Aaron; his wife Ann became Abigail, his daughter Catherine, Sarah. The couple remarried in a Jewish ceremony, after which Aaron Lopez went about learning the business of Newport. Two of his mentors were his cousin Daniel Gomez of New York, and the wealthy Jacob Rodriguez Rivera (the spermaceti candle manufacturer), one of Newport's richest businessmen and a pillar of the Sephardic community. When his wife Abigail died, Lopez married Rivera's daughter Sarah, and with this union his fortunes started to climb. He built up an international shipping business that at its height owned thirty ocean-going vessels and a hundred coastal schooners. He built and ran his own shipyard – the Lopez ships carried rough timber, sperm oil, and mahogany, and brought back dry goods. He also owned a building construction firm in Newport. But the other business, mentioned only quietly today, and one on which many a New England fortune was founded, was the slave trade. Only a minority of the colonists seemed to view the slave trade as the heinous thing it was. The prevailing view in New England at that time had it that life in a civilized and Christian environment, where they could accept Jesus, could only have a beneficial effect on the Africans, though there were clergymen (the beloved Ezra Stiles was one), who saw nothing but an abomination in the institution.

The slave trade was carried on in a huge triangular route. Aaron Lopez was among the traders whose ships would, in the course of a year, carry rum from Newport, where it was made, to the west coast of Africa, where it was delivered to tribal chieftains in return for slaves. From there, the ships would go to the West Indies and trade the slaves for sugar, which was then brought north and made into rum.

Partly because Lopez did much of his business with England in the years leading up to the Revolution, and partly because even in the colony of Roger Williams foreign-born Jews had trouble getting naturalized,

minister, Ezra Stiles, a friend of many in the Jewish congregation Jeshuat Israel (the Salvation of Israel) recorded his impressions: "There were present many Gentlemen and Ladies. The Order and Decorum, the Harmony and Solemnity of the Musick, together with a handsome Assembly of People, in an Edifice the most perfect of the Temple kind perhaps in America, and splendidly illuminated, could not but raise in the Mind a faint Idea of the Majesty and Grandeur of the Ancient Jewish Worship mentioned in Scripture."

The interior of the synagogue, with its eternal lamp and the lustrous light from its chandeliers, proclaims a Judaism that could be practiced in the light of day by Marranos who had had to keep their Judaism a dark secret. It also holds a reminder of their past: a secret stairway goes from the *bimah* (reader's table) to the basement.

A few years after Newport's elite Jewish men's club was formed, Aaron Lopez became a member. The club was modeled after British men's clubs and life therein was a respite from the frantic pace of business. Evenings at the club were orderly – cards (whist, piquet) could be

BELOW
Born in 1759, Isaac Franks served in the Revolutionary War under George Washington, eventually rising to the rank of lieutenant colonel. He died in 1822. This painting is by the famed portraitist Gilbert Stuart.

Lopez – after several attempts in Newport courts – was naturalized in 1762 in Taunton, near Swansea, Massachusetts, where he had a summer home. There is some irony that a Jewish man from liberal Rhode Island had to go to exclusionary Massachusetts, where he became that colony's first naturalized Jew, swearing the oath to His Majesty George III, and crossing out on the petition the words "on the true faith of a Christian," that too often kept the Jews from the full political participation in early America.

Naturalized or not, Aaron Lopez, as *parnas* (president) of the Newport congregation was asked to lay the first cornerstone of their synagogue, known today as one of the most beautiful houses of worship in the country. The preserved building became a national historic monument in 1946. Peter Harrison, who designed King's Chapel in Boston and several buildings in Newport, designed a Georgian synagogue whose symmetry and balance convey the special energy of the enlightened eighteenth-century outlook. When Aaron Lopez, Jacob Rivera, and Isaac Hart were helping to establish Newport's Redwood Library they met and commissioned Harrison.

The synagogue was consecrated on December 2, 1763, the first day of Chanukah. Newport's Congregational

CHAPTER TWO

RIGHT
The classically beautiful interior of the Touro Synagogue in Newport, Rhode Island. The building is a national historic landmark and also the oldest existing synagogue in the United States.

BELOW RIGHT
The Touro Synagogue was designed by the colonial architect Peter Harrison. It was consecrated in 1763. The grace and beauty of the building are representative of the prosperity and taste of the wealthy Newport community.

played for three hours only. If the stakes rose higher than the 20 shillings allowed, the errant member was fined four bottles of fine wine. Toasts were formal, the food elaborate. But much of the conviviality crumbled as the Revolution approached and the Tories – Isaac Hart, for instance – clashed with the staunch Patriots.

When the British attacked Newport in 1777, destroying 480 houses and laying waste to the city, harbor, and surrounding fields, Lopez backed the Revolution and fled Rhode Island. He brought his family to Leicester, Massachusetts to keep them "from sudden allarums and the cruel ravages of an enraged enemy." In his letters to friends and neighbors in Newport, his concerns are solidly with the Patriots.

The Revolutionary War severely limited shipping, while piracy and privateering increased. Soon most of Lopez's shipping business was cut off. By the time he died he had lost a major part of his fortune.

Lopez had stipulated in his will that his Leicester mansion, a stately building with white pilasters, be used to start a boys' school. And it was. Today it is part of the Leicester Academy.

The majority of Newport's Jews were patriots who left the city when the British took it over and never returned. Theirs had been a vibrant life in a city that was never to regain its commercial importance, and which would become the social watering hole for those whose fortunes were made in commercial centers such as Newport might have been. After building up a community, the Jews left mere traces of themselves.

Through the eyes of Ezra Stiles, a minister and a president of Yale College, we get a vivid impression of Jewish colonial life. We see Stiles as he tours churches in New York and finds himself impressed most by the perpetual lamp burning in Shearith Israel. We see the letters he wrote decrying the difficulty his friend Aaron Lopez had in getting satisfaction from Rhode Island courts on his application for naturalization, a prejudice triggered by the Naturalization Act of 1740 passed by Parliament, which granted citizenship to foreign-born Protestants and Jews colonizing British territories. Disturbed at the anti-Jewish prejudice, Stiles wrote that it "forbodes that the Jews will never become incorporated with the people of America . . ."

A New England Congregationalist, Stiles saw the Old Testament as the main spiritual force in what he called "God's American Israel." For the colonial People of the Book he had curiosity and sympathy. We see him forming a friendship with Rabbi Isaac Carigal, who spent some months in Newport in the course of his twenty-year journey to raise money for the Jewish poor of Palestine. The two conversed in Hebrew and read scriptures. When the rabbi left, Stiles asked his friends in Congregation Jeshuat Israel to commission a portrait of the rabbi as a present to Yale. Newport artist Samuel King, who had known Carigal, painted the portrait, and it was hung in Yale College's Public Library.

When Aaron Lopez died, Stiles wrote a most impressive eulogy for his friend, who was so widely beloved in Newport for his generosity. "He did business with the greatest ease and clearness – always carried about a Sweetness of Behaviour, a calm Urbanity, an agreeable and unaffected Politeness of manners. Without a single enemy and the most universally beloved by an extensive acquaintance of any man I ever knew . . ."

Yet there was an abiding belief that Jews cannot be spiritually whole, and accepted into heaven, unless they convert to Christianity. This was echoed mildly in Stiles's memorial to Lopez: "Oh, how often have I wished that sincere, pious, and candid mind could have perceived the evidence of Christianity . . . known that Jesus was the messiah predicted by Moses and the Prophets!" As long as Jews refused to give up their religion for Christianity, the notion that Christianity replaced the covenant between God and the children of Israel was threatened.

Indeed, on the religious front in America, it would take until the mid-twentieth Century for some Protestant theologians to question and re-examine the theological premises behind the drive to convert the Jews, and to acknowledge that Judaism, like Christianity, is an evolving religion. As Protestant theologian Paul van Buren has written, "If God is not faithful to His people, if He does not stand by His covenant with Israel, why should we think that He will be any more faithful to His Gentile church?" This makes for the ability to accept the validity of the "old" covenant as well as the "new".

Whatever the theological questions, for Jews America signified a freedom from the horrors of imposed conversion. No government-sponsored conversion policies suffocated the Jews as they had in Europe. The very nature of America, where competing religious sects learned to trade their desire for hegemony for the security of autonomy, created a democracy like none before. As George Washington, newly elected President of the United States, wrote to the Newport congregation after his visit there in 1790: "May the children of the stock of Abraham who dwell in this land continue to merit and enjoy the good will of the other inhabitants – while every one shall sit in safety under his own vine and fig tree and there shall be none to make him afraid . . ."

BELOW LEFT
Ezra Stiles, learned Newport minister and later president of Yale College, was a great admirer and supporter of the Jews. He was a close friend to Aaron Lopez.

CHAPTER TWO

RIGHT
Judah Monis (1683–1764) settled in Boston in 1720. He was an instructor of Hebrew at Harvard from 1722 until 1760. This book, published in 1735, was the first Hebrew book printed in America.

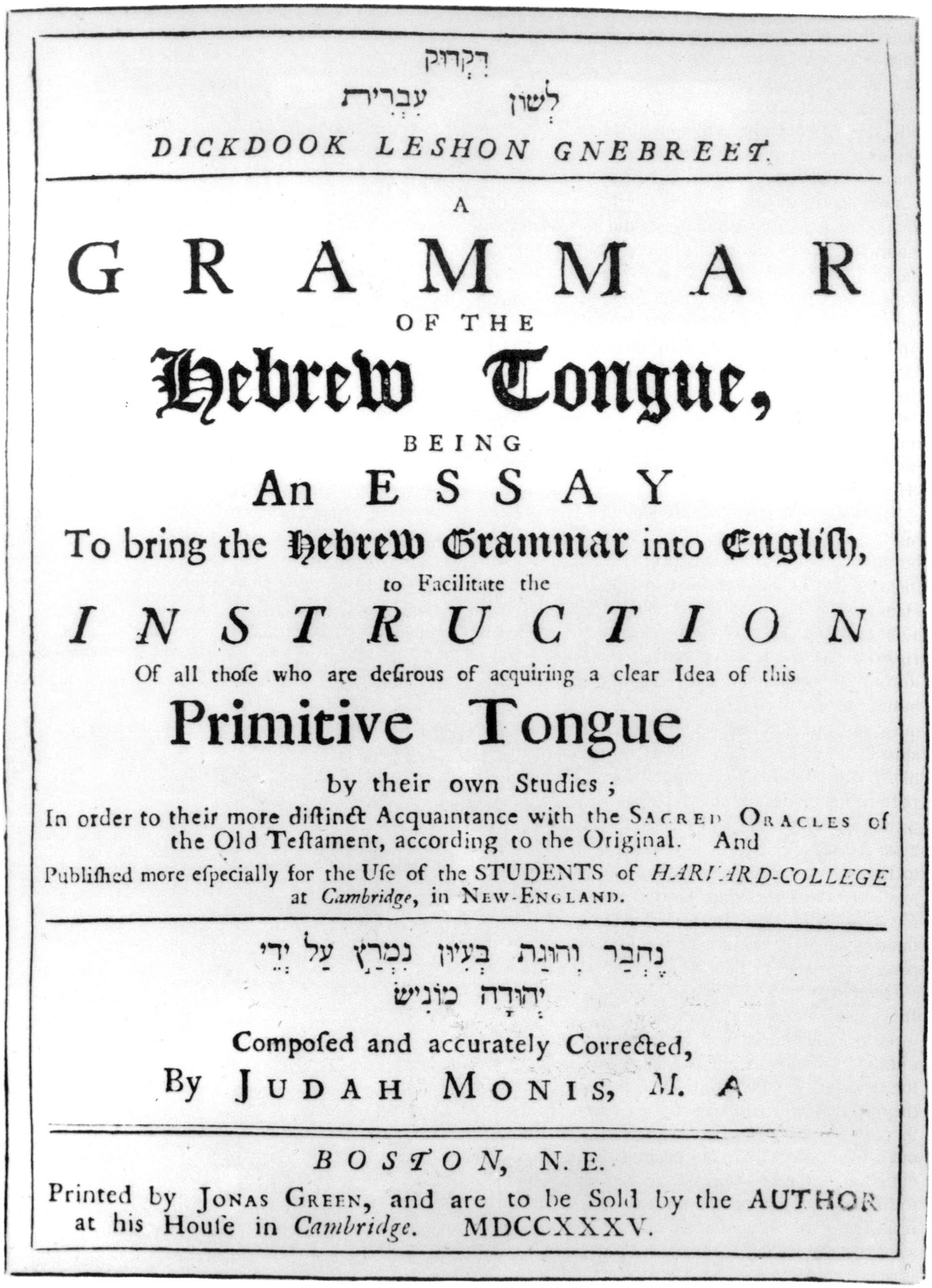

דקדוק

לשון עברית

DICKDOOK LESHON GNEBREET.

A

GRAMMAR

OF THE

Hebrew Tongue,

BEING

An ESSAY

To bring the **Hebrew Grammar** into **Engliſh**,

to Facilitate the

INSTRUCTION

Of all thoſe who are deſirous of acquiring a clear Idea of this

Primitive Tongue

by their own Studies;

In order to their more diſtinct Acquaintance with the SACRED ORACLES of the Old Teſtament, according to the Original. And

Publiſhed more eſpecially for the Uſe of the STUDENTS of *HARVARD-COLLEGE* at *Cambridge*, in NEW-ENGLAND.

נחבר והוגת בעיון נמרץ על ידי

יהודה מוניש

Compoſed and accurately Corrected,

By JUDAH MONIS, M. A

BOSTON, N. E.

Printed by JONAS GREEN, and are to be Sold by the AUTHOR at his Houſe in *Cambridge*. MDCCXXXV.

Washington, like Benjamin Franklin, Thomas Jefferson, James Madison, and Thomas Paine, was a Deist whose religiosity embraced universal ideas. He was a Mason and held the free discussion of religion and philosophy dear.

In this setting, conversion was an individual, autonomous decision. A Jewish settler might venture into the hinterlands and live among Christians; if he converted it was often for want of a Jewish religious context, so far away from the few Jewish centers. Often, for the sake of family unity, intermarriage led him to convert. Contrast the life of Aaron Isaacs, the first Jew in East Hampton, Long Island, New York with that of Aaron Lopez in the synagogue-centered social and religious life of Newport. An East Hampton scholar, Beth Dina Davidson, has unearthed facts about Isaac's life that offer a glimpse into the way of conversion in early America.

Isaacs is on the American map chiefly because he was the grandfather of John Howard Payne, a well-known poet and playwright, and the author of the famous song "Home Sweet Home."

Isaacs was a successful and well-respected member of his East Hampton community. Originally from Hamburg, Isaacs came to New York and was a dues-paying member of Shearith Israel. Soon he settled in East Hampton where he married Mary Hedges (around 1750) and earned his living as a merchant and peddler. He owned a boat that carried goods from New York City to Nantucket, one of the merchants with whom he did business was Aaron Lopez. They corresponded frequently about business, but their friendship does not appear to have been more than formal. Isaacs was versatile. He repaired watches, ran a hauling service, transported hay and livestock, and supplied his customers with spices and furniture. During the Revolution he was a patriot. He took his family from Loyalist Long Island to Haddam, Connecticut to wait out the war. Since he made several visits back to East Hampton at some risk, Miss Davidson raises the possibility that he was spying for the Patriots, or, at the least, picking up secret dispatches from them.

He brought his family back to East Hampton in 1782. It is believed that he had from 11 to 13 children, all of whom were baptized, yet he himself was not converted until at least 14 years after his marriage. Samuel Buell, the East Hampton Presbyterian pastor, writes joyously of the day in 1767 when his diligent efforts bore the fruit of 99 conversions, and describes them as "Children have out of hell's horrors, young people 8, 10, and 12 years old have been converted; among the rest a Jew." That was Isaacs, of whom the pastor also wrote: "I have true reason to think is now a true believer in the Messiah, whom he always despised, 'till within a few days . . ." Isaacs was baptized in the same year that his first son survived infancy, and that could have been a factor. Or perhaps all those years of living among his neighbors slowly and finally caused him to act. Whatever the reasons, there are indications that he kept an identification with Judaism. He named his grandson Richard Mordecai, not one of the names usually taken by the Protestants.

In New York the humble and earnest Gershom Mendes Seixas, the first American-born Jewish minister, and head of Shearith Israel during the Revolutionary War, could not abide staying in a city that would be given up to British control, and urged his congregation to leave. They scattered to Connecticut and Philadelphia. Seixas left on July 4, 1780 with his wife, who had given birth but three weeks before. He took the Torah scrolls from the synagogue with him, and accepted an invitation to preside over the Philadelphia congregation. While he was there, he signed a petition to amend the Constitution so that those elected to office would not have to take the oath of a Christian. Congregation Shearith Israel was in

BELOW LEFT
Gershom Mendes Seixas, born in America in 1745, was the minister of Congregation Shearith Israel in New York for some fifty years. He also helped found the first Jewish congregation in Philadelphia. Seixas was one of the thirteen clergymen who participated in George Washington's first inauguration.

CHAPTER TWO

RIGHT
Benjamin Mendes Seixas (1747–1817), son of Gershom, was a founder of the New York Stock Exchange.

exile for seven years, and when Seixas returned to New York it was to resume a harrowing schedule. As a *mohel,* or someone able to circumcize newborns, his responsibilities took him as far afield as Canada. A trip to circumcize four children in Three Rivers, Berthieville, Montreal and back to New York, took him 34 days, so few were the mohels, and so in need of services were the Jews in the outlands. Seixas was the only Jewish minister north of Philadelphia. He was in charge of Shearith Israel's Hebrew school, and their direct education of its children. Despite claims by the Reform movement that they were the first to introduce sermons into American synagogues, it was Seixas who did that, along with other reforms, many of them designed to create a more orderly service. During the War of 1812, when the congregation was financially pressed – as was most everybody – Seixas had his synagogue obligations, plus 15 children to feed. In 1813 he wrote: "Provisions dear. Hard times . . . Many are living upon black butter-pears, apples and quinces stewed together." (In light of this, it is interesting to note that Seixas played the lottery.)

Seixas was much admired by the Christian community. He was a trustee of Columbia College, and in 1784 was elected by the New York State Legislature as a member of the first Board of Regents of the University of the State of New York. He was asked to preach at St. Paul's Church on the day that the New York City Community Council set aside to commemorate war losses.

What seems most remarkable about Seixas were his inventiveness and his humility. Constantly on call to his congregation, with 15 children of his own, one contemporary account describes him calmly shelling peas while teaching bar mitzvah lessons to his students.

THE PATCHWORK

The Pilgrims left England for Holland in 1604, in the belief that, "It is better to go and dwell in Goshen, find it where we can, than tarry in the midst of such Egyptian bondayge as is among us." They likened their crossing of the Atlantic to the crossing of the Red Sea. The New World was their promised land.

The Congregationalist Puritans and Pilgrims perceived their lives as mirroring those of the ancient Israelites. In a declaration of war against the Indians, for instance, they compared the Narragansetts and their allies to Asher, Amalek, and the Philistines, who warred against Israel. In naming their children and their places the matriarchs, patriarchs, heroes, and places of the Old Testament were their inspiration. The more difficult, or obscure the name, the better. In his book *Jewish Influence on Christian Reform Movements,* Louis Israel Newman recounts the story of a Puritan who "called his dog 'Moreover' because a stray Biblical verse remarks: 'Moreover the dog came and lapped up the water.'"

For the Puritans there was no higher authority than the word of God as it is written in the Bible; they took it as their right to interpret his law. They rebelled against what they considered the Catholic and Anglican impositions of hierarchy on the natural relationship between God and man. *Their* binding authority was the word of God, and their congregations, organized on a New Testament understanding of the church, were autonomous. As had the ancient Israelites, they felt they had a covenant with God. Their Old Testament frame of reference and their reverence for Hebrew, while not affecting their relations with colonial Jews directly, nonetheless exerted a spiritual influence that shows up in court records, and in some ways helped to break down barriers. Jews were dealt with arbitrarily in early New England; one was fined outrageously for operating his boat on the Sabbath, another had his fine reduced because he was one of God's Chosen. Integrating the colonial, contemporary Jew into the Puritan idea of the ancient Israelites, especially alongside the idea of themselves as the spiritual heirs of the ancient Israelites would not have seemed a desirable possibility. But there was, nonetheless, some shared identification.

The Pilgrim Code of 1636 was inspired by Mosaic law. In Massachusetts men like John Cotton were trying to form a theocracy as it had been formed in ancient Israel.

CHAPTER TWO

LEFT
James Oglethorpe (1696–1785) was an English general and philanthropist. He founded the colony of Georgia in 1733 as a refuge for debtors; by defeating an attack by the Spanish in 1742 he assured the colony's survival. The religious freedom offered by the colony (to all except Catholics) quickly attracted Jews.

Their official code, the Body of Liberties (1641), was influenced more by the Old Testament than the common law. Congregational New England's political and legal independence was lessened when the British governors general were sent to preside. But far greater than the influence the small group of colonial Jews could have had in America was the influence of their legal and religious tradition in the forming of American democracy.

THE IDEA OF GEORGIA

The colony of Georgia had its birth in 1733 in James Oglethorpe's reaction to Britain's inhumane and scandalous 500-year-old institution of debtors' prison. He wanted a colony in which the debtors could work rather than languish in disease-ridden jails among hardened criminals where they died in greater abundance than those who were convicted. He convinced King George that a colony between Florida and the Carolinas would help keep Spanish aggression in check. But only too quickly his colony became a place for non-debtors in need of economic opportunity.

In its charter, the Georgia of James Oglethorpe's welfare vision was open to all faiths but the Catholic. On July 11, 1733, just five months after the colony received its first settlers, 12 Jewish Ashkenazic families arrived in Georgia from England. The trustees of Savannah were irate. Twelve Jewish families among Savannah's small population of a few hundred threatened "to make a Jews' colony of Georgia." But the trustees themselves had granted commissions to three London Sephardic Jews – Alvaro Suasso, Francis Salvador, and Anthony De Costa – who already had settlers in mind when they agreed to help raise funds to populate the colony. They were thinking of the German Ashkenazic families who had arrived in London seeking solace and support from the Portuguese Bevis Marks congregation. There were differences between the two cultures: the refined, image-minded and sometimes grandiose manners of the Portuguese, who had been insulated in the upper-class milieu, conflicted with the blunt approach of the poorer Germans, who had been insulated in their ghettos.

It is obvious that the Portuguese wanted to help their coreligionists, but it is possible that they were seeking to do it in a way that would remove the Ashkenazic presence from their midst. A Bevis Marks Committee to procure land grants to settle poor Jews was still operative in 1749.

Soon the Ashkenazic Jews were followed by a ship bearing 40 Sephardic Jews. Oglethorpe was badgered not to give Jews land grants, but he did so anyway. In his territory, which did not countenance slavery or the making of rum, Oglethorpe envisioned a land of wine and silk cultivation and horticultural experimentation.

CHAPTER TWO

RIGHT
The Sheftall family came to Georgia in 1733 and soon prospered as planters and merchants. Mordechai Sheftall Sr. (1786–1854) was a hero of the Revolutionary War. He was captured when the British took Savannah in 1778. He later returned to the city and was very active in organizing the large Jewish population.

Already he had found Jews to be a valuable asset in this. One of the Portuguese, Abraham De Lyon, was an accomplished vintner and horticulturalist in Portugal. De Lyon determined that *Portulan malaga* would grow well in Georgia, and the trustees agreed to advance him money to import malaga vines.

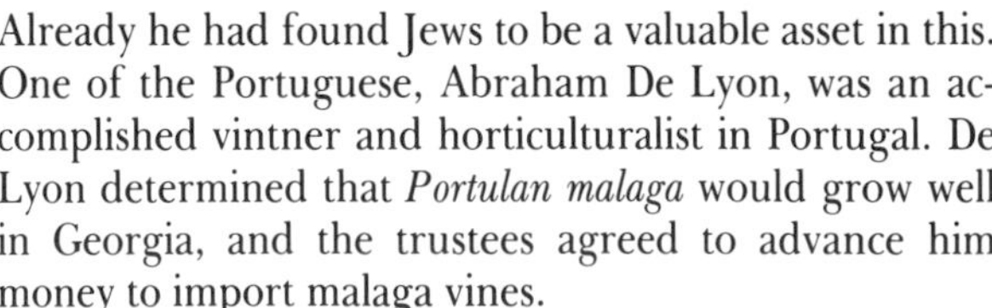

But the climate was never agreeable enough and it soon became apparent that without more farm hands – or the slaves that some in the colony complained were the bulwark of the neighboring agrarian territories – these ventures would not work.

Among the first boatload of Jews was Samuel Nunez Ribiero, a doctor experienced in treating malaria. Oglethorpe wrote to the trustees that Nunez had put a stop to a plague that had taken twenty lives.

Also among the early settlers was Benjamin Sheftall, father of Mordechai, who would later gain a reputation as one of the toughest Revolutionaries. A German-born Englishman, Sheftall, like the Sephardic Samuel Nunez and Abraham Minis (whose son Philip was the first white child born in Georgia), became a wealthy landholder. In 1750, along with Catholic innkeeper Peter Tondee, and Protestant Joshua Smith, Sheftall founded the Union Society, similar to a latter-day community chest. Benjamin's son Mordechai was one of the founders of another organization – the Committee of Safety, which

stole ammunition from the British and sent it north to the troops at Bunker Hill. Benjamin Sheftall was appointed commissary general for Georgia by the Provisional Congress to supply the Continental Army. *His* son, 15-year-old Sheftall Sheftall, was his aide. When Savannah fell, the Sheftalls were captured along with 186 American soldiers. When the colonel realized he had captured Sheftall he put him under special guard. The British commissary general interrogated him, but he would not reveal where American supplies were kept. Finally his interrogator taunted him with the information that Charles Town had fallen two weeks before. Sheftall pointed out that he had a letter from his brother which contradicted this, to which his interrogator said, "Good God, how you poor wretches are deluded by your leaders." Sheftall replied, "If our leaders can deceive wretches, so can yours." He was promptly thrown into jail with his son. They were later sent to Antigua and eventually paroled so that they could arrange their own prisoner-of-war exchange. The custom was to make only equal trades, one general for another. Philadelphia Jews convinced the Continental Army to release a British general in exchange for the Sheftalls and they returned home. Mordechai Sheftall was denounced by the British as a "very great rebel," which put him in the company of two American generals and all the signers of the Declaration of Independence.

One of the notes of discord that marked the settling of Georgia's Jews was the stance of superiority assumed by the Sephardic Jews, who refused to worship with the Ashkenazim. The Ashkenazim sought the company of the recently arrived German Protestants. The German Lutheran pastor, The Reverend Bolzius, wrote to a colleague describing the old hut in which the German Jews were praying, and mentioned that they had asked him to intervene in helping them get permission to build a synagogue. "The Spanish and Portuguese Jews are against the German Jews and they are going to protest the petition by the German Jews to build a synagogue. The German Jews would like to be on good terms with us, and they have done us small favors time and again . . ."

In Pennsylvania William Penn founded his Quaker colony on the land grant he obtained from Charles II as repayment of a debt. The colony was open to other religions, but many, including Jews, were not enfranchised.

For the most part the people who had fled from religious persecution to deliverance on these shores were resistant to the idea of the equally valid deliverance of others. Quakers, whose less formal ways seemed to enrage the Puritans, were banned in Massachusetts. Between 1659 and 1661 four Quaker women were put to death in Boston for preaching. While the Jews were settling and gaining their rights in New Amsterdam, Quakers, Lutherans, and Catholics were banned by the Dutch Reformed colony. Anti-papist feeling ran high, and Catholics were distrusted. In Connecticut no one could take a seat in the legislature without making "a declaration against Popery." And, still smarting from the Anglican excesses against them, the Puritans would not allow Episcopalians to preach in Massachusetts until the eighteenth century. As late as 1868 discriminatory laws in New Hampshire were on the books against Catholics and Jews. The patchwork was, indeed, intricate. Only by granting freedom – through democracy – to the others would each group insure its own. But there was land, there were dreams, there was the sense of building a future – and no impetus to enshrine the European past. Jefferson's "pursuit of happiness" would have been unthinkable in any but the American idiom. As John Adams observed to him: "Your taste is judicious in liking better the dreams of the future than the history of the past."

In the English philosopher John Locke's constitution for Carolina, religious freedom was a main consideration. "If we allow the Jews to have private houses and dwelling places among us, why should we not allow them to have synagogues?" he wrote of the people, a few of whom came up to Carolina from Barbados as early as 1665.

Francis Salvador arrived in South Carolina from England in 1773. A grandson of the Salvador who had raised money to bring Jewish settlers to Georgia, his plantation in South Carolina included land that his father had purchased years before. Like many London Sephardic merchants, the Salvadors suffered great financial losses in 1772 when England and Holland were at war and all trading between them stopped. One of Salvador's remaining assets, his land in the colonies, offered him a chance to rebuild his fortune. Once here, however, the Revolutionary cause became his passion. Building a fortune took a back seat to the political events and the quickening pace of American protest. Within a year after his arrival Salvador was elected to the first Provincial Congress of South Carolina, which met in Charleston to draft grievances to be submitted to the royal governor. The Provincial Congress subsequently became the First Assembly of the State of South Carolina, making Salvador the first Jewish American elected to a popular assembly. Under the state's first constitution, members of the Congress were not required to take the oath of a Christian, so Salvador was not faced with the obstacle that, out of conscience, prevented many Jews from seeking an active political life. When the British governor refused to recognize the congress, its members, who were busily advising the colonists to arm themselves, were in jeopardy.

In a brutal move, the British recruited Indians to massacre colonists inland while they pursued a military strategy on the coast.

CHAPTER TWO

RIGHT
The grave of Reverend Moses Cohen is in this cemetery in Charleston, one of the oldest Jewish cemeteries in America.

Along with his friend Major Andrew Williamson, Salvador raised a force of 500 men and led several campaigns against the Tories and their Indian allies. On August 1, 1776, while probably still unaware that the Declaration of Independence had been adopted – though he had been awaiting news of it daily – Salvador was shot. When he was found lying in the woods still alive, the Indians scalped him. Before he died Williamson was able to tell him that they had routed the enemy. "He said he was glad of it, and shook me by the hand and bade me farewell and said he would die in a few minutes." Salvador's three years of American life were dedicated to strengthening the Patriot cause. He was one of the first Jews to die defending the fledgling America.

In Charleston's City Hall Park a plaque commemorating Salvador reads:

> An Englishman, he cast his lot with America;
> True to his ancient faith, he gave his life
> For new hopes of liberty and understanding.

Another prominent Jewish South Carolinian, Moses Lindo was a technologist, certainly one of the few in the colonies at that time. He was perhaps the foremost expert of his time on dyes, especially indigo, the blue vegetable dye widely used on cotton. He worked on scientific experiments to achieve new dyes, and believed that the indigo plants of South Carolina could produce a better quality dye than he had seen elsewhere. After testifying to this in the House of Commons he went to Charleston in 1756 for the purpose of exporting the dye, and stayed. He had worked for 25 years at sorting and grading the plant, and once here immediately began to promote South Carolina indigo. In 1762 he was appointed Inspector General of Indigo Drugs and Dyes. Largely through his efforts indigo manufacturing became one of the colonies' chief industries.

When Reverend Hezekiah Smith of New England came to Charleston to raise funds for Rhode Island College in 1769, Lindo made a substantial donation, raising money from his friends as well. The school that was to become Brown University did not inquire into the religion of its students – which made Lindo eager to contribute. His own experience as a scholar had been marred because the schools he attended in England would not graduate Jews, and despite his participation in their curricula he was officially considered only an auditor.

After Lindo's generous contribution the trustees read into the charter the following addition: "That the children of the Jews may be admitted into this institution and entirely enjoy the freedom of their own religion, without any constraint or imposition whatever." At that time there were no Jewish students at Rhode Island College.

A Jewish Heritage

ABOVE
The city of Toledo in Spain was a major center of Jewish intellectual life for centuries. The Singagoa del Transito still stands.

ABOVE
When the Jews of Toledo in Spain were expelled in 1492, they left behind the beautiful Sinagoga del Transito.

ABOVE

This thirteenth-century synagogue in Toledo is now the Church of Santa Maria la Blanca.

PAGES 36 & 37

The beautiful interior of the Touro Synagogue in Newport, Rhode Island. The building is now a National Historic Landmark.

ABOVE
The first congregation on the island of the Curaçao in the Dutch West Indies was formed by refugees from Brazil in 1654. The Sephardic synagogue built there in 1732 is the oldest in the Western Hemisphere.

PAGES 38 & 39
The synagogue at Charlotte Amalie, St. Thomas, United States Virgin Islands, is one of the oldest in North America.

ABOVE
The home of merchant Moses Myers, dating from around 1792, is a historical landmark in Norfolk, Virginia. Myers was a wealthy and cultivated music lover who collected music manuscripts and instruments.

ABOVE
Luxurious original furnishings and portraits of family members by Gilbert Stuart and Thomas Sully can still be seen at the Moses Myers house in Norfolk, Virginia.

ABOVE
Kahel Kadosh Beth Elohim in Charleston, South Carolina, was founded in 1749. It is the oldest congregation in the state and the fourth oldest in North America.

ABOVE
The original building of the Adas Israel synagogue in Washington, D.C., was dedicated in 1878.

RIGHT
For thousands of immigrants entering New York Harbor, the Statue of Liberty was a symbol of hope for a new life in the new world.

ABOVE
Immigrants were processed at Ellis Island before being allowed to board the ferry that took them to Manhattan Island. The buildings are now preserved as a national monument.

ABOVE
Thousands of new arrivals flooded into the crowded streets of New York City's Lower East Side. The area today still has a large Jewish population. It is noted around the world for the bargains found in its stores.

ABOVE

One of the principal financiers of the Revolutionary War was Haym Salomon. Born in Poland in 1740, he came to America in 1772. He was an ardent patriot and was crucial in maintaining the public credit of the fledgling United States. Salomon died in 1785.

THE REVOLUTION & AFTER

CHAPTER THREE

An energetic, Polish-born man of 32 arrived in New York in 1772. Haym Salomon had traveled extensively in Europe and spoke several languages. He started out as a dry goods merchant, but in 1776 began an active involvement with the American cause. He accompanied General Philip Schuyler's troops to Lake George as a sutler – supplying them with food and clothes. In September of 1776, when the British controlled New York City, he was arrested as a spy – presumably as a member of the Sons of Liberty, who planned to send fire ships into the harbor to destroy the British fleet. In prison he was made an interpreter by the commander of the Hessian mercenaries (they had hired out to fight for King George) and Salomon translated for prisoners and guards who hailed from all over the European continent. Because of this he was allowed to continue his business (by that time he was again trading) and in 1777 married Rachel Franks, daughter of the prominent merchant Moses Franks. As he went about his prison duties he aided in the escape of American and French prisoners – and in convincing Hessians to desert. When a second arrest became imminent he fled to Philadelphia. There he started his financial trading without even the money to rent an office. Ads in the local paper announced that he could be found at the Coffee House between the hours of noon and two, a low-overhead operation that nonetheless began to yield enough profit so that he could open an office on Front Street. He got the business of the French Minister to Philadelphia, who made him the official broker of all French bills of exchange, and paymaster for French troops supporting America.

During this perilous time, when the Continental Congress couldn't raise enough money through taxes to pay the salaries of Washington's troops, or buy enough supplies, the government had to run on loans from abroad. The financier, Robert Morris, soon to be a founder of the Bank of North America, was put in charge of government financing. Haym Salomon was one of the brokers Morris used to cash the foreign bills of exchange. Salomon kept government currency at a manageable level, and sold bills of exchange at the highest prices to raise money for the war effort.

Salomon was known for his reliability and generosity. Representatives in Congress often went unsalaried and Salomon would lend them money at no interest. As James Madison, who was often in financial straits, wrote, "The kindness of our little friend in Front Street, near the coffee house, is a fund which will preserve me from extremities, but I never resort to it without great mortification, as he so obstinately rejects all recompense. The price of money is so usurious that he thinks it ought to be extorted from none but those who aim at a profitable speculation . . ."

When Philadelphia could no longer take care of its poor, Salomon gave out $2,000. He contributed amply to Congregation Mikveh Israel, and donated Torah scrolls to the synagogue. Many of those who borrowed from him could not repay their loans. Salomon died in 1785 from an illness he had contracted while in prison nine years earlier. He died intestate, his finances in disarray. His assets had depreciated, and after the debts against his estate were paid his family was left with only its furniture intact. Later his son made claims against the government for loans that he alleged were never repaid, but Congress would not act to honor them. Too many financial statements were missing or unable to be verified.

Along with the bonds that Salomon sold for the government, the personal loans that he advanced helped the wheels keep turning for the American effort. He gave his own money to insure that the Spanish ambassador could be maintained by the Revolutionary government at a time when the British had cut communication with Europe, thus helping to keep American credibility undamaged. Of one of Salomon's borrowers, Judge James Wilson, it was stated: "Judge Wilson, so distinguished for his labors in the Convention that framed the Federal Constitution, would have retired from public service had he not been sustained by the timely aid of Haym Salomon . . ."

A statue of George Washington, Robert Morris, and Haym Salomon stands in Chicago. The inscription for Salomon reads:

CHAPTER THREE

RIGHT
A view of the interior of Congregation Mikveh Israel, the first synagogue in Philadelphia. Haym Salomon prayed here.

BELOW
The famed Pinto prayer book, published in 1766. The prayers follow the Sephardic ritual, but are presented in English – a radical departure for the time.

Haym Salomon
Gentleman, Scholar, Patriot
A banker whose only interest was
The interest of his country.

The Jews in colonial America were true to their religious heritage. Emerging from the rabbinical constraints of the ghetto, or the dual Christian/Jewish lives of the Marranos, they managed to pioneer a Judaism that met their needs and allowed them to follow the enduring principles of the religion. Isaac Pinto translated a prayer book for the High Holidays into English, published in 1766, so that his brethren could better understand the service. Gershom Mendes Seixas included sermons in the service; other reforms would be on the way. Synagogue life kept the Jewish communities together and watched that the dietary laws were kept; but at no time did membership put them under the harsher watchfulness that some in Protestant sects endured at home and in their businesses. Many of the descendents of Sephardim and early Ashkenazim fell in love with, and married, Christians but not because they spurned their religion – baptisms were relatively few. Despite the gloomy prediction that with less and less pressure to retain the faith it would be lost, this did not happen.

From the first there was a general regard for religion that had Jews and Christians giving money to needy churches and synagogues. Seven Jews contributed the funds to get the steeple of New York's Trinity Church built. Asser Levy advanced the money for the Methodists to build their first church in New York. When the walls of Shearith Israel's cemetery were caving in, Christian businessmen contributed to help shore them up. And when the British occupation of New York ended and the New York congregation left their temporary residences in Philadelphia and went home, the Philadelphia congregation, now facing financial hardship made a general appeal for funds. Among those who responded were Benjamin Franklin and David Rittenhouse.

The Old Testament was the sacred book of many Protestant sects who, like the Jews, were seeking new freedoms; the sense of coming into and building a promised land sustained them. Both the Massachusetts theo-

PRAYERS
FOR
SHABBATH, ROSH-HASHANAH, AND KIPPUR,
OR
The SABBATH, the BEGINNING of the YEAR,
AND
The DAY of ATONEMENTS;
WITH
The AMIDAH and MUSAPH of the MOADIM,
OR
SOLEMN SEASONS.
According to the Order of the Spaniſh and Portugueſe Jews.
TRANSLATED BY *ISAAC PINTO.*
And for him printed by JOHN HOLT, in New-York,
A. M. 5526.

crats and such men as Thomas Hooker – who has been called the founder of American democracy – used it to support their differing views of government. The Old Testament was very much in the thinking of the Founding Fathers as well. On July 4, 1776, Ben Franklin, Samuel Adams, and Thomas Jefferson were appointed by the Continental Congress to produce a seal for the United States. They chose a design with Pharoah and his men on horseback in the Red Sea, in pursuit of Moses and the Israelites, who stood on the opposite side. The motto was: "Rebellion against tyranny is obedience to God."

Throughout the colonial era Jews were vigilant about their rights. They won religious, civic, and economic rights early on, but political rights were another matter. They voted in some local elections, but in most places could not hold office. As the Revolutionary spirit grew, so did their commitment. Jewish soldiers died for the cause, and Jewish merchants gave up their businesses. After that, the need for full poltical participation became greater. In 1783 Barnard Gratz and Haym Salomon were among the members of Philadelphia's Mikveh Israel congregation who signed a petition to the Council of Censors, asking that the wording of the oath of office be amended so as to include non-Christians. In 1787 Jonas Phillips wrote the only letter on a religious (but by its nature, political) issue received by the Constitutional Convention. He wrote that to "swear and believe that the New Testament was given by divine inspiration is absolutely against the religious principle of a Jew . . ."

The same plucky Jonas, who would give America two famous grandsons, Uriah Phillips Levy and Mordechai Noah, left New York City and his lucrative business when it was occupied by the British. He settled in Philadelphia with his wife and 15 children, and enlisted in the militia as a private. In 1793 he was fined ten pounds in Pennsylvania for refusing to testify on the Sabbath.

If some hopes were fulfilled on a federal level in 1789, with the equal rights assured by the Constitution, it would take years before the individual states changed their discriminatory laws against non-Christians.

Maryland is an example of the massive effort it took to finally get what was called "The Jew Bill" passed.

Barnard Gratz of Philadelphia (signer, along with Haym Salomon, of the Philadelphia petition to amend the oath of office) and his brother Michael were among the wealthiest merchants in the country. Their pack trains and barges brought goods to the farthest settlements. As people pushed westward, so did the Gratz supplies. With his son-in-law Solomon Etting of Baltimore, a director of the Union Bank, Gratz petitioned the Maryland legislature for the "sect of people called Jews . . . to be placed on the same footing as other good citizens."

They were turned down, but Etting persisted, joined by Jacob Cohen, a man whose life history seemed to

CHAPTER THREE

LEFT
German-born Barnard Gratz (1738–1811) was an important merchant in Philadelphia. He was a financier of the Revolutionary War and was very active in Jewish life.

parallel his own. Both were brought up by mothers who were widows, both were railroad directors, and eventually each served as president of the Baltimore City Council. The legislature kept burying the Gratz, Etting, and Cohen petitions, but this state of affairs changed with the appearance on the scene of Thomas Kennedy. The Scottish-born farmer's son was elected to the Maryland legislature in 1817. A diligent man who wanted American democracy to live up to its claims, Kennedy studied the federal and state constitutions and saw that Maryland was denying the right of office to Jews.

Maryland had gone through two major changes in its official religion. Founded by Lord Baltimore in 1632 as a Catholic colony that extended equal rights to Protestants, the colony's religion was changed to Church of England in 1692, three years after William of Orange took the throne of England. Maryland's Catholics were effectively disenfranchised by 1718, when they were forbidden to hold public office. The Revolutionary War changed all that as democracy entered into the relationship between Christians. The Maryland constitution recognized every citizen's right to worship God in ways "acceptable to Him." No qualification was required to hold state office other than "such oath and support of fidelity to the state and a declaration of belief in the Christian religion."

Kennedy felt it was his duty to help the Jews gain the right to hold office. He chaired the committee that introduced a bill, popularly called "Kennedy's Jew Baby," to

CHAPTER THREE

RIGHT
Solomon Etting (1764–1847) was the son-in-law of Barnard Gratz. Etting's persistent efforts to force the Maryland legislature to grant equal rights to Jews finally paid off in 1826.

FAR RIGHT
Rachel Gratz (1764–1831), daughter of Barnard Gratz (one of the wealthiest merchants in the country) was the wife of Solomon Etting.

extend the rights of the Maryland constitution to Jews. Perhaps Kennedy's forthright statement, "I am free to declare that if Christianity cannot stand without the aid of persecution, let it fall; and let a new system, more rational and more benevolent, take its place," did not help matters. The bill was defeated. Issues other than the Jewish one came into play: state government versus strong central government, the general debate about whether America was a Christian country, the new immigrations of 1815 that brought out nativist reactionaries. Kennedy persisted. This time he introduced a more broadly worded bill, describing it as "an Act to extend to the citizens of Maryland the same civil rights and privileges that are enjoyed under the Constitution of the United States." It passed, but as a constitutional amendment it had to be confirmed by the next legislature. Here it ran into trouble again, "Prejudice, prejudice is against the Bill, and you know prejudice has many followers," Kennedy wrote to a friend. Support for the Jews triggered a strong response from those opposed. In the election of 1823, Kennedy lost his seat, but won it back in 1825. The Jews introduced another petition, this time campaigning more actively for the bill and gaining the support of the press. It was passed in January of 1826, with religious overtones. Those taking office had to swear to uphold the Maryland and United States constitutions and "make and subscribe a declaration of his belief in a future state of rewards and punishments."

Perhaps the legacy of the colonial Jewish Americans to their present-day brethren is best summed up by historian Jacob Rader Marcus: "Colonial Jewry wrote the pattern of acculturation which made it possible for the Jew to remain a Jew and to become an American."

The Revolution had put many of the powerful Jewish merchants into bankruptcy. Times were hard in the post-revolutionary era. American exports fell by $54 million by 1814, and the import-export business was no longer a viable occupation. Jews concentrated on land speculation, went more heavily into retail businesses, and began to work for government bureaux as treasury agents, customs inspectors, and the like. In 1815 immigration brought new arrivals who would push westward. Soon Jews from central and eastern Europe would be found settling parts of the wild new frontier.

Thomas Jefferson's dreams for the future included an expanding United States, and he achieved a far greater expansion than he had foreseen. In 1803 he sent his emissaries James Monroe and Robert Livingston to negotiate with Napoleon for the island of New Orleans so that the tiny America could have a port on the Mississippi. When Napoleon offered them the whole Louisiana Territory for $15 million, and with no time to write and await the president's reply, the two signed the contract for the purchase. The vast territory more than doubled the area of the United States.

Now Americans could do what they had relentlessly and characteristically been doing anyway – forge trails and found settlements westward – but without trespassing on French territory.

A year before this greatest of acquisitions, 27-year-old Judah Touro moved from Newport, Rhode Island to New Orleans, the bright, city of many languages and

races. Touro is considered to be America's first full-fledged philanthropist, having crafted a will that bequeathed most of his considerable fortune to causes and charities in several states. He is said by some to have earned his money through great acumen, and by others simply through caution, ploddingly, by holding onto real estate and other investments that accrued as the city grew. He has been described as both a major personality in New Orleans, and a reclusive man. He is today still a man of mystery. But there is something more compelling in the idea of a Judah Touro who lived a tight financial existence and whose will was perhaps the most creative act of his life.

In his famous will, which contained 65 bequests, Touro left money to 15 Jewish congregations in 15 cities. In Boston, where he spent some of his formative years, his money went to Massachusetts General Hospital, asylums for boys and girls, and the Humane Society. In Newport, it went for the building of a public park and the Newport Tower. In New Orleans the funds were spent to fight yellow fever and for the Touro Infirmary. During his lifetime he had provided the funds to rebuild the First Congregational Church of New Orleans, and to build a free public library (the first such in the United States) and a synagogue. In 1840 he rescued the Bunker Hill monument and helped turn it into a national shrine with $10,000. Both he and his brother Abraham, donated enough money to renovate the Newport Synagogue, where their family had once worshipped, and which had all but gone to ruin. Over $483,000 went to charity, an unheard-of sum in that day. In Newport, where he is buried his tombstone reads: "The last of his name, he inscribed it in the book of philanthropy, to be remembered forever."

New Orleans was itself a new frontier for Judaism, for there it was practiced in a unique manner. So many Jewish men had married Christians that when the first congregation was formed in 1828 it simply did away with the Jewish law that in intermarriage only the child of a Jewish mother will be considered Jewish. In New Orleans – thought to be a place of almost religious anar-

CHAPTER THREE

LEFT
Enigmatic Judah Touro (1775–1854) was America's first genuine philanthropist.

FAR LEFT
Michael Gratz, brother to Barnard, had twelve children. Best-known among them were Hyman, who endowed Gratz College in Philadelphia; Rebecca, who began the Jewish Sunday-school movement; and Jacob, who became a politician. Benjamin, shown here, carried on the family business.

BELOW LEFT
Scottish-born Thomas Kennedy fought for political equality for Jews in Maryland. As a member of the state legislature he sponsored several bills, beginning in 1817, but it was not until 1826 that one was passed.

CHAPTER THREE

RIGHT
The father of the state of Texas, Sam Houston (1793–1863), encouraged Jewish emigration to the area.

OPPOSITE ABOVE
Jews fought for Texas in every stage of its struggle for recognition. Dr. Moses Albert Levy was chief surgeon of the Volunteer Army that attacked the Alamo in 1835.

OPPOSITE BELOW
Henri Castro, a French Jew from Alsace, contributed to Sam Houston's fight for Texas independence. He organized the emigration of some 5,000 settlers. Today his memory lives on in Castro County and Castroville.

chy by the staid Northeastern Jews – they made their own rules. The children of Jewish fathers and Christian mothers were accepted as members of the congregation.

In 1815 the forces of change abroad, brought about by the French Revolution and spread by Napoleon's armies, were stilled at Waterloo. With the monarchs re-ascending their thrones, poorer Europeans, who had but too briefly experienced dynamic new freedoms, began to make their way to America. Among them were Jews who had been released from their ghetto existence by Napoleon, but were now without ghetto walls, surrounded once again by repressive laws and restrictions.

Both American-born and newly arrived Jews went west to settle the new territories. Mexico won its independence from Spain and opened its borders to all, though soon it feared the possible encroachment of America and began to limit settlers, sending in a militia to keep watch against Americans arming themselves. Samuel Izaacs arrived in Texas territory with Stephen Austin's party in 1821 as one of the Old Three Hundred, Texas's earliest settlers. He received a land grant, first from Mexico, and subsequently from the Republic of Texas, for his efforts in the fight for Texas independence.

Adolphus Sterne came to the United States from Cologne in 1817, and moved to Nacogdoches, East Texas, in 1826. He managed to thrive by keeping a delicate balance in the shifting affairs between Mexico and Texas until the day when his active support for the Texan cause could come into play. Shortly after settling in, he supported the Fredonian Rebellion, a local Texas uprising of Americans. The Mexicans sentenced him to death for supplying arms to the rebels, but he was saved when the international Order of Masons came to his aid and got him pardoned in return for a pledge of allegiance to the government of Mexico. He became an active Mexican citizen, a mayor, councilman, and city treasurer. He was known for his sharp sense of humor, and could speak several languages, including Indian dialects. But when the Texas revolt finally came, Sterne went to New Orleans to raise money and troops for the cause. After Texas became the twenty-eighth state in 1845, Sterne continued his career in politics, serving in the state legislature where once, during an unrelievedly dull session, he got up and made a speech in Choctaw. When he died in 1852, he was a state senator.

Another Jew who fought for Texan independence was Dr. Moses Albert Levy. He, too, went to New Orleans to raise troops to fight for the cause. He was surgeon-in-chief of the Volunteer Army and one of the men who, in 1836, attacked the Alamo.

As the Lone Star Republic, Texas was independent yet desirous of union with the United States. Its president, Sam Houston, eagerly looked for Europeans to settle the new republic. Henri Castro, a French Jew from Alsace, contributed large sums of money to Houston's struggle. He was made consul general to France and in 1842, was offered a land grant. He set about the arduous task of populating his land with settlers from Alsace-Lorraine, putting much of his own money – over $150,000 – into the project. His colorful notices in French and German praised the opportunities of this wilderness stuck in the middle of Indian territory. Starting with the first settlement, Castroville, up to 5,000 people eventually settled the land. From his own funds Castro paid for the supplies, housing, and farming tools of the first 700. By 1847, a mere five years after he had begun his project, his money was drained. He had expected, as compensation, to receive half of the land settled by each colonist, but was overruled by the state. The settlers kept all of their acreage. Castro was awarded 38,000 acres – worth a mere ten cents an acre. The Comte de Castro, as he styled himself, who had always kept aloof from his settlers, continued in reduced and lonely circumstances to exercise his sense of aristocracy. After his death in 1867, Castro's efforts were recognized when Texas named Castro County in his memory. Today Castroville, Texas, population 2,000, has the nation's largest Alsatian community outside of New York City.

Jews fought for Texas in every stage of its struggle; they were among the merchants who brought goods into Mexico, and operated on the Santa Fe Trail. It is impossible to know precisely how many of them took part, since in the Mexican territories, with their legacy of the Spanish Inquisition Jews were naturally cautious about revealing their religious background.

Jews fought as well in the Mexican-American war, and it was but a moment in time after it ended that gold was

CHAPTER THREE

LEFT
A banker in nineteenth-century Texas, Harris Kempner (1837–1894) was one of the state's Jewish pioneers.

BELOW LEFT
One of the very earliest Texas pioneers was Jacob De Cordova. He was American-born of Sephardic background; otherwise, little is known of him.

CHAPTER THREE

RIGHT
Jews played an important role in the settling of the Southwest, primarily as merchants. Mr. and Mrs. Philip Drachman were among the earliest pioneers in Arizona.

BELOW
The Moise family was prominent in Southern affairs starting in 1791. Columbus Moise was chief justice of the New Mexico Territory in the nineteenth century.

FAR RIGHT
Joseph Jonas (1792–1869) was born in Exeter, England. In 1817 he became the first Jew to settle in Cincinnati, Ohio.

discovered in the California hills. Among the thousands pushing west Jews would play a prominent role in settling the towns and cities that sprang up like instant shrines around that precious metal.

In 1817 Joseph Jonas, a young Jew from Plymouth, England, crossed the Cumberland Gap into Cincinnati. It took him two months to get to the city of 6,000, where he earned his keep repairing watches. The loneliness hung heavily on him until two years later when he was joined by his two brothers and two friends. They worshipped as best they could, indeed, as Jonas himself had done all along, there being no minyan. But within seven years there were enough Jews to form a congregation, Bene Israel – the only one within 500 miles. From the first, out of expedience and respect for one another's needs, the congregation made its own reforms. It was comprised mostly of young people. The men had previously followed German and Polish services, and some of their wives had been brought up in Portuguese congregations. In an interesting example of the struggle between those who wanted to reform the service and those who wanted custom to prevail, Jonas describes the life of the congregation. "We . . . introduced considerable chorus singing into our worship, in which we were joined by the sweet voices of the fair daughters of Zion, and our Friday evening service was as well attended for many years as the Sabbath morning . . . At length, however, large emigrations of our German brethren settled

CHAPTER THREE

LEFT
The Jewish population of Cincinnati prospered and grew. This photograph of the New Jewish Synagogue was taken around 1890.

amongst us; again our old customs have conquered, and the sweet voices of our ladies are seldom heard."

This tug between time-honored ritual and reform was an interesting precursor in a city that was later destined to become the center of the Reform movement.

How to live a fully integrated American life and yet nurture a Jewish religious background was not just a problem in the wilderness. It was a problem for the well-connected, urbane gentleman who could just as easily abandon all ties to Judaism and live his life in a Christian milieu. Many of the Sephardic Jews had begun to do just that. But not Commodore Uriah Phillips Levy. Propelled by a large ego and a mercurial temperament, Levy embarked on a personal Odyssey in which he carefully nurtured a sense of his Jewishness as part of his American character. His great-great-grandfather had been physician to King John V of Portugal; George Washington attended his grandparent's wedding; and his grandfather Jonas Phillips was a stalwart American who stood up equally for his country in war and for his religion when it came time for his country to frame its laws of equality.

No Jew had ever been an American naval officer when the Philadelphia-bred Levy decided, at the age of ten, that an illustrious naval career would be his life's goal. He ran away to sea, served for two years as a cabin boy on a merchant vessel, and came home in time to prepare for his bar mitzvah. At 14, despite the protests of his parents, he was back at sea, and, in March of 1817, the 25-year-old Levy began his rise from the ranks, and got his commission as a lieutenant in the Navy. He was the Navy's second Jewish officer (Levi Charles Harby was the first).

Levy's career, in fact, was a campaign in itself. The anti-Semitism he encountered and his own fiery temperament were such that only his great tenacity brought him through six court martials to the rank of commodore. When Levy first witnessed a flogging he vowed to work toward getting the Navy practice abolished. That resolve was viewed as counter to the spirit of a good Navy man. But in 1831, as commander of the *Vandalia,* he informed his crew there would be no corporal punishment on his ship. He eventually wrote letters to the newspapers against the practice, and lectured against it as well. By the 1850s the issue was ripe for national debate. Factions were formed, and soon the issue was taken up in Congress by Senator John P. Hale of New Hampshire, who got the practice abolished.

Levy's quick temper, his readiness to pursue insults (which by turns may have attracted them), his many well-publicized trials in which it became obvious that anti-Jewish feeling was a motivation for much of his trouble, raised the issue of anti-Semitism in a public manner that dismayed the quiet Sephardic families. Their breeding made them uneasy about calling attention to themselves in any way. But Levy's passion for seeing Jews treated

CHAPTER THREE

BELOW RIGHT
One of the more colourful characters in American Jewish history is Uriah Phillips Levy (1792–1862). He went to sea as a boy, fought in the War of 1812, and eventually became flag officer of the Mediterranean fleet, at that time the Navy's highest post. His untiring efforts eventually brought about the abolition of corporal punishment in the Navy. Levy also purchased Thomas Jefferson's home in Virginia, Monticello. His son gave the home to the nation to be preserved as a national monument.

equally stayed with him. He made eloquent speeches at his trials in which he attacked the anti-Semitism of his fellow officers.

He won, although slowly and at great cost, all his battles with the Navy. The last one, in 1855, was against the Navy's Act to Promote the Efficiency of the Navy, by which Levy and 200 other officers were declared incapable of further service. The act was apparently aimed at those who had created problems for the brass. In a petition, Levy's lawyer, Benjamin Butler, stated the Navy's real objections to Levy: He had come up through the ranks, he had spoken out against corporal punishment, and he was Jewish. Anti-Semitism in the armed forces had been revealed, and some attempt to deal with it would have to be made. By the time he died, Levy was a commodore in his beloved Navy and had been given command of the entire Mediterranean fleet.

Mordecai Manuel Noah, Uriah Phillips Levy's first cousin, was the leading light in the social and political life of New York. Diplomat, journalist, newspaper owner and editor, playwright, he too sought to solve some of the problems Jews faced. He was perceptive about some of the long-range issues, and some of his ideas were ahead of his time. But others were spurred by self-promotion and an outrageous ego.

Born in 1785 and orphaned at age seven, Noah went to live in Philadelphia with his grandfather, Jonas Phillips. Noah became the editor of a Charleston newspaper that supported James Madison and when Madison became president Noah was appointed United States consul in Tunis, the first Jewish-American diplomat in an official post abroad. By all accounts he performed his duties in an exemplary manner. An example of his skill, very much in line with his own idealism, was evident in a challenge he received from his counterpart, the British consul in Tunis. In 1812, when Britain and America were at war, the British consul complained to the ruler of Tunis that Americans had disposed of the British vessels they had captured. He maintained this was against Tunis's treaty with England, which prohibited such disposals by Christian countries. Noah pointed out – with successful results – that the American treaty with Tunis stated, "The Government of the United States is in no sense founded on the Christian religion."

While in Tunis, Noah ransomed American sailors held captive by pirates. There was some question as to whether the French-speaking sailors were American citizens, as claimed, but with no way of gaining actual proof and with lives at stake, he effected the rescue. Having done his work so successfully, Noah was mystified and enraged when he received a cryptic letter from Secretary of State Monroe, stating that while his religion was not thought to be an obstacle when he was assigned to Tunis, it would now "produce a very unfavorable effect." Since he was held in high esteem by the Tunisian ruler and the other consuls, Noah could only think this a matter of anti-Semitism. In later years, Madison assured him that his religion was not the reason for the recall; it remains an unsolved mystery. But this incident, combined with what he saw of the impoverished and limited lives of Jews in North Africa, made Noah more keenly aware of the difficult circumstances of many of the world's Jews. He began to nurture the dream of Jews reclaiming their homeland in Palestine.

Back in New York, Noah achieved great success as a playwright, with efforts that he readily admitted were mediocre. His best-known play, *She Would Be a Soldier* (1820), has some importance because it was an American patriotic play put on at a time when English imports were standard fare in American theaters.

Noah's plan to help the Jews involved settling Jews in need from abroad in their own colony in the United States, where they could then learn to farm in preparation for settling later in Palestine. He managed, with a contribution from a friend, to get land on Grand Island, near Buffalo, New York. He began to see himself as a redeemer, assuming the grandiose self-image of a Jewish prophet. The American Jewish community did not give him much support, but he made much of the opening of his city, called Ararat. His loyal friend A. B. Seixas was beside him on the day he officially declared before the world that Ararat was open to Jews everywhere. He put on a splendid parade, dressed in royal robes. His speech – in which he declared himself governor and judge of Israel – was laced with royal commands: "It is my will

that a census be taken . . . those who do not wish to settle are permitted to stay in their own countries . . ."

Was it the stuff of delusional fantasy, or the self-promoting showmanship of a newspaper owner? After the opening ceremonies he left his place of refuge, returned to New York, and the project was abandoned.

He was spirited, though. When he was serving as sheriff of New York an outraged bigot said to him: "Fine thing that a Jew should be hanging Christians!" The sheriff answered, "Fine Christians, to need hanging by anyone!"

Not all of Noah was outrageous vanity. He continued to lecture and write about Jewish resettlement in Palestine, basing much of his argument on concrete facts. The United States, he pointed out, supported the independence of Greeks, Africans, and South Americans. Why not the Jews?

He was direct in voicing his displeasure with Christian missionaries who put such effort into helping Jews in order to evangelize them. He assured the missionaries that the Second Advent for which they so fervently yearned would more likely come about with the Jews settled in Palestine as Jews, the way Jesus had left them.

He felt that Christian help, including that of the missionary societies, was essential in establishing more Jews in Palestine, but he wanted this to be given on humanitarian grounds, not with the aim of conversion. Many Jewish leaders were incensed, however, that he could turn to the missionary societies, who had never desisted in their conversion efforts.

Rebecca Gratz's concern for Jews and Judaism was abiding. The daughter of Michael Gratz, she was born into the leading Jewish family in Philadelphia; her legendary beauty is preserved in portraits painted by Thomas Sully and E. G. Malbone. She was brought up in luxury in a house where statesmen, scholars, and philosophers regularly dined. Her own friends were serious writers and painters, including James Fenimore Cooper, William Cullen Bryant, and Washington Irving. But her religion always took precedence. She was disapproving of Jews who had no interest in their religious heritage, and wrote a cautionary letter to her brother, Joseph, who was about to visit New Orleans. ". . . At New Orleans, there are many who call themselves Jews, or at least whose parentage being known are obliged to acknowledge themselves such, but who neglect those duties which would make that title honorable and then respected . . ."

She was a gifted organizer for Jewish and nonsectarian causes, and played an important role in the nineteenth-century movement to bring some unity into the separate Jewish congregational existences. But her most important contribution was in strengthening Jewish education in America. She saw how faulty it was, with no proper prayerbooks for children, and no context in which they could learn about their heritage. In March 1838, along with Louisa B. Hart, Ellen Phillips, and Sim'ha Peixotto, she founded the Jewish Sunday school movement. They began with 50 pupils, and before long were training teachers for schools in other areas. There is a memorable story of how Gratz, with few resources, had to use Christian Sunday school bible books. She would carefully paste paper over the objectionable passages, which no amount of prying by the giggling students would loosen.

Her concern for social welfare started early. By the time she was 20, she was secretary of the Female Association for the Relief of Women and Children in Reduced Circumstances, Philadelphia's first nonsectarian society to aid the poor. She helped found the Philadelphia Orphan Asylum, and started the Female Hebrew Benevolent Society. Gratz's Jewish philanthropic organizations were formed independent of the synagogue, a trend that would burgeon until, in another departure for the Jews in America, the major Jewish charitable organizations would be run by laymen.

Part of the Rebecca Gratz legend resides in the story of the writing of another legend: *Ivanhoe*. The author Washington Irving was once engaged to one of Rebecca's closest friends, Matilda Hoffman, the daughter of a judge in whose office Irving had studied law. When Matilda contracted tuberculosis, Rebecca nursed her day and night, but despite these efforts she succumbed to the disease. Some years later Irving visited Sir Walter Scott in England and told him all about the beautiful Rebecca and her devotion. She became the inspiration for the character Rebecca in his novel *Ivanhoe*.

Rebecca herself never married, supposedly because she had been in love with young Sam Ewing, whose father was provost of the University of Pennsylvania, but would not marry out of her religion.

LEFT
Among the dozen children of Michael Gratz, the highly successful Philadelphia merchant and financier, was Rebecca (1781–1869). Well known for her charitable works, she was the founder of the Jewish Sunday school movement. She is also the supposed model for the character of Rebecca in Sir Walter Scott's novel IVANHOE.

ABOVE

The Reform movement in American Judaism began with the Reform Society of Israelites in Charleston, South Carolina. Isaac Harby (1788–1828), editor and author, was one of the founders.

AMERICAN JUDAISM GOES NATIONAL

CHAPTER FOUR

BELOW LEFT
Isaac Leeser (1806–1868), the minister of Congregation Mikveh Israel in Philadelphia, was the first to introduce sermons given in English to the American synagogue. He was also an important educator and the editor of THE OCCIDENT *and* JEWISH ADVOCATE, *an influential Jewish newspaper. Leeser is often considered the father of the Conservative movement in America.*

Jewish religious reform in America began naturally, on a small scale, as people adjusted to conditions of life on the new continent. Isaac Harby, of Charleston, South Carolina, was a journalist and literary critic, and a member of Congregation Beth Elohim. In 1824 he drew up a petition with 47 signatures that proposed changing the Sabbath service. It was then three hours long, there was constant repetition of prayer, and the congregation was often restless. Harby wanted more English in the solemn parts, and a weekly sermon, also in English so that those who didn't understand Hebrew could gain more knowledge of their Jewish religious heritage. A shorter service and an organ to accompany the singing would make for a more spiritual experience. The petition was rejected. Shortly thereafter Harby and eleven others started their own congregation, the Reformed Society of Israelites. The Society proclaimed that its members "are their own teachers, drawing their knowledge from the Bible and following only the laws of Moses, and those only as far as they can be adapted to the institutions of the society in which they live and enjoy the blessings of liberty." They stopped wearing yarmulkes, installed an organ, and did not pray for the arrival of the Messiah. It was a short-lived experience, nine years in all, but it influenced other Jewish communities.

In 1828, the New Orleans congregation made its own decision to admit the children of Christian mothers and Jewish fathers.

By the middle of the nineteenth century Jewish religious leaders were coming from Europe to head congregations. Some were part of the Reform movement that had developed in Germany, a Judaism that took into account social forces and modern-day life. It sought to eliminate that part of ancient ritual which did not seem relevant to the day. Scientific, historical truth was important, but not necessarily faith in miracles, the coming of the Messiah, or the resurrection of the dead. With the help of the German Reform rabbis, American Reform Judaism began to grow in importance, but it had already had its beginnings in native American circumstances. In the beginning it was a bare-bones Judaism that was practiced: God and minyan. Coming here and surviving called for men and women of action, not scholarship, and action was individual, expansive, lonely. Families branched out, sending brothers and sisters to start businesses in other towns, trekking through the wilderness with wares, and often improvising through memory their religious rituals. Most important, they were free of the Old World belief that tragedies were punishments from God.

The European rabbis had a lot to learn about America before they could adapt their ideas to their congregations, and they were quick to realize this. Their own Americanization, and that of the recently arrived Germans in their flock, was of the utmost importance. The American Jewish congregations were autonomous. They had grown out of the fabric of everyday, newly democratic, rabbi-less life. But the European rabbis were skilled organizers and saw the need for the widely scattered American Jewish communities to be made aware of each other and perhaps to act together on national issues that affected them as Jews. That contribution, which took time and nurturing, was of inestimable value.

CHAPTER FOUR

RIGHT
The father of Reform Judaism in America was Isaac Mayer Wise (1819–1900). An energetic, controversial, and deeply influential figure, he was the founder of the Union of American Hebrew Congregations and of Hebrew Union College.

Two leaders, Isaac Leeser and Isaac M. Wise, shared this goal. Leeser was a traditionalist and Wise a reformer; they tended to get in each other's way.

Isaac Leeser was the minister of Congregation Mikveh Israel of Philadelphia, to which Rebecca Gratz belonged. In fact, he was instrumental in urging her to start the Sunday school movement, and provided her with much help. This was but one of a multitude of tasks he undertook to bring the scattered American Jewish communities together. He was only 18 when he came to Richmond, Virginia from Westphalia in 1824. He worked as a clerk in his uncle's mercantile business, and at night studied English and added to his religious education. He gained attention when he responded to anti-Semitic articles published in the London *Quarterly Review* with a spate of his own in defense of Jews and Judaism. They were published in the local paper, the *Richmond Whig*, and to Leeser's surprise the Philadelphia congregation, Mikveh Israel, was impressed enough to ask him to become its minister. For 23 years he served the congregation, and worked to bring the American Jewish community into awareness of itself as an entity. He started the first major Jewish publication in the country, the *Occident,* which carried news of Jewish communities abroad, and of all those he could visit or correspond with in the United States. He translated a Hebrew prayer book into English; it was standard issue until the early twentieth century. He saw the paucity of Jewish education in the U.S., and wanted Jewish day schools to be an established part of the community; many Jewish children were being educated in Christian parochial schools. He foresaw the day when American academies would train and ordain rabbis. More importantly, he saw how a lack of communication between the congregations impeded Jewish religious and community growth.

As Leeser visited communities he reported his findings in the *Occident*. The Hebrew Benevolent Society of New Orleans was collecting funds in New York for the yellow fever epidemic that was ravaging their city. Shearith Israel contributed $469, but Philadelphia's congregation was not even informed of the collection. This was tragic lack of organization.

On a visit to New York in 1853, he suggested that leaders of the city's 17 congregations should meet to take joint action on issues that affected their members.

In Norfolk, Virginia, he reported that Jews had prayed together for the High Holy Days, and that one had offered to be *shochet* (ritual slaughterer) so that the others could have kosher meat.

He saw that Louisville, Kentucky, had one German and one Polish congregation, and thought they could have united.

In the *Occident* he took on the Society for Meliorating the Conditions of the Jews and other missionary groups for their attempts at conversion. The American Tract Society sent one of their number to Leeser's synagogue for the Sabbath service. After the service, the man posted himself outside the door and handed departing worshippers copies of a tract that argued against the basic tenets of Judaism. In a letter in the *United States Gazette* (1836), Leeser warned that another such violation might well invite physical ejection from the synagogue.

His crowning moment in a work-filled, ascetic life (he never married and became more introverted after smallpox disfigured his face) was when, through his efforts, Maimonides College, an institution to train rabbis, opened in Philadelphia in 1867. Lacking national support, it closed after six years. But taking Maimonides' lead, other schools subsequently opened.

Perhaps the best chance for unity among the Jewish congregations came with the formation in 1859 of the Board of Delegates of the American Israelites, the first countrywide meeting of American Jewish religious leaders. It was formed by Rabbi Samuel Isaacs in the aftermath of the Mortara case in Italy. In this incident, agents of the Pope kidnapped a Jewish child whose nurse had had him secretly christened when he was ill. The Church refused to relinquish the child on the grounds that since he was baptized he must be brought up as a Christian. This case, like the Damascus Blood Libel of 1840, in which Damascus Jews were accused of ritual murder, leading to the torture and imprisonment of 13, strengthened Jewish resolve in general. Particularly in America, gained the sympathy and support of Christian as well as Jewish Americans on behalf of Jews in other countries.

CHAPTER FOUR

LEFT
Hebrew Union College in Cincinnati was founded by Isaac Mayer Wise in 1875; he served as president from then until 1900. In 1947, HUC established the American Jewish Archives to further the study of American Jewish history.

Isaac Leeser, the traditionalist, and Isaac M. Wise, the Reform leader, were active members of the Board of Delegates, but their intense rivalry and the qualms of the Sephardim, who were by this time heavily outnumbered in America by the Ashkenazim, prevented any fruitful results. The enormous task of bringing together co-religionists who came from more countries, and were separated by more languages and cultures than all the other religious or ethnic groups in America, was becoming apparent. Some of the newly arrived immigrants were fearful of making common cause on public issues; Roman Catholics had the accusation of un-Americanism hanging over them by the Know Nothing crusade.

Isaac Mayer Wise, Reform's great leader, received his religious training in his native Bohemia and became leader of a congregation in Albany in 1846. Like Leeser, Wise traveled around the country, lectured, and published his own paper. In Albany he introduced reforms – sermons in English, a choir of men and women, the family pew to replace the segregated seating of men and women. Some in the congregation took exception to the changes. The opposition grew steadily until the president of the congregation, Louis Spanier, claimed that Wise was an unbeliever and violator of some religious laws. He was not permitted to defend himself against the charges, and the opposition withheld his back salary, claiming he had been dismissed. Wise was determined to stay in office. He went to the synagogue to perform his duties. It was during the High Holy Days, and the synagogue was packed. As Wise stepped forward to recite the customary prayer, Spanier stood up and struck him. The congregation erupted into a brawl that spread out into the street and could not be stopped even by the sheriff and his men.

Wise's supporters organized a congregation where he could freely express his views. Then, in 1854, he went to Cincinnati to head Congregation Bene Yeshurun, a young progressive group lacking the prejudices he had encountered in the East. Here he published his prayer book, *Minhaq America,* or *The American Rite,* which became widely used and was the basis for the Reform prayerbook used in later years. Here too, he started *The American Israelite,* a paper presenting the Reform point of view. Wise included novelizations showing the emotional heartache that sticking to the old folk ways and old country values could bring to the relations between parents and children.

After 20 years he succeeded in making Cincinnati the center of the Jewish Reform movement. He established the Union of American Hebrew Congregations for Reform rabbis and laymen, in 1873, and in 1875 founded Hebrew Union College, which became the most important institution of American Reform.

B'NAI BRITH IS FOUNDED

German Jewish immigration, which began in earnest after 1815, swelled when the Revolution of 1848 turned into a victory for the conservative, repressive forces; to many, Europe had become a bankrupt territory, overpopulated and devoid of freedom and economic opportunity. They came to America.

CHAPTER FOUR

RIGHT
In the tradition of Jewish and American self-help, B'nai Brith (Sons of the Covenant) was founded as a fraternal organization in New York City in 1843. Today it is an influential international organization with members in dozens of countries. Here Frank Goldman (far right), president at the time, meets with President Harry Truman.

BELOW RIGHT
B'nai Brith president Jack Spitzer meets with President Jimmy Carter.

BELOW FAR RIGHT
President Ronald Reagan meets with B'nai Brith president Gerald Kraft.

CHAPTER FOUR

LEFT
In 1856 anti-slavery crusader John Brown formed a militia group in Kansas. He was joined by three Jewish men – August Bondi, Jacob Benjamin, and Theodore Wiener. All three went on to serve in the Union Army during the Civil War; Bondi later became a judge.

Jewish fraternal orders began to spring up to meet the worldly needs of the Jewish community, and to hasten the process of Americanization. B'nai Brith, or Sons of the Covenant, was formed in 1843 by Henry Jones and others in a New York working-class community. It offered social life and mutual aid. Its lodges borrowed rites from the Masonic orders to which many of their members belonged, and took their titles from Jewish lore. By 1860, B'nai Brith had a membership of 50,000; it brought together people with differing views of Jewish religious practice, for B'nai Brith was a social, not religious, organization. It was to develop into the key organization fighting discrimination against Jews and others through the establishment of its famed Anti-Defamation League. In 1923, B'nai Brith established Hillel chapters on campuses for college students.

With B'nai Brith and other Jewish fraternal organizations, an important shift occurred: they took over some of the important fund-raising formerly done by the synagogues. More and more, through the efforts of such as Isaac Leeser, Rebecca Gratz, and Isaac Wise, the function of the synagogue, which had traditionally been a place for social gathering, education, and the dispensing of sedakah as well as religious observance, had changed. It was now primarily a place of worship.

THE CIVIL WAR

The 1859 meeting of the Board of Delegates of the American Israelites had another tension added to those between the Reform and traditional movements: the impending war. Jews were as divided on the issues as was the nation. The majority of Northern Jews were for abolition; there were Jewish abolitionists in the South as well, but no prominent Southern Jewish politicians spoke out against the institution. Slaves had been part of well-to-do households since colonial times. Forward-looking Christians and Jews whose humanism made them embrace many a just cause were often oblivious to this one.

Mordecai Manuel Noah, with his experience in foreign service, was concerned not just about the fate of Jews in North Africa, but of other groups abroad, as well. Yet, his New York newspapers were pro-slavery. Among the eloquent and strong voices against slavery, however, was another Jewish newspaperman, Moritz Pinner, owner of the German-language *Kansas Post.*

Many Southern Jews who were against, or at least ambivalent, about slavery took to liberating their slaves in their wills. The Jews of Charleston often did this. When liberation was made unlawful in the South, they paid the slaves the wages they would have gotten if free; some of them simply refused to own other human beings.

In his will, probated in 1806, land speculator Isaiah Isaacs of Virginia freed his slaves – although it would happen not only over his dead body but 14 years after his death, presumably to make his children's lives easier until then. Since many Southern Jewish wills contained provisions to free slaves, historian Anita Lebeson wonders: "Was it due to a basic ambivalence in attitude that in life they condoned slavery and in death wished to be free of the stigma of slave ownership?"

Kansas became a territory on May 30, 1854 – an open field for the tensions between North and South. Anti-slavery homesteaders came in from the East and Midwest, pro-slavery groups came from the South and neighboring Missouri – movements that were sure to meet in conflict. In May of 1856, some pro-slavery border ruffians were at work, hoping to extend slavery into the territory by keeping the abolitionists in check. Three Jewish business partners, August Bondi, Jacob Benjamin, and Theodore Wiener, had just settled in Pottawatomie, Kansas, when a pro-slavery force raided an anti-slavery settlement 50 miles away in Lawrence. Bondi was friendly with the sons of outspoken abolitionist John Brown, who lived on a neighboring ranch. On May 28, he and Wiener rode with the awesome Brown in a company of 11 men. They were in hot pursuit of marauders who had burned down Bondi's cabin and stolen his cattle. Though much outnumbered, the small but determined group of Brown's riders won the day. In the next skirmish, on August 30, 400 Missourians attacked, killing four men, one a son of Brown, and burning the town of Osawatomie. Brown's free-soiler militia was regrouped and ready to fight again when a truce was declared.

During the Civil War all three partners served in the Union Army. In 1866 Bondi moved to Salina, Kansas, where he became a judge (probate and police), postmaster, and at age 63, a lawyer. Reflecting on his early years with Brown, Bondi wrote, "He admonished us not to care whether a majority, no matter how large, opposed our principles and opinions. The largest majorities were sometimes only organized mobs, whose howlings never changed black into white or night into day. A

CHAPTER FOUR

RIGHT
Reform Rabbi David Einhorn (1809–1879) was a prominent abolitionist after he came to America in 1855.

FAR RIGHT
Just as the nation was torn by the Civil War, so was Judaism. Rabbi M.J. Michelbacher was a prominent pro-Southern rabbi in Richmond, Virginia, the capital of the Confederacy.

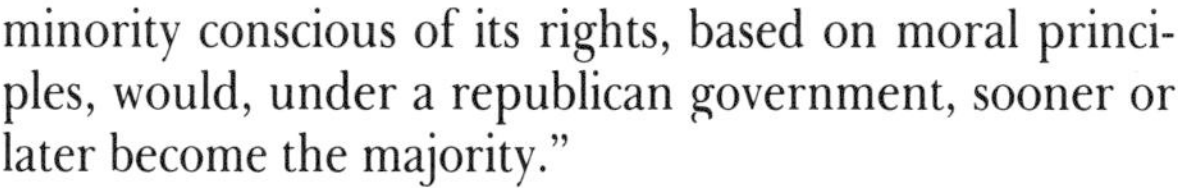

minority conscious of its rights, based on moral principles, would, under a republican government, sooner or later become the majority."

In October of 1859, John Brown captured the U.S. arsenal at Harper's Ferry, Virginia. There he hoped to get the weapons to lead an insurrection of slaves in the South. Robert E. Lee, then a little-known U.S. Army colonel, recaptured the arsenal; Brown was captured and hung.

By February of 1860 tensions were so great that Congress still had not elected a speaker. It was becoming a matter of urgency. The tension hung over the chamber on the day that a rabbi was invited to give the opening prayer for the first time. Morris Jacob Raphall, rabbi of New York's Orthodox Congregation B'nai Jeshurun, walked into the thick atmosphere, a calm figure in velvet skull cap and prayer shawl. As he prayed, "... thou who makest peace in the high heavens, direct their minds this day that with one consent they may agree to choose the man who, without fear, and without favor, is to preside over this assembly ..." heads bowed, the room was stilled. Raphall's eloquent prayer and commanding voice were credited with breaking the tension that made the election of the speaker possible on that day.

But Raphall himself created a furor when, a year later, he was queried about Jewish law on slavery and found biblical justification for it. Other rabbis and Jewish scholars hotly disputed this. Rabbi Sabato Morais, now head of Congregation Mikveh Israel in Philadelphia, spoke out against slavery and Raphall's interpretation, despite the feelings of his board that it was best to keep the dispute out of the synagogue. Rabbi David Einhorn of Baltimore was the most vociferous, speaking out not only against slavery but doing so in a city in a border state that just barely maintained its anti-slavery consensus. He knew he was placing his life in danger. When locals threatened to kill him he would not leave town until the police convinced him that they could not guarantee the safety of his family.

Among the voices raised against slavery was that of Ernestine Rose, a Polish-born reformer who became known in America as "Queen of the Platforms." To William Lloyd Garrison, she was one of the most admirable women of her day. She was born in 1810, the daughter of a rabbi. Like many Jewish women activists and reformers – Emma Goldman, Golda Meir – she broke out of the confines of her home situation at an early age. She was 16 when her mother died, but her youth did not stop her from waging a lawsuit against her father over her mother's estate. She won the suit and then, supposedly, gave the property to her father with the explanation that it was justice, not money, that made her wage the fight. She traveled throughout Europe, married an Englishman, and in 1836 came to New York. She was a key figure in the annual women's rights conventions, and a formulator of policy. The year she arrived in America she petitioned for a bill that would give the married women of New York state the right to own property. Her campaign gained momentum. It took 12 years to bring it about, but in 1848 New York state's Married Woman's Property Act was passed. The act served as an impetus for a national women's rights movement.

For Ernestine Rose the issues of women's rights and slavery were closely connected. She took them both on. The Bible was enlisted by many to justify slavery, and it was used, as well, as ammunition against the suffragists.

What this eloquent lecturer said about women's rights applied as well to the rights of the Negro population: "When the inhabitants of Boston converted their harbor into a teapot, rather than submit to unjust taxes, they did not go to the Bible for their authority, for if they had they would have been told from the same authority to 'give unto Caesar what belongs to Caesar.' . . . No! On human rights and freedom – on a subject that is as self-evident as that two and two make four, there is no need of any written authority . . ."

Tensions kept mounting. In December of 1860 South Carolina seceded; other states did likewise, and declared ownership of the federal property within their borders. Wanting to avoid being the aggressor, Lincoln made it clear that he was sending ships to provision, not attack, Fort Sumter. When Confederates attacked the fort, April 12, 1861, the war was on.

As the country was pulled apart, so were families. In 1861 Major Alfred Mordecai, a North Carolina-born descendant of a colonial family, resigned his commission. He was a leading expert on weapons (he wrote the Ordnance Manual for the United States Army), and a military scientific researcher. His family was both nurtured on, and nurtured, the Southern way of life. His father, Jacob, established the first private school for girls in the south in 1809 in Warrenton, North Carolina. Jacob's children, who taught at the school before entering the professions, were doctors and lawyers, and Alfred, the military man, was graduated first in his class from West Point. Alfred Mordecai resigned his commission the year that *his* son, Alfred Mordecai, Jr., graduated from West Point to fight in the Union Army. Alfred senior could not bear the idea of taking up arms against his family. Nor would he fight for the Union. Alfred Jr. went on to become a brigadier general and the most widely respected ordnanceman in the army.

The man who rarely lost his calm, was Judah P. Benjamin, Jefferson Davis's right-hand man. Benjamin's great resilience helped him weather the reverses in fortune that being a main player in the short-lived Confederacy brought. He was born in 1811 in St. Croix, of Anglo-Jewish parents, and brought up in Charleston, South Carolina. By age 21 he became a lawyer, settled in New Orleans, and married Natalie St. Martin, a French Catholic. In the practice of law – as his later years proved – he was almost without peer. His first famous legal summary was a guidebook through the legal maze of problems of Louisiana, a state that went from Spanish to French to American control. He made the definition of Louisiana laws his speciality. In ten years he had earned enough money to leave his practice and buy half-ownership in a sugar plantation. There he lived the good life and had the time to work on such scientific pursuits as finding the best methods of extracting saccharine from sugarcane.

CHAPTER FOUR

LEFT
Major Alfred Mordecai, descendent of a prominent Jewish family in North Carolina, was the leading weapons expert in the U.S. Army at the start of the Civil War. He resigned his commission rather than fight against his family, but would not fight for the Confederacy. Interestingly, Mordecai purchased only one slave in his life – for the specific purpose of setting her free.

His political career started when he was elected to the Louisiana legislature in 1842; in 1848 he was a Presidential elector and Whig party member.

He lost a fortune when his 1852 sugar crop was ruined by flooding, and had to sell his share of the plantation. He recouped his losses by becoming the South's leading lawyer. He was elected to the United States Senate in 1852, and began to be recognized as an orator every bit as gifted as Daniel Webster. In his speeches in defense of the South and slavery he put forth the Southern argument that slaves were property and that the Constitution provided for slavery.

When Jefferson Davis became provisional president of the Confederacy, he made Benjamin attorney general; in September of 1861, Benjamin became acting secretary of war. As such he was in the untenable position of having to fulfill the impossible. As a civilian, he was the target of army men for not supplying them with proper weapons, even though there were few to give. Benjamin took the blame, especially when he was unable to supply enough guns in the battle that led to the fall of Roanoake Island. This was doubly hard on Benjamin, since his plan to raise money for munitions by selling cotton to the English before hostilities began had been rejected. To counter further moves against Benjamin after the Roanoake debacle, Davis appointed him secretary of state.

With Richmond about to fall in 1865, the president and his secretary of state fled the capitol; Benjamin made a perilous escape to England. Unable to return to the United States, 54 and penniless, he became a naturalized Englishman, and within six months was appointed to the bar. In 1868 he published the famous *Law*

CHAPTER FOUR

RIGHT
David Camden de Leon of South Carolina was known as "the fighting doctor" of the Mexican War. When the Civil War began he resigned his commission in the U.S. Army and became surgeon general of the Confederate Army. This portrait is by Jewish artist Solomon Nunes Carvalho.

BELOW RIGHT
Born in the West Indies in 1811, Judah P. Benjamin became a lawyer in New Orleans. He became secretary of state of the Confederacy in 1862. After the war he successfully reestablished his legal career in England, dying there in 1884.

of Sale of Personal Property, known far and wide as "Benjamin on Sales." He was appointed Queen's Counsel, and was able to amass another fortune practicing law.

In the South of the Civil War anti-Jewish sentiment began to be evident. There were barbs against Benjamin, who was called "Judas Iscariot." It would be advantageous, one newspaper proposed, to "widen the gulf between President Davis and the descendant of those who crucified the Saviour." Preachers railed against Jews. It was partially hard-times prejudice, for the South was demoralized and looking to fix blame, but there was also a markedly different group of people running things. The plantation aristocracts and their city cousins, whose children had married those of the old-line Jewish settlers, had given way to a new class of small businessmen of meager education. Emotionalism was having its day. In their eyes, to be Jewish wasn't to practice a particular religion, but to mysteriously spread some kind of evil, or take some kind of advantage. The usual wild and cowardly claims were made. The Jews were accused of owning most of the property in the South. This remarkable rumor, no doubt a negative compensation for all the South did lose, was especially ironic, since along with most everyone else who had businesses before the war, the Jews were economically devastated. Some Southern grand juries, with no proof,

condemned Jewish hoarding and black marketeering. Confederate officers tried to prevent Jews from getting promotions. A somewhat cynical if not repugnant measure of change could be seen in the Ku Klux Klan. In its early days, when its aggression was directed mostly at carpet baggers it admitted Jews and Catholics. But given the nature of its vigilantism it was inevitable that it would turn against Jews and Catholics as well as blacks.

Between 1840 and 1860s the Jewish population of America rose from about 15,000 to 150,000. Most came from Germany, particularly Bavaria, and Alsace, and to a lesser extent from eastern Europe. Not only did they have to adjust to the new country, but many were immediately pulled into the war, being recruited as soldiers sometimes as they stepped off the boat.

Some 7,000 Jews fought for the Union, about 1,500 for the Confederacy. The surgeons general of both armies were Jewish. Twenty-three Jews were staff officers in the Confederate army, 12 in the navy. Seven Jews – all enlisted men – received Congressional medals of honor. Major General Frederick Knefler was the highest-ranking Jew in the Union Army, in which there were four full Jewish generals.

Max Frauenthal was so spirited and courageous a Confederate soldier that when one soldier spoke of another as truly brave he would use the term a "real Fronthall," as the name came to be said. Jews served in both armies in greater proportion than their numbers, but nonetheless it was convenient for the emerging anti-Semites to deny their participation.

There was always one man who could be relied upon to reverse the missteps and prejudicial decisions involving Jews – the most powerful man in the Republic, President Abraham Lincoln. He was their beacon of justice. When the laws in the North seemed to proscribe Jewish participation as chaplains (Jewish men eventually served as chaplains on both sides) Lincoln stepped in to help. When General Grant issued his infamous Order #11 barring all Jews from territory under his control because he believed that the cotton buyers dogging his army – many of whom were Jewish – were interfering with troop movements, it caused a furor. Rabbi Isaac Wise was in a delegation that went to see the President. He later quoted Lincoln in *The Israelite*: "I don't like to see a class or nationality condemned on account of a few sinners." Lincoln had the order revoked, and Grant himself, who had no prejudice against Jews, regretted his action, much of which was based on faulty information.

On April 14, 1865, a Passover night when Jews were celebrating the exodus out of Egypt and giving thanks for the end of the war, President Lincoln was assassinated. More than 50,000 mourners, 7,000 of them Jews, marched in funeral processions. The synagogues were places of mourning. At Shearith Israel in New York, the Sephardic prayer for the dead – the Hashkabah – was said for Mr. Lincoln, the first time such a prayer had been offered for someone not of the faith. The body lay in state in Chicago's Court House; the canopy shielding it bore the words of David's lament for Saul, "The beauty of Israel is slain upon the high places."

That day Louis Moreau Gottschalk, New Orleans-born son of an Anglo-Jewish doctor, and the first American composer of international reputation, was on a concert tour that had taken him across the nation, 80,000 miles through both mining camps and large cities. The pro-Union Gottschalk played his piano on the train in tribute to Lincoln for all who would listen. His Creole melodies, African and South American rhythms, and the regional folk tunes in his music, were a synthesis of the country's experience as a nation. He, like his country, had come a long way. When he had first applied to the Paris Conservatory as a young boy he was informed that America was "only a country of steam engines" and was summarily dismissed. He went on to study with Hector Berlioz and was saluted by Frederic Chopin as "the king of pianists." He made people take notice of the culture – distinct from Europe's and formed out of so many vibrant influences – that was America's.

Below left
Genral Ulysses S. Grant created a controversy when he issued his Order #11 banning all Jews from territory under his control. President Abraham Lincoln forced Grant to rescind the order.

ABOVE
Levi Strauss went West to find his fortune, not as a gold miner but as a supplier. The heavy-duty denim trousers he invented are often called Levi's – or blue jeans.

THE GOLDEN WEST

CHAPTER FIVE

BELOW LEFT
Author Bret Harte (1836–1902) was the grandson of Benjamin Harte, secretary of the New York Stock Exchange. His colorful stories of Western life were extremely popular.

Bret Harte (whose Jewish grandfather, Bernard, had been secretary of the New York Stock Exchange) wrote stories filled with the local color of the West: the language and lawless predispositions of mining-camp characters. Harte popularized – indeed helped create – the distinctive American short-story form. When he published the tale "The Luck of Roaring Camp" in the *Overland Monthly* in 1868 he gained a bonanza of recognition.

A Jewish artist who recorded the American experience, and did so at great personal risk, was Solomon Nunes Carvalho. Born in Charleston, South Carolina, Carvalho was a portrait painter who also knew how to make daguerreotypes. He lived quietly with his wife and children, a good enough painter to support them with his art, until the day when he met Colonel John C. Frémont. The famous soldier, politician, and explorer was planning an expedition to the West to assess the viability of constructing a transcontinental railway along the 38th parallel. Carvalho was so impressed with Frémont that he agreed to document the journey photographically. Before that brief interview in August of 1853, Carvalho was to recall, he wouldn't have agreed to go to California even by the safer "emigrant route."

Carvalho's task was formidable. He had to make daguerreotypes under the roughest conditions. He spent hours climbing to get the best view, and hours setting up and repacking the cumbersome equipment. He kept a diary of his impressions. At first he was in awe of the beauty he saw; later, he worried as supplies began to run low. Freezing weather, rough terrain, unfriendly Indians, and finally a lack of food – they had to eat their pack animals – took lives. When they reached a Mormon settlement in Utah, Carvalho had scurvy, frost bite, and chronic diarrhea. His daguerreotypes, however, were clear and in good shape. The party was cared for by the Mormons, and upon recovery, Carvalho went to California. There he helped organize the Hebrew Benevolent Society, the first such Jewish organization in Los Angeles.

In the 1850s, some of the heartier German immigrants arrived from Europe, took one look at the East, and quickly sought the great adventure out West. A fine example is 19-year-old Adolph Sutro, who left his mother and siblings in Baltimore and made his way to San Francisco. Too late to cash in on the mining lodes there, he went into the clothing business with a cousin, some 50 miles from San Francisco. But restlessness dogged him. He opened a tobacco shop in San Francisco, then two more. Soon success allowed him the increased capital to support his next adventurous impulse. He was 29 when the Comstock silver strike drew him to the Sierra Nevada. There, using a process to extract metal ore from quartz rock that he developed with a chemist partner, he opened his own mill. With profits as high as $10,000 a month he took the time to learn about the mines around him. The mines were pervaded by noxious gases. Ventilation was poor and there was dangerous flooding. He conceived of building a tunnel that would protect miners from these health hazards. The Sutro Tunnel took 13 years to build, and

CHAPTER FIVE

RIGHT
Many American Jews made their fortunes in the rough-and-tumble of the frontier. Adolph Sutro (1830–1898) caught the silver fever of the Comstock Lode and went West in the 1850s. He built a ventilation and drainage tunnel in the Sierra Nevada that was a true feat of engineering. He is shown here, third from the left.

BELOW RIGHT
Adolph Sutro engages in conversation with miners of the Comstock Lode in an uncomplimentary cartoon from 1874.

CHAPTER FIVE

LEFT
The commercial development of the Western territories was greatly aided by Jewish merchants and traders. Isidore Elkan Solomon, founder of Solomonville, Arizona, is shown here in his banking office sometime in the 1870s.

was hailed as an engineering feat. But by that time the lode was already running dry. Sutro sold his interest for a hefty profit and returned to San Francisco. There he bought considerable city real estate (at depressed rates), and began, in the 1880s, to build his own luxurious mansion and also a resort, public gardens, and baths, on Sutro Heights overlooking the Pacific Ocean. In 1894 he was elected mayor of all he could survey.

Levi Strauss was another who got the gold fever. Orphaned at 17, he left his native Bavaria for New York, where he and his brothers were peddlers. Soon he was on a schooner making its way around Cape Horn to San Francisco. On board were a wide variety of goods that Levi had carefully chosen for their scarcity in San Francisco. Like many other '49ers he knew that in the anarchic "rush" atmosphere he might have to fall back on what he knew best. His stock sold out immediately and he was soon supplying merchants in mining areas with goods that he shipped to them on pack trains. Levy Strauss and Company prospered and opened a four-story headquarters on San Francisco's Battery Street. In a venture with Jacob Youphes, a Russian tailor who had found his way to Reno, Nevada, Levi Strauss began to manufacture sturdy denim trousers with pockets held on by metal rivets. So popular and durable were these trousers that today the name Levi's is synonymous with blue jeans around the world.

Jews played a major role in opening the West. They were in the grain and livestock businesses. They were cowboys and ranch owners; they built railroads and mines. Here, too, many got their start as peddlers, working the mining camps and railroad construction sites. One of the most successful ranchers in Wyoming, Harry Altman, started that way. Since the distances in the West were vaster, peddling was less common than in the East. Those dealing in dry goods would save enough capital to open their own stores. In the West a new general store might be one of the first structures in what would soon grow into a small town. It easily became the center of the settlement, and the man who was industrious enough to pick his spot and build his store and provide a place for his customers to meet and talk might well become sheriff or mayor. This happened with some frequency to young Jewish men. As a crossroads developed into a settlement, the storekeeper planned ahead. His was a sane voice amid the drifters and restless souls living from day to day who were used to wafting through towns that had shriveled in the sun after a brief period of usefulness.

Implicit in the nature of his business was the storekeeper's sense of order – and this included helping to keep the social order, which was a way of protecting his own business. So, he might take on the duties of sheriff. Imagine the contrast for some of these Jewish men: fleeing countries ruled by oppressive autocrats,

CHAPTER FIVE

CENTER ABOVE
Many thousands rushed to the gold fields of California, the Southwest, and the Yukon, but few struck pay dirt. Many Jewish merchants realized that there was more profit to be made in outfitting prospectors than in prospecting themselves. The firm of Cooper & Levy was a busy one in Seattle near the turn of the century.

CENTER BELOW
The interior of the I.S. Solomon Commercial Company store in Solomonville, Arizona, probably around 1880.

they arrive in a wild West where laws are written on the wind – and in the natural course of developments, they begin to help keep order.

In the late 1800s and early 1900s, Jews were mayors of such towns as Butte, Montana; Boise, Idaho; Burns, Oregon; Tucson, Arizona; Prineville and Portland, Oregon; Port Townshend, Washington; Santa Fe, New Mexico; Deadwood, South Dakota; Sacramento, California. The first Jewish congresswoman, Florence Prag Kahn, of California started to serve in 1924, and was elected for six terms thereafter. Edward Salomon, a civil war hero was appointed governor of the Washington territory by President Grant in 1869. Moses Alexander was elected governor of Idaho in 1915.

In the cities as well as the small towns, vigilante groups made up of concerned citizens patrolled and made arrests. Gangs called Sydney Ducks, who had come from the convict colonies of Australia preyed on San Francisco, and Jewish merchants – Jesse Seligman for one, who would eventually rule over his Eastern family's banking business – joined forces with a few hundred men who drew up their own guidelines for law enforcement. For a few months they sat in judgement, pronounced sentences, and executed four men. Soon civil libertarians, and the office-holders whose functions had been usurped, helped end the vigilante reign, but not until stricter law enforcement was in the offing.

By the 1880s some 30,000 Jews were living in San Francisco. The older-established German- and French-Jewish families were related through intermarriage and business. They had built up much of the city, formed a social elite, and lived comfortably with the ease of social acceptance in the larger community.

Almost the first thing young Jesse Seligman noticed upon arriving in San Francisco in 1850 was the wood – almost all the buildings were made of it. Back East, Jesse had run a store in Watertown, New York that had caught fire. Once was enough. To store the $20,000 worth of dry goods, food stuffs, and clothing he brought to sell in the gold rush town, he rented a brick building. He also joined the San Francisco volunteer fire department. In the massive fire of 1851, Seligman's was the only general store to survive.

During the gold rush San Francisco was a town where a quart of whisky fetched $20 and the smaller necessities of life were also outrageously expensive. Seligman's Western addition to the family pot – some $900,000, including gold bullion shipped east – helped provide a basis for the family's leap from retailing to investment banking. On the frontier, extending credit, dealing in bullion, and accepting IOUs were a sort of informal banking anyway.

The West played a pivotal role for several German-Jewish families who would eventually head Eastern-based investment banking and mining concerns.

CHAPTER FIVE

BELOW LEFT
Financier Bernard Baruch first sought his fortune in the mines of Colorado. He later went on to a successful career in finance and as a public official and economic advisor to Presidents, especially Franklin Roosevelt.

The Guggenheim family, originally from Switzerland, began peddling goods in Pennsylvania in 1848. Meyer Guggenheim, the oldest son, looked beyond the hard-earned percentage of profit over cost. To increase earnings he decided to make one of his products, stove polish himself. Stove polish irritated and stained the hands of housewives. Meyer had a chemical analysis done; based on this he made his own nonirritating, nonstaining polish. He added other household products – lye and bluing, for example – and profits were accordingly increased.

By the 1880s the Guggenheims were importers and distributors of household goods; the family also owned lacemaking factories in Switzerland. Meyer was into his 50s and had seen his family through to sure prosperity. Suddenly the bounty of the West came to his doorstep, disguised as a risky, if not losing, proposition. Through Charles H. Graham, a Pennsylvania storeowner, Meyer came to own a third of two lead and silver mines near Leadville, Colorado. This was not part of a natural business progression. Meyer knew nothing about mining, so he went to Leadville to see for himself. The mines were flooded. He had them pumped out, an expensive undertaking offset somewhat by the profits from the goods he had brought with him to sell. The pumping continued at a money-draining rate. The rich strike of silver and copper was unexpected. But smelting copper ore was costly. Meyer rallied his sons. Two came to Leadville to study metallurgy. The others ran the dry-goods busi-

CHAPTER FIVE

RIGHT
The Guggenheim family became prominent through mineral wealth. Patriarch Meyer (1828–1905) came to own mines in Leadville, Colorado. He brought in his seven sons to help make the mines pay, and pay they did.

BELOW RIGHT
The success of the Guggenheim enterprises allowed Meyer's sons to pursue extensive philanthropic interests. Daniel (1856–1930) endowed foundations for the study of aeronautics and social welfare.

CENTER
Solomon R. Guggenheim was a well-known patron of the arts, especially modern fine arts. The Guggenheim Museum, housed in a famed building designed by Frank Lloyd Wright, is in New York City.

ness, and looked into finding a cheaper way to smelt the copper ore. A very young Bernard Baruch told Meyer about a process developed by Richard J. Gatling, the inventor of the rapid-fire machine gun. Others had been dubious, but Meyer gave the process a try. It worked, considerably lowering the price of refining copper.

The family went on to buy and build smelters in Colorado and Mexico, and to form a trust of their own, thus bringing all their mining operations together. Stock was issued. The family bought more mines – tin, gold, diamond, nitrate – in Bolivia, Alaska, Africa, and Chile, and became an international mining giant, with a fortune rivaling the Rockefeller's. Meyer Guggenheim, in fact is credited with laying the foundation of the United States copper industry.

By 1880, the town of Leadville had a population of 15,000, at least 200 of them Jews. David May, founder of the May Stores chain, opened a small department store in Leadville in 1877. At the time young Bernard Baruch was loading ore and worked on a blasting crew in nearby Cripple Creek, while shrewdly investing in the mines. There was a B'nai Brith lodge, a Reform congregation, and a Jewish cemetery. By 1884 a synagogue had been built, and later an Orthodox congregation would rent a building. The Shoenberg Opera House was a focal point of cultural activity. After 1893, when the price of silver plummeted, Leadville rapidly shrank to a virtual ghost town.

Jews were involved in all phases of the cattle

CHAPTER FIVE

LEFT
Simon Guggenheim (1867–1941) was U.S. Senator from Colorado from 1907 to 1913. In 1925 he established a foundation to endow fellowships for research and creative studies.

BELOW RIGHT
Daniel Guggenheim's son Harry Frank, born in 1890, served as American ambassador to Cuba from 1929 to 1933.

business on the Western range. Louis Kaufman and Louis Stadler formed the Stadler Kaufman Meat Company. The famous sketch *Waiting for Chinook (Last of the 5,000)* depicts the effects on the Kaufman and Stadler herd of a devastating winter on the range, and was drawn by their ranch manager, the renowned artist Charles M. Russel.

In rough-edged Sitka, Russian territory before the Alaska purchase of 1868, Jews were whisky dealers, saloon-keepers, and principals in American fur companies doing business with the Russians. Because of the bitter Russian anti-Semitic policies of that era the Jews were careful to put forward the names of their Christian partners. But in 1868 at least 20 hard-bitten Jewish adventurers met for Sabbath services in one of Sitka's wooden-planked huts.

Of the many Jewish store-owners and merchandisers in the West, a few gained national prominence. The fourth-generation Senator Barry Goldwater, Episcopalian-born, is descended on his father's side from Jewish frontier tradesmen and local politicians whose ventures culminated in a large Phoenix, Arizona department store. Starting in 1864, the German-born David May ran stores in Indiana, Leadville, Denver, and St. Louis, building up to what became one of the country's largest chains, the May Department Stores Company.

Mary Ann Magnin arrived in San Francisco with her family in 1875 and resolved to build a business in luxury

CHAPTER FIVE

RIGHT
Building a synagogue was a high priority among the Jewish communities of the West. Temple Emanu-El of Helena, Montana, was erected in 1891.

BELOW RIGHT
The original Adas Israel synagogue in Washington, D.C. is now a museum of Jewish history. The cornerstone of the building was laid in 1876; President Ulysses Grant attended the ceremony.

CENTER
One of the oldest synagogues in America is the Lloyd Street Synagogue in Baltimore, Maryland. As this photo of the interior shows, the synagogue is austerely beautiful.

retailing. While her husband worked as a wood carver, she made clothes for the children of rich women, then extended her creations to bridal gowns and lingerie. In 1877 she and her husband Isaac established I. Magnin. True to her plan, the store catered to the tastes of the upper crust and was decorated accordingly. It was also her aim to have each of her seven sons working in the business, and Mary Magnin (nicknamed Queen Victoria by her children) had her way. One son, Joseph, broke away to start his own store chain.

In the nineteenth century railroads was the name of the game in the world of business speculation. Railroads sprouted towns. The country was being linked end to end in a typically American way – through fierce competition between railroad magnates, the likes of Edward Harriman and James J. Hill and Jay Gould. Joseph Seligman, whose firm was the first of the German-Jewish banking houses to deal in railroad securities, made sure that one of his railroad lines ran through the Missouri farm of his dear friend Ulysses S. Grant, though he would later complain of the illogical way in which railroads were laid out.

To insure the growth of their retail businesses, investors built narrow-gauge railroads, short lines, and extensions. Jewish frontier businessmen built up whole areas by forging roads through rough terrain, connecting mining camps with towns, and opening up the flow of supplies.

In the 1880s, immigration to the United States increased so rapidly that it alarmed some Americans. This was but one of the tensions that propelled the first national trend of social anti-Semitism across the country. In the Western towns and cities where Jews had been elected to represent the general population, they would soon be elected as representatives of a Jewish constituency that had become more guardedly aware of the need for protection from those who would try to close the doors of opportunity to them.

From the 1600s to about 1870 European arrivals who put down roots in unpopulated American territory were settlers. After that, the end of the Western frontier and the beginning of mass immigration dramatically changed the status of newcomers. Now they were immigrants, first and foremost.

THE PACE QUICKENS

THE GILDED AGE

In the nineteenth century the railroad was the force that linked America from coast to coast, making possible the settling of the frontier. During the Civil War, North and South vied for railroad routes: to control them was to

CHAPTER FIVE

LEFT
Congregation Beth Shalome, in Richmond, Virginia, traces its origins back to before 1790.

BELOW LEFT
The first synagogue in Boston was Ohebei Shalom; the building was erected in 1851.

control the new West. Railroads created cities – Chicago, Omaha, Kansas City. Railroads swelled the fortunes of the new millionaires, the moguls of the Gilded Age – Jay Gould, Edward Harriman, James J. Hill, the powerful J. P. Morgan. And for the German-Jewish investment houses such as J. & W. Seligman Brothers, and Kuhn Loeb, railroads, too, were key.

The industrial age was gaining momentum, and it tilted the balance: the political clout of the industrialists became greater than that of the farming majority. Railroad owners were granted choice land cheap. Manufacturers got protective tariffs.

With the railroads, speed became part of the daily American experience. Within a few years after the Civil War, Americans were a growing population on the California coast, it had taken 250 years for them to get from the Atlantic coast to the Missouri River. Fortunes seemed to amass with the flickering speed of kinescopes. Alongside the old, inherited wealth ran the first generation money men: the former clerks, John D. Rockefeller and James J. Hill, and the former telegraph operator Andrew Carnegie.

The number of millionaires in the U.S. in the 1840s is estimated to have been 25. After the Civil War, there were several hundred in New York City alone. There were few restraints on the new captains of industry, and much rampant exploitation and strong-arming by them. Since a goodly number of the industrialists who would dazzle the age started out in humble circumstances, they were seen as examples: the common man could make it in America! And so the average citizen, steeped in the ideal of equal opportunity, gave credence to Rockefeller's statement: "The growth of big business is merely a survival of the fittest," an attitude expressed with little variation by several other of the moguls. Charles Darwin's *Origin of the Species*, published in 1859 and misapplied to the economic pyramid, had the rich, and those identifying with them, attributing their wealth to their greater fitness to be wealthy.

Some of them went about demonstrating this with abandon – building palaces, giving lavish balls and outrageous banquets. One such sit-down for 72 at Delmonico's restaurant had as its centerpiece glitter and splash to blind the eye – swans swimming in water! Next to that the imposing but quiet chopped-liver swans of bar mitzvah fame run a sedate, if not sedentary, second.

With the same great speed it had created itself, the new society felt the need to age itself. This could best be done by drawing a circle about its members and announcing their exclusiveness. And so, in the form of a Mr. Ward McAllister, there came into the American

CHAPTER FIVE

RIGHT
Laying the cornerstone of Temple de Hirsch in Seattle, Washington, in 1901.

lexicon the "social arbiter." The homegrown ladies who ran the social lives of the cliques in their separate cities across the country were one thing. But the preferred people would be The Four Hundred, a magic number based on the amount of people that Mrs. William Astor's ballroom could hold. McAllister's Four Hundred was a marriage of the old families – some with more American history than money – and the new industrial rich. The social arbiter's task was to create an image for a group that was avid to be seen as an aristocracy – most particularly like England's, to which they yearned to belong. McAllister was protective of his group. When their extravagance added steam to the growing movement to impose an income tax (2 percent on incomes over $4,000), he railed against it, threatening to leave the country. In a speech in the House of Representaives William Jennings Bryan remarked: " . . . I have never known one [man] so mean that I would be willing to say of him that his patriotism was less than two per cent deep."

In 1888 McAllister's *Social Register* was published, a listing of some 2,000 mostly Anglo-Saxon Protestant families. This handy book spelled out which friends it would be important to make in the world. In 1892 , the same year in which America adopted the Pledge of Allegiance, McAllister brought out his exclusive Four Hundred listing. With McAllister's publications the new aristocracy was at last spared the burden of anonymous greatness. The very rich German-Jewish families, however, who had made their fortunes in the same speculative markets and deals as had the new Protestant moguls, were not included in the *Social Register*. Like the low-key and more socially secure Sephardic descendents of colonial Americans – who were also excluded – they would, in time, come to prefer their anonymity. But now, a formal separation between Gentiles and Jews – one that had not existed in the higher social spheres of early America – was being insisted upon. Flushed with the success of his undertaking, McAllister suggested that "our good Jews might wish to put out a little book of their own – called something else, of course."

However frivolous these social vanities, the *Social Register* telegraphed an important message: This aristocracy would define itself not by a social vision that would include Americans of merit and culture from other backgrounds and, so make for a sounder, more cohesive America, but by whom they excluded. The parvenues needed distinctions to assure themselves that their rapid ascent was real. This need had been in the formative stages for at least two decades. The much publicized Hilton–Seligman Affair of 1877, in which America's best-known Jewish banker was denied entry to a hotel he had frequently patronized, began a trend in which hotels hoped to gain distinction by refusing admittance to Jews. Soon children of the German-Jewish families were being refused membership in clubs to which their parents had belonged and sometimes had a hand in starting.

Up until the 1860s Jews in America met with a fairly broad social acceptance. Society's aggressions were directed mainly against Catholics, especially the new Irish immigrants. From 1815 on, and particularly after 1848, German Jews had spread out, settling in small towns along the Erie Canal, the Great Lakes, the Mississippi River, and in the 1870s in increasing numbers in California. After the failure of the Revolution of 1848 in Germany Jewish immigration to America rose sharply: from 4,500 in 1830 to 50,000 by 1850. The economic conditions in Europe were dire. Peasants were leaving the countryside, and so, too, the small Jewish retailers who had been their suppliers. Restored monarchies were hunting down revolutionaries, Jewish and Gentile. German Jews living in Slavic territories became suspect as bearers of German culture. Many young, educated German Jews had fought in the revolution and its defeat was a final disappointment. If they wanted democracy, they'd have to find it elsewhere. Lazarus Straus and Adolf Brandeis (father of Supreme Court Justice Louis Dembitz Brandeis), were among those who emigrated. Of America Brandeis wrote to his future bride. "To your own surprise you will see how your hatred of your fellow man, all your disgust at civilization, . . . will drop away from you at once. You will appreciate that these feelings are solely the products of the rotten European conditions."

Though the German Jews were venturesome and had spread out across America, by the 1880s the pattern of Jewish habitation had changed. Depression affected the agricultural economies on which the small towns were built. Populism and a religious fundamentalism hostile to Jews held sway. The Jews left the small towns of America for the quickly expanding industrial cities; they were on their way to becoming a metropolitan population.

JEWISH ARTISTS

ABOVE
Photographer Alfred Stieglitz (1864–1946) was a pioneer in making photography into an accepted art form. This photo of the MAURETANIA was taken in 1910.

RIGHT
Artist Max Weber (1881–1961) came to America from Russia at the age of ten. Starting around 1917, his work often dealt with Jewish themes. The coloured woodcut, called PRIMITIVE MAN, *dates from 1918.*

ABOVE
Bronze figure by Jacques Lipchitz (1891–1973), created in the period 1926–1930.

LEFT
Despite a lack of formal training, sculptor William Zorach (1887–1966) created works of remarkable simplicity and beauty. This piece is called MOTHER AND CHILD*; it was made in the period 1927–1930.*

ABOVE
Artist Ben Shahn was born in Lithuania in 1898; he came to the United States in 1906 and died in 1969. Shahn often expressed social and political themes in his work. This tempera painting from 1946 is called FATHER AND CHILD.

LEFT
Leonard Baskin's 1952 woodcut, A MAN OF PEACE. Baskin is known for his powerful graphic works.

ABOVE
Mark Rothko (1903–1970), came to America from Russia in 1913. This painting, RED, BROWN, AND BLACK, dates from 1958.

PAGES 88 & 89
NO. 10,
a monumental 1950 canvas by Abstract Expressionist Mark Rothko, is probably his best-known work.

VIR HEROICUS SUBLIMIS,
a representative painting of Barnett Newman's style. Newman (1905–1971) forms a link between Abstract Expressionism and color field painting.

THE POOL,
a 1956 work in mixed media by Larry Rivers.

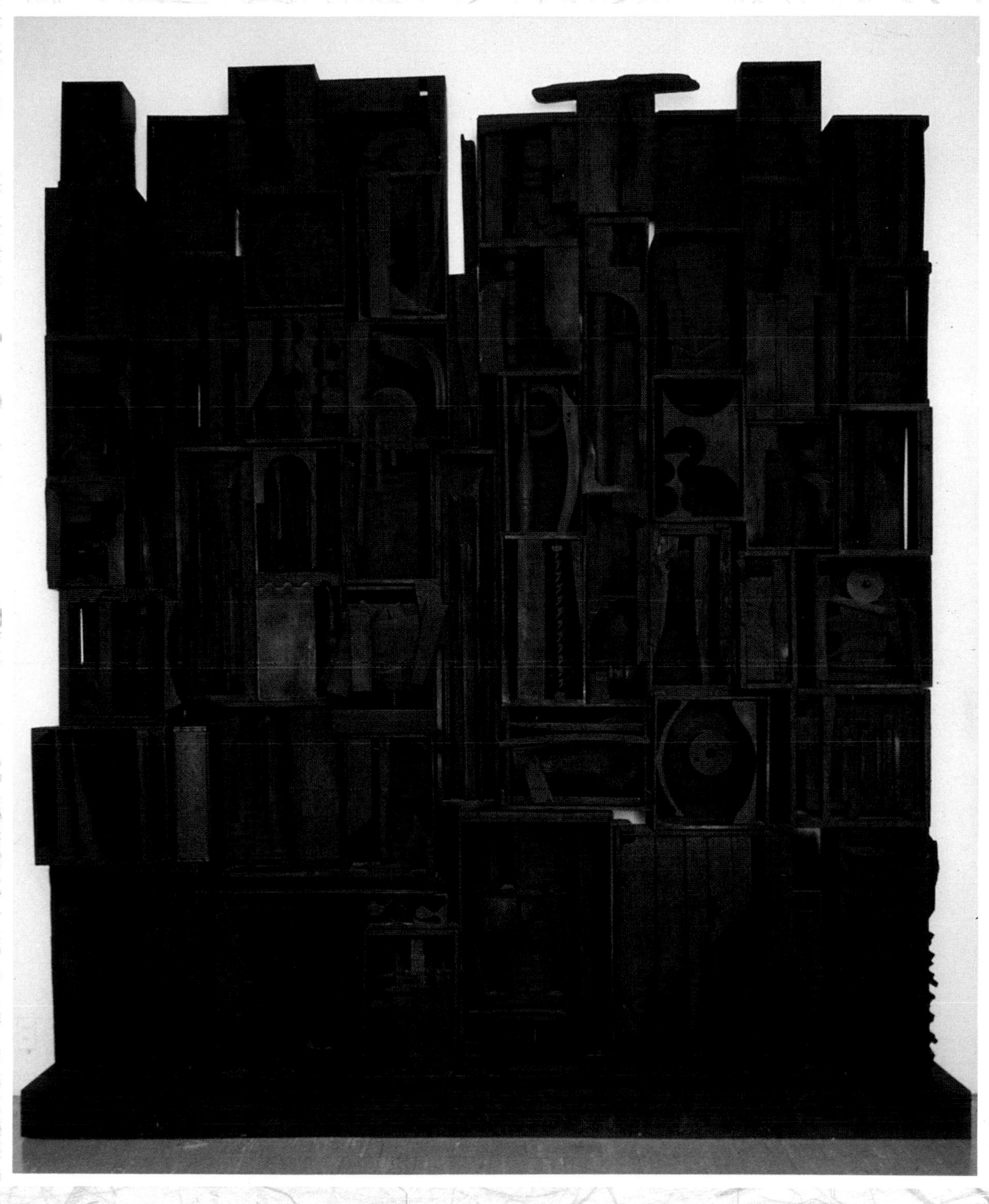

SKY CATHEDRAL,
a sculpture by Louise Nevelson dating from 1958.

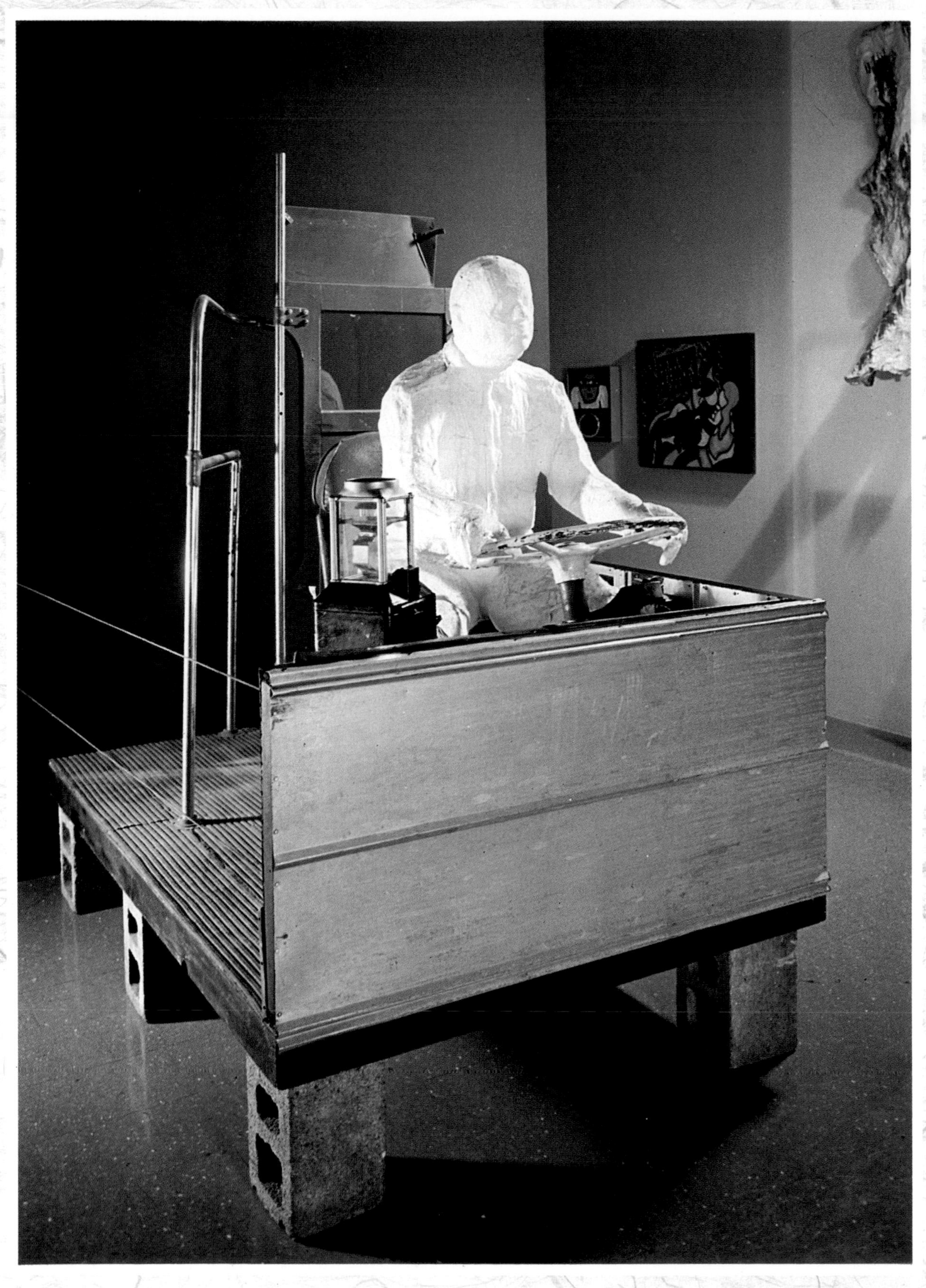

ABOVE
Sculptor George Segal is known for his plaster statues of ordinary people in everyday situations. BUS DRIVER *dates from 1962.*

ABOVE
George Segal's works can be amusing and incisive. This sculpture is called PORTRAIT OF SIDNEY JANIS WITH MONDRIAN PAINTING. *It dates from 1967.*

ABOVE

The towering figure of Jacob Henry Schiff (1847–1920) influenced Jewish affairs for decades. His philanthropic activities were wide-ranging and included the American Jewish Committee, the Jewish Theological Seminary, educational institutions in Palestine, and much more.

CHAPTER SIX

THE GERMAN JEWISH CONTRIBUTION

It happened between the 1830s and 1870s. Among the increasing number of German-Jewish immigrants to the United States, a few families would amass great fortunes and become the architects of an organized philanthropy that would serve as a model for later Americans.

In industry, the German-Jewish clothing manufacturers, tailors and salesmen were well represented among those who shaped an American ready-to-wear garment industry that helped democratize American society. Starting with army uniforms, which were for the first time mass produced according to standard sizes, to the mail-order houses servicing prairies and plains, the new industry brought to farmers, clerks, and housewives affordable clothes like those in the custom-made tailor and dress shops. Soon dressing well was no longer solely the province of the rich.

The times were providential for businessmen: the Civil War and its demand for uniforms, and the needs of government finance, created a dynamic atmosphere in investment banking and manufacturing.

Joseph Seligman, the most famous Jewish American of his day, offers one of the best historical examples of the life of his times. He went through all of its phases – an American Everyman who fulfilled the dream. He went from peddler to retail store chain owner, then investment banker, and finally head of an international investment-banking concern. If he grew and changed along with America's changing business community, he did so in relation to his social environment as well. Brought up an Orthodox Jew, he became president of Temple Emanu-El, the Reform congregation, and in later years supported the efforts of Felix Adler's Ethical Culture movement. From peddler to financial adviser to president – Seligman's life was an Horatio Alger story. Indeed, as a millionaire banker he would not send his children to an elite New York private school for the German-Jewish rich. Instead, he hired Alger to tutor them.

Joseph Seligman was the oldest of 11 children born to a weaver and his spirited wife in the small German village of Baiersdorf. His mother was ambitious enough to set up shop selling the blankets and fine materials she had brought as her dowry, and to save the money to ensure that her brilliant eldest son went to university, a rare experience for a Jewish boy of little financial means. America was part of his mother's plan for Joseph. After graduating at 17 with honors in the classics, Joseph left for America. One day in the early fall of 1837 he began the hundred-mile walk from New York to Mauch Chunk, Pennsylvania, where his mother had a relative. There he met the town's most prominent businessman, 29-year-old Asa Packer, a builder of canal boats, who befriended the young man and hired him as his cashier. Packer would go on to become president of the Lehigh Valley Railroad, and to found Lehigh University.

As Joseph's environment became clearer to him, so did his future plans. When he had saved enough money to put his sales experience and trained eye for goods to use, he left the boatyard and began peddling in the countryside. Soon there was money enough for passage for his brothers. From peddling they rented a building to warehouse their goods; by 1843 they were merchandising in stores in the South as well as the East. At the Watertown, New York store, a favorite stopping point for the locals, they played cards with a young army lieutenant, Ulysses S. Grant, who would become a lifelong friend.

In 1848 Joseph combined his first business trip back to Germany with a *Brautschau* – a bride search – as was the custom among prosperous German-Jewish men. In Baiersdorf he met and married a first cousin, Babet; they returned to New York to set up house.

A fortuitous move was made when Joseph's brother William purchased a clothing factory. When the Civil War began, the brothers could woo government contracts for Union Army uniforms. But as desirable as the step may have been, it was also risky. The United States treasury was depleted. Southern money had been withdrawn from Northern banks, and American credit overseas was getting tighter by the day. As part payment for the uniforms Joseph accepted several hundred thousand dollars worth of three-year treasury bonds at the high rate of 7.3 percent interest. In Europe, where he went to

CHAPTER SIX

sell the bonds, these high interest rate fueled rumors of the dreadful state of the government's finances. Seligman found himself caught in a cycle of selling bonds so the government would have more money to buy more uniforms from him.

Several historians have made the claim that Seligman's bond-selling efforts were crucial to the Union victory. William F. Dodd called the efforts of the Seligmans "scarcely less important to the Union cause than the Battle of Gettysburg." But others, such as writer Stephen Birmingham, point out that there are too many incomplete or lost records to justify such claims. What is certain is that Seligman sold over $60 million government notes in 1865, and that his unflagging efforts and success at selling the bonds on the European market was a critically important contribution.

Seligman now began to make his mark as a banker. In an era bent on maintaining exclusive preserves, the old-line Protestants were plugged into the choicer, more secure companies by their old boy networks. The German-Jewish and Protestant newcomers to banking had to back the speculative, riskier companies. There were disadvantages, there were challenges, and there was excitement.

When the Civil War ended, Seligman threw his energies into expanding his New York-based banking house into an international one based on the Rothschild model: brothers and nephews ran offices in Paris, London, Frankfurt, San Francisco, and New Orleans. It came as a surprise to Joseph when, in 1869, the newly elected Ulysses S. Grant offered him the post of Secretary of the Treasury. He declined, as he had declined other offers, including an approach to run for mayor of New York on the Republican ticket.

Instead of the political arena, Seligman got into the game that drew the era's monied players into dramatic competition: railroads.

The lives of Joseph Seligman and August Belmont, the financier and social lion of that fabled era, make for a striking contrast. Belmont's approach to success was markedly different than that taken by most of the German-Jewish men who built huge fortunes in America.

He was born in 1816. His father, Simon Schönberg, was a struggling merchant in the Rhineland. August left home at 13, and got himself apprenticed to the Rothschild office in Frankfurt. Rudeness was said to characterize him, but that and his lack of education would not hinder him; the Rothschilds were quick to recognize his gift for finance and he was dispatched to outposts where his bad manners would be less of a liability. America was one of these. He was but 21 when he arrived in New York in 1837, but he was already an experienced Rothschild agent with access to huge sums of money. He traveled first class all the way. There was no hundred-mile walk such as Joseph Seligman, with his first-rate university education (at graduation he had delivered his farewell oration in Greek; he spoke five other languages as well) had undertaken in the same month and year. It is interesting to note that among the restrictive laws that hindered Jews in Germany was one that barred them from selling goods they could not carry with them. And so, while Jews were restricted to peddling from backpacks and pushcarts in Europe, in America, as in Joseph Seligman's case, peddling became the basis upon which these men could build the capital and experience to enter into a more solid occupation.

August Belmont's America would be comprised of a glittering social set in a city that was just beginning to tap its potential. New York did not yet have a class of idle gentry, but it had become the financial capital of the country. It was an open field with much money around – hundreds of millions were being invested in the stock and credit markets. Commercial banks were not taking advantage of these circumstances. Belmont saw that the climate was right for private banking and set up a firm. During the Panic of 1837 he won respect all around when with loans from the House of Rothschild he saved several banks from failing.

While still in Europe his social self-image had prompted him to change the German name Schönberg, meaning beautiful mountain, to Belmont, the French equivalent. Also before arriving in America he met the first prerequisite for entry into the new society by changing his religion and worshipping in the Episcopal Church. Once in New York, Belmont perceived the nature of the social climate as well as he did the financial one. He cultivated the impression of an exalted family background and a "continental style." Kissing the hands of his hostesses, he would look directly and challengingly into their eyes, an experience he knew they found pleasurable. In 1848, he married Caroline Slidell Perry, daughter of the famous Commodore Matthew Perry, who had opened up trade with Japan. It was a marriage of the Perry social distinction and Belmont's great wealth. Ensconced in his new mansion, with the largest ballroom of any in New York, Belmont was soon setting the social pace. Servants wore the Belmont livery, maroon coats with scarlet piping; the Belmont crest was on buttons and carriages.

Belmont was a connoisseur of good food. He helped bring "cuisine" into the home – or rather the mansion. His dinner parties – sometimes for 200 – included gifts of precious gems for the ladies. In this he was not unique. Some tycoons went so far as to leave formidable amounts of cash under the plates of their guests. This cash-under-glass was more than just another outrageous display of affluence, however. It was an outright buying of guests in the scramble to entertain those most sought-after. It is ironic, but perhaps not so puzzling, that as

CHAPTER SIX

LEFT
This sympathetic caricature of the Grand Union Hotel affair appeared in PUCK *in 1877.*

anti-Semitism grew, some in the new Protestant upper class – those who had not taken stock of themselves – would justify their exclusiveness on the grounds that Jews were materialistic.

One can sum up Belmont's success in this narcissistic society with the old saying, "It takes one to know one." The leading German-Jewish families, the ones calling themselves the One Hundred, or Our Crowd, were not taken in by Belmont, but they were respectful of his business acumen and amazed at his social mobility. Belmont was someone to watch carefully, but not to follow. Embracing America was one thing; apostasy quite another. As the century moved into the 1870s, people started making distinctions between Hebrews and Jews. The descendents of Colonial Sephardim were Hebrews, society's phrase for Jews of breeding. Dilemmas of self-definition seemed to abound for the immigrants of 1848 and after, many of whom still spoke English with a German accent. As they scored successes in America, and as anti-Semitism increased, they too wanted to be thought of as Hebrew; they wanted to avoid being lumped together with Jews who came from other countries, cultures, ethnic groups, and poorer economic strata.

A NETHER WAY TO THE TOP

Not of course, that there weren't poor German Jews. A majority were lower- and middle-income earners. And some, small in numbers, joined the ranks of the criminal professions where the "entrepreneureal spirit" had fuller play. The most professional and successful fence in all of New York City was Fredericka, or Marm (also known as Mother), Mandelbaum. Between 1862 and 1882 she is said to have passed up to $10 million of stolen goods.

The 250-pound Marm also started out as a peddler, but in a markedly different tradition. She went from house to house selling goods stolen for her by the top burglars and gangs. In those days a gang was likely to have hundreds of members, so it can be seen by today's standards that Marm was one of the best networkers in her business. In fact, she was managerially inclined; she kept her lawyers on annual retainer, and adopted some basic business practices. One was to put her burglars on salary so she could be sure of getting all they stole. But too many of her employees proved to be bad team players and funneled the loot to competitor fences. For a while she tried educating the young. She supposedly ran a school for boys and girls where pickpockets and other thieves lectured on their areas of expertise.

When the reformers came into power in City Hall in 1884, and the underworld could no longer depend upon the police and city officials who had been on their payroll for years, indictments for receiving stolen goods came down against her. Marm's practical business sense had her skipping bail and setting up housekeeping in Canada. Through clever transferences of property her holdings were kept from the intrusive arm of the law.

CHAPTER SIX

THE GRAND UNION HOTEL AFFAIR

Joseph Seligman was at the height of his career when he was asked, along with other eminent bankers (including August Belmont), to devise a plan to "refund the Government's war debt." Seligman's plan was deemed the best, and was implemented with excellent results. It was after this feverish flurry of work in June, 1877 that he decided to vacation at the Grand Union Hotel, which he had frequented before. Built on seven acres in Saratoga Springs, the Grand Union was where the rich promenaded in a seemingly endless array of fashion; the Saratoga trunk was designed for this purpose. Seligman was shocked to be told that the hotel's new proprietor, Judge Henry Hilton, had left word that no "Israelites" would be welcome. He immediately dashed off a letter to the hotel and a copy to the newspapers. So great was his belief in America that he seemed to have no gnawing doubts about what the public's reaction to such discrimination would be. The responses were divisive. Most condemned the exclusionary policy, but many welcomed it.

Hilton rebutted with a letter to the papers affirming his policy "notwithstanding Moses and all of his descendants." The incident caused a sensation. In an announcement in the *New York Times*, Hilton implied that Seligman was not held in respect by his colleagues on Wall Street. But the companies, Morgan-Drexel, First National Bank, and August Belmont, ran a paid statement to the contrary.

The Grand Union had been losing its clientele to other resorts, such as Cape May and Long Branch. Through appeals to their sense of specialness, Hilton sought to woo the loyalty of the society swells. Excluding Jews was one method. But there are indications that he was engaging in a personal vendetta against Seligman. Hilton was a member of the Tweed Ring, and Seligman was a member of the Committee of 70, a group of prominent citizens chosen to investigate and rid New York of this notorious group, which had defrauded the city of millions. Hilton was the executor of the estate of Alexander T. Stewart, who owned the largest retail store in New York, and whose estate included the $2 million interest in the Grand Union that gave Hilton proprietorship of the hotel. Both Stewart and Seligman had been on the board of directors of the New York Railway Company, of which Henry Hilton was president. When Seligman became a member of the Committee of 70, the A. E. Stewart Company stopped getting its bills of exchange from Seligman's firm. Stewart was avid for a political appointment. After Seligman turned down Grant's overture for Secretary of Treasury, Grant offered the post to Stewart. But because of his affiliation with Hilton and other Tweed Ring members, he was not confirmed. And, finally, when Seligman turned down a bid to run for mayor, Stewart, who craved that job, exclaimed: "Who does Seligman think he is? He seems to think that politics is only for tradespeople."

As things got even uglier, with anti-Semitic slurs scribbled on walls, the newspaper editorials decried prejudice, and ministers based their sermons on the incident. Seligman took but little comfort from his friends. Some of his faith in America was shaken. His close friend, the Reverend Henry Ward Beecher, the most famous minister of his day, described the Saratoga snobs as "men who made their money yesterday selling codfish." "A man may be annoyed by a mosquito," he told Seligman, "but to put on his whole armour and call on his followers to join him in making war on an insect would be beneath his dignity."

A large indignation meeting was planned, but as the controversy grew more shrill, Seligman decided to have it called off. However, 100 leading Jewish merchants boycotted Stewart's department store and eventually helped bring about its decline. Fearful of losing some of the huge fortune over which he had proprietorship, Judge Hilton responded by offering $1,000 to Jewish charities. The gesture was laughable. *Puck*, the satiric magazine, stated, ". . . the Jew has stood up like a man and refused to condone the gross and uncalled-for insults of this haphazard millionaire, merely because he flings the offer of a thousand dollars in their faces . . ."

There is a ghoulish irony in the fact that the following year the remains of A. E. Stewart's body were taken for ransom by bodysnatchers, who usually sold less renowned corpses to medical students. The snatchers demanded $200,000. Hilton's top offer was an unyielding $25,000. Negotiations dragged on for almost two years, during which time Stewart's widow would gladly have paid much more to end the agony of her husband's unsettled remains.

The Hilton–Seligman Affair advertised a discrimination that until then was tacit. Justifications for it were now blithely offered in public debate. Since public opinion came down squarely against the exclusionists, the episode could be viewed as an opportunity to clear the air in the best democratic tradition. And most important, this was America, where exclusion has no government sanction.

But the incident spotlighted a change in values that had been germinating for a long time. A Protestant establishment that had Sephardic and German Jews and Irish and French Catholics among its ancestors, closed ranks. The diminished fortunes of some of the old aristocracy, the rise of brash new millionaires, and the steady increase in immigration throughout the century helped fuel the bent for exclusion. The social anti-Semitism of Germany, which in the 1870s gained

respectability within German politics was an influence too. The times were charged with faddish scientific theory. Eugenics and the new philosophies of race had everyone checking and classifying what were assumed to be inborn traits. Skulls were precisely measured. The skull size of Anglo-Saxons, for instance, was found to be superior to other groups. Exclusion now gained a so-called scientific justification, at least until Franz Boas, the famous German-Jewish anthropologist, came to America. In a study for the U.S. Immigration Commission, he demonstrated that environment plays an important role in determining physical traits such as head size, and that head size has nothing to do with intelligence.

But socially the intent was clear. The new value system was gaining momentum. What counted now was caste, not class. After the Grand Union closed its doors to Jews, other posh hotels and resorts followed suit. Of course, there were people of sensibility and wit, such as the philosopher William James, who upon receiving a flyer from a hotel advertising that Jews were not allowed, sent it back with the note: "I return the boycott." The private clubs were next. Joseph Seligman was a founder of the Union League Club; his brother Jesse was a member. In 1893, when Jesse's son was put up for membership – his sponsors were Elihu Root and Joseph Choate – he was rejected. Jesse resigned, but the membership committee refused to accept it. The rejection, they said, "was not a personal matter in any way . . . the objection is purely racial." Out West, too, territories in which but 30 years before everyone was a welcome stranger, had a new set of rules. By 1881 the Denver Club – a chess and literary society among whose organizers was frontier merchant Fred Z. Salomon – was closed to Jews.

Now lines were being drawn by everyone. In what has come to be called the Second Battle of Saratoga, Jews set about building hotels there and in other resorts, for Jewish clientele. Nathan Straus built his own hotel in Lakewood, New Jersey, bigger and better than the one next door that had refused him admission. German Jews founded more of their own clubs, and created their own "Hebrew select." This not only met their social needs, but it served as a class barrier against the East European Jews who started to arrive en masse in the 1880s. In time though, the barriers between the two groups would lessen considerably. Other immigrant groups also began to form societies and clubs.

The majority of Jews worked hard earning a daily wage and had more pressing needs than luxury hotels and private clubs. But when the professions closed their doors – the New York Bar Association started blackballing Jews in 1878 – and the colleges instituted informal quotas, it was another matter. Even in the poorest East European Jewish families the value of learning was in the grain; in America a college degree was a way to prosperity. But now there were exclusions that would affect the East European newcomers harshly.

Things would loosen up a bit with World War II, but it would take the civil rights movement of black Americans, the country's most excluded minority, and the election of an Irish-Catholic president in 1960, before the country would really begin to open up to its diverse population.

Near the end of the nineteenth century America was

CHAPTER SIX

LEFT
Another partner in the firm of Kuhn, Loeb was Otto Hermann Kahn (1867–1934). A noted patron of the arts, Kahn was chairman of the board of the Metropolitan Opera Company in New York from 1903 to 1917, and then president from 1917 to 1931. This picture was taken around 1909.

BELOW
One of the founders of the banking firm of Kuhn, Loeb, and Co. was Abraham Kuhn. He is shown here in the banking office he established in Ogden, Utah, in 1868.

CHAPTER SIX

RIGHT
Jacob Schiff was a generous contributor to the Jewish Theological Seminary of America, founded in 1886.

FAR RIGHT
John M. Schiff continued many of his father's charitable works. He is shown here in 1939 with New York Governor Alfred Smith.

changing rapidly. The sense of place, of traditional religions and social affiliations, were weakened. The railroads, soon to be eclipsed by the automobile, allowed families to move easily to other parts of the country. Patterns of worship changed: richer Protestants worshipped in the Episcopal Church; richer Jews in the Reform branch of Judaism. The link with the Old Testament that observant Jews and the descendents of Puritans had in their daily lives was lessened too. Old Testament first names were less frequently given to the children.

Those days in the South of the 1880s that writer Harry Golden recounts, of young Orthodox peddlers who stopped overnight with Southern Fundamentalist families who delighted in hearing their Jewish guests recite the morning prayers in Hebrew, and who were careful not to serve them pork and pork products, would soon be gone.

Part of the American past, too, was Harriet Beecher Stowe's memory of her grandfather praying: "My grandfather always prayed standing . . . [The prayers] were Hebraistic in their form; they spoke of Zion and Jerusalem, of the God of Israel, the God of Jacob, as much as if my grandfather had been a veritable Jew; and except for the closing phrase, 'for the sake of Thy Son, our Saviour,' might have been uttered in Palestine by a well-trained Jew in the time of David."

JACOB SCHIFF & JEWISH PHILANTHROPY

He was a force that kept Jewish Americans aware of their obligations to each other, of the ancient Jewish principle that each Jew is responsible for every other Jew. This was especially important during the time of the East European immigration, which the established German Jews saw as a threat to their balance of American secular existence and Reform Judaism. He was short, with piercing blue eyes that even in old black-and-white photos seem to rivet the viewer; they tell a story of mastery, toughness, and acuity. Jacob Schiff was born in Frankfurt, Germany in 1847. His father was a broker on the stock exchange. His upbringing was one of affluence, education, and religious piety. Jacob was a restless child, strong-willed and good at going it alone. By the age of 18 he was in New York, working for a brokerage house; then he attempted to start his own, with two young partners. The partnership was not successful and he returned to Germany, where he tried and was bored by commercial banking.

Traveling in Germany's Jewish investment circles, which had close ties to U.S. families, Schiff soon met Abraham Kuhn, a founder of the firm Kuhn, Loeb. He suggested that Schiff contact his partner, Solomon Loeb, in New York. It was a fortuitous idea. Schiff started to work for the firm at 26; within a year he was married to Solomon Loeb's daughter, Therese. He had already begun to enhance the fortunes of the firm by specializing in railroads. Railroad speculation was the main financial game of the time, and backers could be found for even the most speculative lines. But Schiff wanted to be more than an investment advisor to the railroads. He assured his success by taking an active role in the management of the railroads he backed. He rode the lines, querying the engineers, porters, and everyone else. His first bold undertaking was a collaboration with Edward (Ned) Harriman, who had just bought the bankrupt Union Pacific line. The two set about reorganizing the railroad that financier Jay Gould had left in shambles. Few had faith in its revival, but within three years they made it profitable.

Schiff and his client Harriman worked together for

CHAPTER SIX

LEFT
The Warburg Mansion on New York's Fifth Avenue was built in 1909. It was donated to the Jewish Theological Seminary of America in 1944 by Mrs. Felix Warburg. The mansion opened to the public as The Jewish Museum in 1947.

twenty years of some of that era's most intense financial battles. Most notable was the so-called Battle of the Giants. This struggle for control of the Chicago, Burlington and Quincy Railroad pitted Harriman and Schiff against James J. Hill, a long-time friend of Schiff and a man who echoed the spirit of the age when he said, "The fortunes of the railroad companies are determined by the law of the survival of the fittest." Hill's banker was J. P. Morgan. Harriman wanted to buy the Chicago line to eliminate competition with his Union Pacific. In the famous square-off, Schiff kept promoting the idea of compromise. Harriman, he knew, would be satisfied with an interest in the line and a seat on the board. But Hill and Morgan wanted no part of Harriman: they bought the line without him. Harriman and Schiff countered. Since he could not get the Burlington line, Harriman decided to go after the parent company and buy out Hill's Northern Pacific. He and Schiff bought up large blocks of shares. Hill got wind of the plan and started buying shares to keep them from his rivals. The struggle caused massive insecurity in the market, and other stocks plummeted.

At a crucial point, Hill – who had proved to be untrustworthy before – betrayed his friend Jacob's trust. He called a halt to the struggle by promising Schiff he'd give Harriman a seat on the board of the Burlington. Then he turned around and bought up 150,000 more shares of Northern Pacific stock.

It would be hard to determine who was "fittest" here. The stock value of both sides was near even. To protect Hill's interests, Morgan formed the Northern Securities Holding Company, due in large measure to Schiff's ability to focus on long-term interests, Harriman was given a seat on the board of the new company.

Through just such clear-headedness in troubled waters, Schiff led his firm to become the largest, most prominent of the Jewish investment-banking firms. Kuhn, Loeb financed mining companies, helped the Guggenheims gain control of the embattled American Smelting and Refining Company, aided Western Union Telegraph, and for 40 years financed the Pennsylvania Railroad through to its entry into New York and the building of the original Pennsylvania Station.

When he had firmly set the direction of Kuhn, Loeb, Schiff turned over his day-to-day business responsibilities to his younger partners, including his son Mortimer, son-in-law Felix Warburg, and Otto Kahn, and devoted himself to the needs of Jews worldwide. Once the East European immigration was inevitable, he was a formidable intercessor with authorities, especially immigration authorities, on their behalf. He had the will and resources to get things done. No one carried more weight in the Jewish community.

Schiff's philanthropy is notable not only because of his largesse – he gave somewhere between $50 and $100 million to Jewish and secular causes, but because it was given in the spirit of sedakah. Ten percent of everything he gave was a tithe, society's due. Only what was given beyond that did he consider philanthropy. And, in the tradition of sedakah, his contributions were almost always anonymous. He was a main benefactor of the Henry Street Settlement in New York City. The project closest to his heart was Montefiore Hospital, also in New York City, of which he was president. He spent Sundays visiting patients. He supported many educational institutions, including the Tuskegee Institute and a number of other Southern black schools. He gave buildings to the Young Men's Hebrew Association, to Barnard College, and to the Jewish Theological Seminary. He gave the Semitic Museum to Harvard. Along with Seth Low (president of Columbia University), J. P. Morgan, and financier James Speyer, he started a humanitarian pawn shop that was precursor of the Provident Loan Society. By charging 1 percent interest instead of the then high rate of 3 percent that pawnbrokers were permitted to charge, they were able to bring down the interest rates in the immigrant communities.

It was in keeping with the spirit of sedakah, too, that Schiff and the relatively small number of millionaires in the German-Jewish establishment began to support worthy causes as soon as their earnings permitted. This was a departure from the habits of almost all of the other millionaires so comfortably lionized in that gilded era. The philanthropic foundations built from fortunes made in the period from after the Civil War to 1900 were – as historian Richard Hofstadter points out – almost all created after 1910. Among Gentiles, Andrew Carnegie, who believed that "few millionaires are clear of the sin of having made beggars," was an exception.

ABOVE

Henry Morgenthau (1856–1946) came to America from Germany as a child. He made his fortune in New York City real estate and banking. He was U.S. ambassador to Turkey from 1913 to 1916, a position he used to protect Jews in Palestine.

THE EAST EUROPEAN INFLUX

CHAPTER SEVEN

Up until the nineteenth century, people could travel from country to country with a fair amount of ease. The right of asylum was honored, and exiles were accorded respect in their adopted countries as intellectuals, people of conviction, or because they were monied or offered new skills. But starting in the late nineteenth century, and in full force by World War I, passports and visas were required; borders were now fixed and closed. A new misery was added to the world – one that would befall millions of people with increasing frequency throughout the twentieth century: statelessness. As growing nationalism led to the expulsion of minority groups from newly formed countries, as thousands upon thousands of civilians were caught in the battlegrounds of the Austro-Prussian and Franco-Prussian wars, as peasants were uprooted by the Balkan wars, and as Russian and Rumanian Jews, who had been forced into poverty by government restrictions against them trekked toward western Europe, they became populations on the road to no man's land.

The first major exodus of Jews out of Russia was in 1881. They fled from the pogroms that were being incited throughout the Pale of Settlement, and encamped in Brody, an Austrian border town where authorities were known to be less exacting, and where they could slip across the border illegally. By 1882 more than 20,000 refugees swelled the population of this town of 15,000 residents; it was but an indication of things to come.

The May Laws, so called because they were passed on May 3, 1882, were designed to make the Russian-Jewish population virtual prisoners in their shtetls and villages. They were forbidden to move. If they left their town or village for even a few days their homes could be confiscated. Relatives in other villages were not permitted to dwell with them. They were not permitted to inherit family businesses based in other towns. They were cut out of education and the professions by strict quotas. They had to undertake various subterfuges to make life worth living. One of the most perverse instances was of Jewish women who, to get the education they craved, had to register as prostitutes, the only condition under which the mocking authorities would allow them to travel and live in university centers. When the police saw they were not practicing their "registered" trade, they were thrown out of a city. The May Laws had the desired effect: Russian Jews streamed into West Europe, and from there to America.

In Europe the Alliance Israélite Universelle, then the world's largest Jewish philanthropic organization, and the Baron de Hirsch Fund helped to feed, house, and transport the immigrants to ports of embarkation. But the West European Jews were soon overwhelmed by the massive and costly immigration. The Jewish middle classes of West Europe were unprepared to deal with the influx. After the initial expressions of joy and gratitude by the first refugee groups the larger flow of refugees from the Ukraine began to complain of the inadequate provisions. They sat on benches or slept in the streets of Brody and other towns. Out of a habit of open expression developed in the close, cramped quarters of the Pale – and especially after the rigors of their journey – they voiced criticisms of their richer – and culturally different – benefactors. It was a habit they would bring with them to America. A reaction set in. The directors of the Alliance, and other German and French Jews, began to believe that their philanthropy, rather than dire poverty and persecutory restrictions, was the incentive for the Russians to flock to the West. Official greeters at the Brody train station attempted to bribe them to return to Russia, but to little avail. When the Alliance, acting on pressure from the Board of Delegates of American Israelites, wanted to limit American immigration to males, the Russians in Brody wired to Paris, "Would rather starve than leave families."

In the U.S. too, the first impulse of the German-Jewish establishment was to try to limit the immigration. In 1891, Jacob Schiff went to Europe in an effort to convince the Jewish establishment to channel the immigrants away from America. For European and American Jews, the desire to help was pitted against a fear of jeopardizing their own positions as Jews who were more than ever before integrated into the national lives of

CHAPTER SEVEN

CENTER
This cartoon appeared in JUDGE *in 1892. It depicts old-line Americans being forced westward by Jews from East Europe.*

their countries. There was also a simple lack of resources. In the 1880s, American-Jewish charities did not have enough money to sustain the immigrant poor. A concern of another nature was that the sheer numbers of East Europeans flocking to the tenements of America's cities could make them a controlling factor in city elections. And were that to happen, the German Jews feared, it could cause an uproar. Perhaps they also sensed it could eventually deprive them of their leadership in the Jewish community.

From 1870 to 1891 the feeling in America was generally favorable to immigration. Immigrants were still needed in the labor force. It was the American Jews who wanted to limit, unofficially and through Jewish agencies, the immigration. But what is remarkable is that in a short period of time, and for a range of reasons, they not only changed their position, but undertook to facilitate immigration for as many as wanted to come. As a new American mercantile class, the German Jews felt honor-bound to help their poorer cousins. The rising social exclusion at the upper reaches of Gentile society had made them rethink some of their more idealistic notions about America. There was the realization that as immigration increased, all Jews were being thought of as new immigrants, the distinctions between Hebrew and Jew, of class and cultures, were meaningless. Finally, there was true sympathy for their displaced co-religionists. They resolved to solve the problem through a well-organized philanthropy that would have as its goal the quickest possible Americanization of the seemingly backward, difficult East Europeans. There were some, such as Jacob Schiff and Julius Rosenwald, who would act out of the principle of sedakah; others acted out of a condescending noblesse oblige. But no matter the reasons, they – and later the Russian Jews who brought with them organizing skills honed in the Pale, where more than 40 percent of the Jews survived through sedakah – built a huge philanthropic structure that has never been rivaled in the U.S. A system of responsibilities between the West European and American agencies was set up. Refugees were accompanied on trains, met at borders, given kosher food and medical attention; con men and thieves, who from the first preyed on refugees, were fended off. Kosher kitchens were set up on ships, and agency officials dealt with European immigration authorities to aid those caught in red tape – as did the American Jews at their end.

When the Immigration Restriction League, founded in 1884 by Boston Brahmins, began to rattle the bones of American nativism and gain popular support, the American Jewish establishment was prepared to fight them, tactic for tactic.

In 1891 the League was able to get an extension of an 1882 law that excluded, along with the mentally handicapped and "morally undesirable, paupers . . . or anyone

whose ticket or passage is paid for with the money of another." It was a law that would have made it harder for the impoverished Jews of the Pale to gain entry were it not for the legal skills of such organizations as the Hebrew Immigrant Aid Society (HIAS) in defending immigrants on a case-by-case basis. HIAS was founded and run by Russian Jews, who learned much about American politics, lobbying, and legal defense tactics from the German-Jewish organizations.

In 1896 the League proposed literacy tests that would require all adult immigrants to read forty words in any language, a test that would, as historian Abraham J. Karp has commented, "have excluded one-fourth of the Jewish and far more of other immigrants then arriving."

This law was turned down twice by Congress and by three different presidents: Cleveland, Taft and Wilson. Each time it came up – in 1898, 1902, 1906, 1913, and 1915 – the various immigrant communities rallied in opposition.

Whenever possible, Jacob Schiff used his formidable financial skills to ease the plight of Jews worldwide. He did this through philanthropy and by refusing to float loans to countries that legitimized anti-Semitism.

In 1904 Baron Korekiyo Takahashi, financial commissioner of the Japanese government, went abroad to raise money for Japan's war with Russia. Schiff went into action, underwriting half of the total needed, $50 million. It was his expression of hatred for the per-

CHAPTER SEVEN

sistently anti-Semitic Russia. He made it his policy to discourage other American bankers from lending money to Russia. His daughter, Frieda, explained, "It was not so much my father's interest in Japan, but rather his hatred of Imperial Russia and its anti-Semitic policies, that prompted him to take the financial risk." With the Japanese victory the risk happily turned to huge profit. In all, Schiff was to arrange loans to Japan totaling $200 million. The Japanese government bestowed high honors on him, including the Second Order of the Sacred Treasure, the Order of the Rising Sun, and an invitation to lunch with the emperor – the first foreign citizen to have that honor.

Schiff viewed the Russia of his day with a clearer eye than those who believed that unofficial discussion could make a dent in Russia's anti-Jewish policies. His friends encouraged him to meet with the Russian diplomats who came to the U.S. to work out peace terms with the Japanese. He refused. He saw only one condition upon which to base any favorable dealings with Russia, and that was the bestowal of civil rights on the Jewish subjects. Until those civil rights had *actually* been given, Schiff saw no point in entering into any business dealings.

Even at the expense of large profits, Schiff remained true to his views. During World War I, in 1915, Lord Rufus Reading, head of the Anglo-French Commission, came to the U.S. to negotiate a loan for the Allied cause. Russia was an ally of England and France, but pogroms were a fact of everyday life in that country. It was, no doubt, an interesting meeting between the former Rufus Isaacs, an observant Jew, who was named Lord Chief Justice of England in 1913, became ambassador to the U.S. in 1918, and was appointed His Majesty's Viceroy for India in 1921, and the stalwart leader of the American Jewish community. Schiff's son Mortimer, and Otto Kahn, both Kuhn, Loeb partners, were eager to participate in the loan. Schiff, too, wanted to help the Allies, but only on the condition that none of the money he raised would go to Russia. This, of course, was impossible for Lord Reading to guarantee. Schiff declined to participate, even though his refusal to do so would be widely interpreted as a sign that – especially as a German-born American – his sympathies were with Germany. Nothing was further from the truth, but he kept to his position. At a momentous meeting in the Kuhn, Loeb offices he said: "I cannot stultify myself by aiding those who in bitter enmity have tortured my people and will continue to do so, whatever fine professions they may make in their hour of need. I cannot sacrifice my profoundest convictions. This is a matter between me and my conscience." Some years later, after a wild misquote of a statement he made was printed in the press and caused a furor in New York's Russian-Jewish community, he asserted that for 25 years he had struggled singlehandedly against "the invasion of the Russian Government into American money markets and to this day have staved them off."

When Japan entered the war on Russia's side, he resigned with dispatch from the Japan Society, although he was a founding member.

THE AMERICAN JEWISH COMMITTEE

FROM BOLD ACTION TO QUIET DIPLOMACY

Troubled by events abroad – the Dreyfus case in France, German anti-Semitism, and the Kishinev massacre in which 49 Jews were killed, 500 wounded, and 700 houses and businesses destroyed (all justified by the Russian government), Jabob Schiff and his friends in the Jewish establishment began to meet and discuss what could be done. Protests were held across the country, senators and governors expressed their outrage, and it was hoped that the U.S. government would condemn the Kishinev atrocity. That did not happen. The German Jews realized they had to assume leadership and create a national organization to represent Jewish interests, one that could rally enough support to bring about government action. They were afraid, too, of the role the vocal new Russian immigrants, with their im-

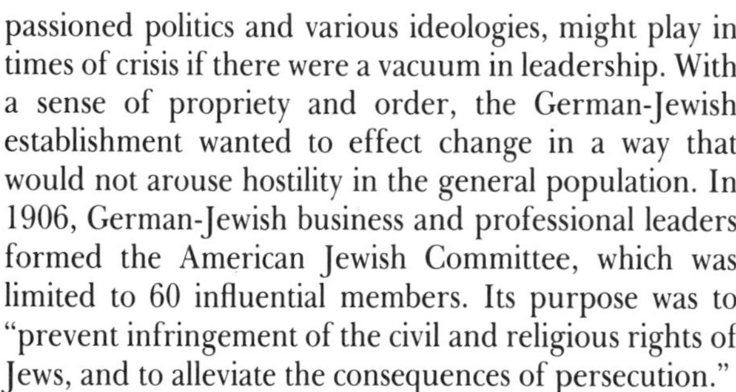

A FUTURE CRŒSUS.

ROSENSHEEN—"Mein sohn, you vas tervendy-one to-day, unt I maigs you a bresent."
ISIDOR—"Vell, vat vas it?"
ROSENSHEEN—"I dakes you into bartnerships."
ISIDOR—"Unt you vas goin' to fail nexd veek?"
ROSENSHEEN—"I vas."
ISIDOR (*falling on his father's neck*)—"Fader, dot vas munificend!"

CHAPTER SEVEN

RIGHT
Jewish immigrants from East Europe found themselves the target of prejudice and exclusionary laws, starting in the 1890s. This anti-Semitic cartoon appeared in the "humor" magazine JUDGE *in 1890.*

passioned politics and various ideologies, might play in times of crisis if there were a vacuum in leadership. With a sense of propriety and order, the German-Jewish establishment wanted to effect change in a way that would not arouse hostility in the general population. In 1906, German-Jewish business and professional leaders formed the American Jewish Committee, which was limited to 60 influential members. Its purpose was to "prevent infringement of the civil and religious rights of Jews, and to alleviate the consequences of persecution."

Its first big campaign, in 1911, was to lobby for the cancellation of the Russo-American treaty of 1832, an important issue. Over the years the Russians had used clauses in this treaty of commerce to exclude or restrict certain American citizens – Protestant missionaries, Catholic priests, and all Jews – from the freedom of travel that was otherwise mutually assured the residents of both countries. Russia sought to impose on all foreign Jews traveling within its borders the same restrictions and disabilities it imposed on native Jews in the Pale.

The American Jewish Committee argued that this was onerous for all Americans, not just Jews. The treaty allowed a foreign government to discriminate against certain Americans. The renowned constitutional lawyer Louis M. Marshall posited that if the passports of Episcopalians or Presbyterians were not honored by the Russians, the U.S. should surely and rightly take it as an insult to all Americans. And, indeed, since these restrictions affected the Jews, even though they were very few, then representing America in the foreign service, they symbolically affected all America. When diplomat Oscar Straus was about to end one of his several tours as minister to Turkey, he was invited by the Russian ambassador to Turkey to come to Russia on his way back to America. Straus reminded him of the passport restriction; the ambassador then presented him with a passport that read: "The Jew Oscar Straus is permitted to enter Russia for three months." Needless to say, Straus did not make use of his "privileged" passport.

The U.S government took heed of the American Jewish Committee's campaign and issued protests through diplomatic channels to the Russian government; Congress denounced the Russian position but still nothing was done. Economic considerations outweighed all others: Russia was a potentially strong trading partner, a market for U.S. goods. The Department of State informed passport applicants that Jews and all former Russian subjects would be issued passports only with the consent of the Russian government.

Jacob Schiff urged a bolder approach. The newly elected President William Howard Taft supported the State Department position, but Schiff was undaunted. Through rallies, articles, and lobbying in the House and Senate, the Committee presented its case to the American public. It won. On January 1, 1913, the 80-year-old treaty was terminated. But there were repercussions: the expected loss of trade, Russian reprisals against its Jewish population, and bitterness from other Americans against Jewish Americans.

The usually decorous members of the American Jewish Committee distanced themselves from their bold action. From now on they would act with quiet diplomacy, a conclusion that was perhaps a rationalization that allowed them to fall back upon a style with which they were naturally at home.

With the outbreak of World War I, the resources of the American Jewish Committee, and all Jewish charitable organizations were needed. When Turkey entered the war on the side of Germany against Britain, France and Russia, the safety of Russian Jews who had fled to Palestine, then under Turkish rule, was threatened. Schiff and other members of the American Jewish Committee were asked, in an urgent telegram from the U.S. ambassador to Turkey, Henry Morgenthau, Sr., to contribute toward their relief. They raised the money requested. Through the contributions, and more importantly through the influence of some of the American Jews, such as Morgenthau with the Turks, 55,000 Palestinian Jews were saved. But the American Jewish Committee realized that the financial need of the masses of uprooted Jews was far greater than any one of the organizations could handle. The Turks conscripted Jews in Palestine; Jews not born in the Ottoman territories were expelled. The entire Jewish population of Jaffa was routed. Thousands were forced into boats bound for Alexandria, Egypt, where they desperately awaited help to immigrate to America. There was a need to coordinate the efforts of the various agencies and charities. Schiff and the American Jewish Committee met with representatives of forty of the largest organizations. At the meeting one hundred Jewish leaders were chosen to comprise the American Jewish Relief Committee. After an agency was set up by Felix Warburg to disburse funds to Europe, this group became the amazing Joint Distribution Committee. It was soon disbursing over $15 million yearly so that Jews in Europe could have the freedom of choice: They could use the financial aid to ease their daily lives in their countries, or they could use it to emigrate. This rescue operation incorporated the luxurious American values of opportunity and choice.

Jacob Schiff and his fellow philanthropists had a spiritual agenda. Aiding in the survival of beleaguered Jews worldwide meant the survival of the Jewish mission. "As Jews," Schiff said, "we have something precious of high value to mankind in our keeping, that our mission in the world continue and with it our responsibilities of one for the other."

This sense of obligation between coreligionists who are not related by country or class has been called a Jewish phenomenon. Judaism, like Christianity, is a religion made up of diverse ethnic groups. But as author Charles Silverman has pointed out, it is a religion that defines itself existentially, as does a race. One does not *become* a Jew. One *is* a Jew, whether born or converted. That is why a Jew who converts to another religion and wants to return can do so without converting back. The wonder is that so many diverse groups of people from so many different parts of the world have remained part of this historic mission.

The Growth of Reform Judaism

The elite, successful men in the American Jewish Committee shared similar beliefs and opinions. They belonged to the same congregation, Temple Emanu-El. In 1870, when their gleaming new synagogue on New York's Fifth Avenue was built, the *New York Times* wrote of their congregation that it was "The first to stand forward before the world and proclaim the dominion of reason over blind and bigoted faith."

Reform Judaism sprouted in the pre-Civil War era in an atmosphere when individualism became a driving force for religious change. Protestants were also breaking off from the established churches, and Jews were continuing an American chain reaction that began with the break from the enforced – often legislated – religious orthodoxy of Europe. Reform Judaism could fit easily into the American landscape, and especially with the declaration, made at the Reform Pittsburgh conference in 1885, that they considered themselves a religious community and not a nation. Their emphasis was on Judaism as the religion of a people with a universal mission: to bring the word of God to the rest of mankind; a Judaism, as they wrote in Pittsburgh, that preserved "the God-idea . . . the central truth for the human race."

Their reform congregation would keep only that part of the Jewish tradition that was compatible with reason and experience. As Judaism stresses ethics over doctrine, and as it is not as credal as many other religions, Reform congregations viewed the changes they made as being within the bounds of the tradition. To be a Jew is a birthright, or a matter of conversion. Accordingly, some stopped the practice of circumcision. Some stopped reading prayers in Hebrew, since it was found to be a principle of Judaism that prayers can be said in any language. They stopped performing bar mitzvahs and began to hold services on Sunday. They accepted the moral laws of Judaism, but not the ones restricting diet or dress; they no longer wore yarmulkes.

It is believed by some that Reform practice was able to become so spare so quickly because even those in the Reform camp who wanted less radical change knew – or perhaps hoped – that this new form of religious worship would hold little appeal for the East European immigrants, who they wanted to keep at a distance.

But history – however forward-looking its spiritual readers – has a way of going back on itself. The amended service was so spare as to be dry. The prayers were rendered into an English that lacked spirituality. Soon the grandchildren of the Reformers, and the second American generation of East European Jews, who joined Reform congregations, brought a spiritual dimension to the service. Some prayers were said in Hebrew. Boys and girls were bar and bat mitzvahed, services were switched from Sunday back to Friday night and Saturday.

But even in the early stages of the Reform movement, definitions of Judaism and Jewishness were being put to the test by two men who were raised in the Reform tradition. In fact, they were sons of Temple Emanu-El rabbis.

Felix Adler studied for the rabbinate in Germany; it was hoped he would accept a pulpit at Emanu-El. Instead, he founded Ethical Culture in 1876, with help from Emanu-El's president Joseph Seligman. Adler aimed to take the religious liberalism of Reform Judaism and make it universal through public action. In Sunday lectures open to Christians and Jews alike he focused on the problems and ethical issues that had arisen in an increasingly industrial society; the plight of workers was a great concern. He set up schools and a free kindergarten for children of working people. He called attention to living conditions in the tenements, and got action for the tenement dwellers. He was the impetus behind a company that built model apartment houses for the Russian immigrants. He wanted ethical standards applied to daily life in accord with the Ethical Culture motto: "Deed, not creed."

Richard Gottheil, son of Rabbi Gustav Gottheil, became a Zionist leader, heading the Zionist Organization of America for many years. Zionism put the German-Jewish instinct for caution on alert. The majority were opposed to Zionism, fearing it would focus attention on Jews and make room for those who would accuse them of lack of loyalty to their native country.

Gottheil was one of a few eloquent voices within the

German-Jewish community – Louis Brandeis was another – to argue that there was no contradiction between Reform and Zionism. He claimed that the fear of being accused of dual loyalty had no place in a country where so many other groups maintained ethnic and religious identifications abroad; he argued that the state cannot expect "any group to give up its historic associations." Zionism went counter to the notions of many of the German Jews. America was their Zion. Emanu-El was called temple, not synagogue, to signify the rebuilding of the temple in America, their new Jerusalem.

Though they would not embrace Zionism, the German philanthropists did not hold back funds from the Jewish pioneers in Palestine. Jacob Schiff provided $100,000 for the Technium in Haifa, and funds for many other undertakings in Palestine, which he came to see as a center of Jewish learning and a homeland for Jews, though not a potential nation.

OSCAR STRAUS & AMERICAN DIPLOMACY

Lazarus Straus came from Bavaria to the American South, where he peddled goods to plantation owners who awaited his visits with eagerness and hospitality. In return he would, as was the custom, have just the right gift for the lady of the house. In this way he got to know the social habits and distinctions of the rural and small-town residents.

In 1854 he settled his family in Talbotton, Georgia. The Civil War and its attendant tensions sent a rash of anti-Semitism across the South that was echoed in the newspapers and, most damaging of all, in the courts. Grand juries, including one in Talbotton, made a blanket condemnation of Jewish merchants as unprincipled and unpatriotic. The well-liked Straus picked up and moved to Columbus, Georgia, despite the protestations of his neighbors that the indictment had nothing to do with him personally.

The family suffered the financial reverses typical in the post-Civil War South. Lazarus moved to New York, where he and his sons Nathan and Isidor began merchandising china and glassware. They rented display space in the basement of R. H. Macy's. Eventually they bought the store and built it into the world's largest, using the most modern merchandising methods yet devised for an American department store.

Oscar Straus, the youngest of the Straus brothers, was also the most famous. There were a number of firsts in his life. He was the first Jewish member of a presidential cabinet, serving as Secretary of Commerce and Labor under Theodore Roosevelt. The post was an honor, but did not wield much power; that was still reserved for members of the Protestant establishment. Straus was also the first Jew to be appointed an ambassador. After serving for two tours as minister to Turkey – where he managed in this relatively minor posting to defuse several major crises – he was given the rank of ambassador on his third tour. He was a founder in 1874 of the Young Men's Hebrew Association and in 1894 became the first president of the American Jewish Historical Society.

His political life began in 1882 when he worked for the re-election of W. R. Grace for mayor of New York against the Tammany Hall candidate.

By 1884 he was campaigning hard for Grover Cleveland for president. At the same time he was studying the origins of American government and formulating a thesis connecting ancient Hebrew democracy and the development of American democratic government. The development of religious liberty and democracy in America, and the ancient Jewish influences on them, were for him a lifelong interest.

In 1885 he published *The Origin of the Republican Forms of Government*, in which he traced the influence of the Hebrew Commonwealth at the time of the Judges on the formation of American democratic institutions. "When all of Western Europe was an untrodden wilderness . . . the children of Israel . . . established a free commonwealth, a pure democratic republic under a written constitution . . ." He believed that the "American spirit and the spirit of American Judaism were nurtured in the same cradle of liberty and were united in origin, in ideals, and in historical development." In his studies of the Puritans he concluded that "Moses was their law giver, the Pentateuch their code, and Israel under the Judges their ideal of popular government."

In 1894 he published *Roger Williams, the Pioneer of Religious Liberty*. He saw Williams as one of the world's great reformers, a man who not only believed in religious liberty, but who, he later wrote, had the "courage and wisdom . . . to found a purely secular state."

Straus sent his book on the origins of American government to members of Congress. Senator A. P. Gorman, who admired it, put the author forward as minister to Turkey. Though Straus had earned political credits by working for President Cleveland's election, and though Cleveland admired Straus, he hesitated. He wanted to be certain that the Protestant missions in Asia Minor would be comfortable with a Jewish diplomat looking after their interests.

By the late nineteenth century, the American Protestant missionary tradition abroad had become extremely influential. It had resonance in the secular as well as the religious realm. The religious spirit that saw the colonization of the New World and the expansion westward as having divine blessing was echoed in the

secular belief that the spreading of democracy was part of a national mission. Thus, as the U.S. expanded, so too, it was believed, did democratic freedom.

The Protestant missions abroad introduced American material values and living standards to their flocks. They provided religious and secular education, opened hospitals, and improved farming and cooking methods. In Turkey, for example, they baked a more nutritious bread for health and profit using hop yeast, and it was, in fact, called "Protestant bread" by the students. They became practical doers justifying for themselves and for the business sector the belief that industrial expansion abroad created more civilized and progressive societies – the model of civilization being, of course, the American one. "That which is good for communities in America is good for the Armenians and Greeks and Mohammedans of Turkey," went a statement made in 1881 by the American Board of Foreign Missions.

Through trade agreements and other diplomatic endeavors the government smoothed the way for U.S. industry abroad. The American missions too began to demand diplomatic help and protection in carrying out work which was often vulnerable to the changing political climate and territorial wars. Protecting the Protestant missions in Turkey would become a major preoccupation for Straus.

A letter from Reverend Henry Ward Beecher to President Cleveland reportedly clinched the appointment for Straus. He wrote: "We are Jews ourselves gone to blossom and fruit, Christianity is Judaism in evolution and it would be strange for the seed to turn against the stock on which it has grown."

Implications of a stagnant Judaism aside, Beecher was an active supporter of Straus and of appointing a Jew to the post. He wanted to demonstrate that the deeply rooted European prejudice against Jews had no place in America. "I would urge his appointment as a fit recognition of this remarkable people who are becoming large contributors to American prosperity, and whose intelligence, morality, and large liberality in all public measure for the welfare of society, deserve . . . such recognition."

Straus's appointment served in particular as a statement to Austria-Hungary, which had rejected an American for a ministerial post because his wife was Jewish.

In 1887 Straus became the third Jewish diplomat to serve in a ministerial post abroad. He set about to woo and win the confidence of the Turkish ruler. Through patience, tact, and perseverance he was successful, and got the Turkish government to stop harrassing American missionaries and mission schools. Through his auspices Robert College (built with contributions from the New York railroad magnate Christopher Rhinelander Robert) received permission to erect more buildings. He eased the way for Americans to pursue archaeological excavations in Babylon. The threat of his influence with the sultan helped make the often brutal local authorities in Palestine stop persecuting and imprisoning foreign Jews.

The Turkish massacre of Armenians in 1897 caused a world outcry. President McKinley asked Straus to return to Constantinople to help sort out the problems and antagonisms that had arisen in Turkish relations. The sultan was refusing to make restitution of the American property destroyed during the massacre, and the lives of American missionaries in Armenia were still in danger. Straus was able to obtain guarantees of their safety. Knowing that international arbitration of the property disputes would prove the sultan's participation in the massacres, Straus suggested it. The sultan then agreed to settle the property claims and to rebuild the destroyed schools. Thus the cries from Americans in Turkey for warships to back up their claims were silenced before the crisis could escalate.

Straus played an important role during the American occupation of the Philippines when he got the sultan to convince the Moslem tribes in the Philippines to cooperate with U.S. occupation forces. He did this – harking back to the days of Mordecai Manual Noah – by reading to the sultan the 1796 treaty with Tripoli, which states that the U.S. "is not in any sense founded on the Christian religion," thus sparing the American troops from having a religious war foisted upon them.

In 1906 President Roosevelt appointed Straus Secretary of Commerce and Labor. Immigration fell in his bailiwick, and with it the problems of East European migration. Straus was a watchdog for the immigrants against those immigration officials who chose to interpret the general "public charge" classification too widely.

When he returned to Turkey under President Taft,

LEFT
Isidor Straus (1845–1912) and his brother Nathan built their father's china and glassware business into R.H. Macy's, the world's largest store. He served as U.S. ambassador to France from 1933 to 1936.

CHAPTER SEVEN

RIGHT
Zionist leader Rabbi Stephen Wise (1874–1949) established the Free Synagogue in New York City in 1907. He founded the Jewish Institute of Religion and also the American Jewish Congress. Famed as a speaker, Wise was considered one of the most influential American Jews of his time.

the post was upgraded to ambassador. The Turkish revolution of 1908 had left the minorities there vulnerable; Straus set about protecting the right of the Americans. He was able to get American cultural institutions out from under Turkish supervision. When a promised major ambassadorship didn't come through, Straus resigned.

In 1912 Straus agreed to run for governor of New York as part of Theodore Roosevelt's Progressive Party bid for the presidency. Straus, it was thought, would draw the Jewish vote. He had, along with Jacob Schiff and Cyrus Sulzberger, headed up the relief committee for the Russian victims of the second Kishinev pogrom. The gubernatorial race was a three-way one that all but insured the Democrats of victory. Straus's intention wasn't necessarily to win, but to use his campaign as a way of gaining support for Roosevelt.

The Jewish immigrants of New York City's Lower East Side were just beginning to make themselves felt as an electoral force. They had a hard choice to make between Straus and the Progressive Party and Congressman William Sulzer, a Democrat who had introduced a resolution in Congress that challenged Russia's passport rule, and called for the cancellation of the Russian-American treaty. Sulzer was elected; but Straus got the majority of Jewish votes, and made a stronger showing in New York State than Teddy Roosevelt.

Straus took a leading role at the Paris Peace Conference concluding World War I; prior experience had prepared him well. Starting in 1901, when he was appointed by President Roosevelt, Straus held successive posts as a member of the Permanent Court of Arbitration at the Hague; the last appointment there began in 1920.

Oscar Straus died in 1926 at age 75. In 1947 a memorial was erected to him in front of the Department of Commerce in Washington D.C. At its dedication President Truman said: "He did more for the Christians in Turkey than all the ambassadors we had there up to that time put together. A wonderful thing – a wonderful thing! Oh, that we had more like him! I wish we could raise some more of the same stock."

THE BALFOUR DECLARATION

For the Allies and for many others the Paris Peace Conference held after World War I was seen as an opportunity to put the Wilsonian principles of international cooperation and justice into practice. Some politicians were skeptical, but as they awaited the arrival of Wilson and the American delegates, hope was everyone's guardian. For American Jews, especially, this was a significant time.

On the agenda was the Balfour Declaration, Britain's promise of support for a Jewish national home in Palestine which was now under British control. In attendance at the conference were representatives of the American Jewish congress, the first major organization to represent the outlook of the East European American Jews.

Prior to the end of the war a revolution had taken place in the American Jewish community. The East Europeans were intent on helping to solve the problems of their relatives in the East-European war zones, but as usual, the American Jewish Committee, with its largely German-Jewish membership, expected to speak for all American Jews at the peace conference. The AJC leaders were men who were far removed – no matter their good intentions – from the hopes and needs of the Jews in East Europe.

Stephen Wise, founder of the Free Synagogue, world-famous Reform rabbi, and champion of Zionism, rallied the opposition in speeches on the "oligarchic" nature of an American Jewish Committee that had made itself the sole representative of American Jews, even though the majority had divergent interests. In 1917 an election was held in which over 130,000 Jews voted for representatives of an American Jewish Congress; the representatives in turn elected delegates to the Paris Peace Conference. The election emphasized the undemocratic character of the American Jewish Committee, presented with a *fait accompli*, the Committee agreed to work with the Congress and present a united front at the Conference. Judge Julian Mack, who belonged to both organizations, headed the delegation to Paris. Finally, the East Europeans had outgrown their fear of representing themselves within America. The Congress was subsequently made a permanent body to promote Jewish rights and interests, similiar to the aims of the Committee, but with a specific commitment to Zionism.

At the Peace Conference the Congress delegates contributed vital knowledge as they worked with Committee members to hammer out a secure future for the Jews of East Europe. Of prime importance, however was the Balfour Declaration.

The authors of the Declaration had a mixture of motives. Chief among them was the British desire to maintain control of the Suez Canal. Britain had wrested Palestine from the Turks, and wanted to secure strategic advantages for the future. The Balfour Declaration provided a moral justification for Britain's maintenance of the territory. Some, like Lord Balfour, who had been steeped in the Old Testament as a child, felt that the Christian world had ignored its debt to Judaism, an opinion influenced, in some part, by George Eliot's writings. Chaim Weizmann, the prominent Russian-born Zionist, formed a strong friendship with Balfour. It was agreed that if Britain issued the Declaration, Weizmann would then request that Britain be made the mandatory power in Palestine.

Weizmann perceived that only with autonomy would the Jews of Palestine be able to control immigration; indeed, unrestricted immigration was crucial to the Jews and Palestine. He submitted to Prime Minister David Lloyd George and his cabinet a memorandum outlining an autonomous national home for the Jewish people in Palestine, including unrestricted Jewish immigration. It is believed that the memorandum would have been approved were it not for the ferocious objections voiced by Edwin Montagu, the only Jew in the cabinet. His views were those of some of the most highly placed Jewish families in England: They were anti-Zionist, fearful that their gains as upper-class English nationals would be compromised by a Jewish state. There was also a class issue, for what did the impoverished East Europeans stand to lose from such a state? The fear of the dual-loyalty accusation that made obstructionists of an educated class of Jewish rich struck many outsiders as odd, especially in an era of revived nationalism. Despite Montagu's objections, there was a Declaration. But because of Montagu, it was left vague. It left the Jews of Palestine vulnerable to questions of autonomy, including what would become quite literally a life-and-death issue: Jewish immigration. Nor would it help much that Lloyd George, Balfour, and others later went on to record that it was their intention that a Jewish state ultimately be formed.

With President Wilson's approval of the Balfour Declaration American Jewish anti-Zionists found themselves in the untenable position of having their own government support a Jewish Zionism they were too insecure to countenance themselves. Through Chaim Weizmann's insistence Palestine maintained contacts with, and opened itself to, the help of non-Zionists as well as Zionists.

At the Paris Peace Conference new countries were carved out of old empires. Former minorities became sovereign and inherited their own minorities in turn. Poland became the fifth largest state in Europe, with minority groups of Ukrainians, Germans, and Jews. Rumania became the largest state in the Balkans with Hungarians, Ukranians, Bulgarians, Ruthenians, Jews, Serbs, and Poles for minorities. Hungary was diminished in size by two-thirds.

All the minorites – except for the Jews – had states made up of their nationalities bordering on or near the ones in which they lived. This provided them with protection in the event that their rights were violated. The East European Jews in America were aware of this, and were determined to get legal guarantees of safety, of state-subsidized education, community projects, and the rights of national language (Yiddish) for their people. President Wilson agreed that these guarantees were in keeping with the American belief in self-determination. Louis Marshall, Rabbi Stephen Wise, and Judge Julian Mack gave eloquent and persuasive testimony on behalf of the East European Jews. The American Jewish delegation knew how volatile national rivalries were in the newly formed states, and thus how important state protection could be. Finally, because the guarantees of freedom were a condition for their sovereignty, the new nations agreed to them. Jewish equality was established in some as a matter of international law. But who would enforce it?

The American efforts – spurred by idealism – did not hold. Once the old rivalries began again, with each new state jealous of its territory and afraid of being overrun by its neighbor, there was no mechanism to prevent or punish violations of the minority treaties. And the violations centered mostly on the Jews, who, the states knew, had no nation-state of their own to protect them. The period after World War I saw the Poles invade the Ukraine and slaughter Jewish communities. Poland stopped funding its own Jewish community, and separated the Jews from participation in the Polish economy. The Rumanians took citizenship away from Jews who could not prove ten years of residence inside the country. The Hungarians reduced to a pitiful number the amount of Jews they would allow to partake of higher education.

By 1920 the Joint Distribution Committee knew that the state of the Jews in Poland was desperate in the extreme, and in the Ukraine it was even more hopeless. The Jews were being used as scapegoats in the struggle between the Poles and Bolsheviks – each side told the populace that the Jews were responsible for the country's ills. The Joint Distribution Committee sent $45 million to relieve the distress, but even so people in refugee camps died in great numbers. All told, a million Jews died.

ABOVE
Philanthropist Nathan Straus (1848–1931) was best known for his efforts on behalf of public health. He fought successfully for mandatory pasteurization of milk and gave over $2 million for health care centers in Palestine.

SUCCESS & PHILANTHROPY

CHAPTER EIGHT

From the end of the Civil War through the 1890s the working man's standard of living had improved, though not by much. The depression of 1893 knocked out the gains. Factories, mills, and banks closed. By 1894 four million people were out of work. In the clothing industry, women workers were toiling for 60 hours a week for five dollars. There was a surplus of goods and a population that couldn't buy them. America looked to overseas markets and economic expansion for a way out of the crisis. It was becoming distressingly clear that private charity and public relief could provide little aid. The homeless and unemployed marched on Washington. The most famous march, led by "General" Jacob Coxey, was organized in the hope of getting the government to back work programs for the jobless. President Grover Cleveland's response was hardly sympathetic. The marchers were arrested for trespassing on the grounds of the Capitol.

It was the ravages of this depression that convinced Lillian Wald, the privately educated daughter of a wealthy German-Jewish family, to devote her life to the immigrant poor on the Lower East Side of New York City. She started the Visiting Nurse Service and founded the Henry Street Settlement. It was she who got Eleanor Roosevelt and many other society women involved in social work.

The depression of 1893 was a spur to action for the socially concerned: Nathan Straus, who eased the plight of thousands of New Yorkers, and men such as Joseph Fels and Julius Rosenwald, whose businesses first began to flourish in that fateful year. They helped in ways that reflected their best, and very different, abilities.

Nathan Straus was New York City Parks Commissioner from 1889 to 1893. Called Nathan the Kind, he came up with a system of public relief that aided impoverished New Yorkers without taking away their self-respect. He provided them with coal at five cents a bucket and disposed of 1.5 million buckets in the winter of 1892 alone. He charged the same amount for the thousands who fed and housed at the bed-and-breakfast lodgings he established. His interest in public health was the impetus for his most lasting legacy: the campaign to bring pasteurized milk to New York City. In 1897 he was Health Commissioner of New York; despite politics and the opposition of ignorance, he was able to start a sterilization plant on Randall's Island. Other cities followed suit. Straus started a Pasteur Institute in Palestine, where he also sponsored programs to prevent trachoma and malaria.

Most Jewish philanthropists were pragmatists with a social conscience. But Joseph Fels was possessed of an idealism every bit as strong as the pragmatism that enabled him to build his business. He was famous in his time as the strongest backer of Henry George's Single Tax Movement, which became the means through which its advocates worldwide hoped to eradicate poverty.

He was born in 1853 in Halifax Court House, Virginia. The family moved to Yanceyville, North Carolina where his father, Lazarus, ran a warehouse. He made fancy soap, as well. Little capital was needed for the soap business: kitchen ware, pots, household help. After business reverses, the family started over in Baltimore, where Joseph and his father became the agents for two soap manufacturers in Philadelphia. In 1876 Joseph bought the Thomas Worsley & Company Soap manufacturing firm of Philadelphia for $4,000. By 1890, the company was manufacturing 107 different soaps, but fancy soaps were not to build his fortune. A man named Charles Walker Stanton had developed a soap that answered the housewife's quest for a good grease-cutting product. His soap contained a naphtha or benzine solvent. Stanton was a poor money manager, often in need of capital, Joseph Fels supplied it when he bought an interest in the enterprise in 1893: shortly thereafter, he bought the whole company. To his line of 107 soaps he added the soon-to-be-famous Fels-Naphtha Soap. Fels and Company existed until the mid-1960s when it was acquired by the Purex Corporation.

As Fels began to build his fortune, the country plunged deep into economic depression. He concerned himself with bringing to Philadelphia the relief program started by Detroit's Mayor Hazen S. Pingree, which turned vacant lots over to the unemployed for the culti-

CHAPTER EIGHT

RIGHT
In the late nineteenth century and well into the twentieth, political power in New York City resided with Tammany Hall. Although the politicians were often Irish, they served all immigrants. This picture shows Tammany Hall in 1914; note the Yiddish signs for High Holy Day services in the door.

vation of vegetables and subsistence farming. The *New York Times* called the Detroit plan, "The greatest scheme yet to help the poor;" Fels was among the fifty Philadelphia philanthropists who solicited land and money. He contributed generous amounts of his own money, and instituted a matching grant program to bring in more contributions. He began to consider the problems of poverty with a focus on the land and the financial exploitation of it through ownership. Soon he became a staunch supporter of Henry George's Single Tax Movement.

Henry George was a Philadelphia-born, self-taught economist and philosopher who had spent years at various jobs in different parts of the country – farmhand, tailor, reporter – often suffering from joblessness and hunger. When he first went to New York he was struck by the sharp contrasts between "monstrous wealth and debasing want." In California he saw unsold land being held for speculative purposes, a cause, to him, of the tragically unequal distribution of wealth. His book *Progress and Poverty*, published in 1879, was circulated in the millions. Believing that a period of poverty always follows on times of progress, George contended that in good times, and as the population increased, landlords raised their rents, but that wages didn't keep up with the raises. The rising rents then bring about more land speculation until rents go so high that the renters stop producing; depression ensues. George wanted to make the land common property, as a God-given natural resource. One way to do this was to end all taxes except for a single tax on land values.

George's popularity among urban dwellers almost won him election as mayor of New York City. He ran in 1886 against Democrat Abraham Hewitt and Republican Theodore Roosevelt on the United Labor Party ticket – a fusion of trade unionists, radicals, and liberals. Henry George clubs sprouted on the Lower East Side; as this left-winger garnered support, Tammany Hall leaders stood up and took notice of his Jewish following. It is generally agreed that with an honest count (not necessarily the custom then) George would have become mayor. Hewitt won with 90,000 votes; Roosevelt registered 60,000 to George's 68,000 votes. With this threat from the left signaling that the times were changing, Tammany Hall services to Jewish voters miraculously improved. Later, when Socialist candidate Morris London was sent to Congress, Tammany Hall would have even stronger reasons to keep on its toes. The George candidacy was a sign of the voting strength that the Lower East Side Jewish community could muster when it organized, and a measure of its social dreams.

By the late 1890s Fels began to help finance single tax colonies. He was the leading patron of one in Fairhope, Alabama. In his efforts to champion the movement abroad he moved to England, where he also set up offices to promote Fels and Company sales. Once sales were successfully launched, he turned his attention to the single tax. Soon the business, which was being run in America by his brother, took second place to his passion to see a poverty-free world. In fact, he severely strained the resources of his business and more than once was close to bankruptcy. But for the protestations and management of his brother, it might have been lost altogether. What Fels said in 1910 characterizes his attitude: "We cannot get rich under present conditions without robbing somebody. I have done it, you are doing it, and I am still doing it; I propose to spend the damnable money to wipe out the system by which I made it."

Fels counted many leading philosophers and social scientists among his friends. He knew Walt Whitman and was friendly with the famous lawyer and orator Robert Ingersoll. He admired modern forward-looking men who, he said, "were trying to understand themselves, without any of the damned nonsense of trying to

understand their grandfathers". No builder of dynastic myths, Fels questioned, as only a few in his time did, the romantic notion of the self-made man. To him it was folly not to acknowledge the role of accident in the fortunes of an individual.

For all his modernity, however, he once lost the interest of a potential business partner when it was revealed that although he had automatic wrapping machines he employed women who, at considerable expense to the company, hand-wrapped the soap. He explained that he would keep the hand-wrappers until they were ready to leave of their own accord, and only then would he add more machines.

With the single tax a constant motivation, Fels initiated a friendship with Israel Zangwill, the English playwright who headed the Jewish Territorial Organization. The aim of the organization was to acquire territory wherever conditions seemed most favourable for Jewish settlement. Zangwill's organization enraged the other Zionists for whom Palestine was the only true goal. But aside from Palestine, where the Turks refused to sell land to the Jews, Zangwill was considering territories in Africa and South America. The first time Fels went to see Zangwill, he offered him $100,000 if he would agree to establish the new Jewish state on a single-tax basis. Zangwill was sympathetic to Henry George's view, but Zionism came first. His priority was to acquire land; since he could not anticipate the circumstances under which this would happen he could not tie his hands by making such an agreement. Buying the land was frustrating. There were endless negotiations and arbitrary responses from different governments. Meanwhile the Russian Jews languished, and had to be helped to get out of Russia. As a concrete way to help the Russian Jews Zangwill helped Schiff work out the Galveston Plan. The Jewish Territorial Organization had joined with Jacob Schiff's Jewish Immigration Information Bureau to funnel Russian immigrants into the U.S. through Galveston, Texas and other ports west of the Mississippi. This allowed some thousands more to enter the country, and relieved New York and other East Coast cities of some of the influx. The Immigration Bureau welcomed the plan in the beginning, but later responded to the protests of organized labor and ruled that the contract labor law was being violated. Schiff and his forces battled it out legally and through public opinion, but the process was not smooth going. Nativist immigration officers provided their own obstructions – the old financial means test was a popular one. Such was Schiff's influence that they usually waited until he was out of the country to refuse admission to Jewish immigrants. Once, when a shipload of Jewish passengers were rejected and sent back to Europe for having "poor physique" while Schiff was in Alaska, Fels and Zangwill pursued the steamer to Bremen. There Fels hired a photographer to take pictures of the lot and show, as Zangwill recalled, "How many muscular giants the party contained."

Julius Rosenwald built Sears, Roebuck into the largest retail merchandising company in America. He attributed his success to luck and hard work, rather than to superior business acumen. But his imaginative approach to philanthrophy – he gave away a third of his fortune – would tend to belie this modest assessment of his talent. His approach to giving money was innovative and geared to reaping immediate results. And if he has been called the greatest philanthropist of his era, it may be because he felt it wasn't just his duty to make other people's lives easier, but his pleasure.

A native of Springfield, Illinois, Rosenwald and his brother-in-law, Aaron Nussbaum, each bought a quarter-share interest in Sears, Roebuck, the Chicago merchandiser, in the depression year of 1893.

Richard Sears, the founder started out as a railroad agent. He accumulated the capital to begin his business

CHAPTER EIGHT

after he was enlisted into a profitable selling ploy of the time. Jewelry manufacturers would send shipments of watches to stores that had not ordered them. The manufacturers would then persuade the railroad agents to buy the unsold watches, instead of freighting them back, and to sell them to other agents down the line. There was a quick profit in this and soon Sears started his own watch company in Minneapolis, using the same "marketing methods." He hired a man named Roebuck to run the watch repair end and began to advertise in catalogues, developing the ad copy for which he had a genius and for which he became notorious.

In his copy he made exaggerated claims for the inventory of general items he was selling. The careful buyer had to read the small print – very small – carefully. He bought discontinued items cheaply and sold them at reduced rates but always – as an assurance to the customer – with a money-back guarantee.

Mail-order catalogues were a perfect medium for the practical, present-minded Americans. In remote areas they were, and still are, called wish books, or dream books. Farmers and those living in isolated areas made as much practical use of them as the Puritans used to make use of the Bible. They were used in country schools to teach reading, spelling and, through the pretend buying of items, arithmetic. Even those who could not afford the items in the catalogue felt that its presence enriched their homes. It brought them in touch with the outside world and made them feel part of the rest of the country. The chatty letters they sent with their orders were answered by hand instead of by typewriter so as not to seem impersonal. Rural free delivery, which was organized between 1893 and 1898, was a boon to mail order, as was the parcel post service starting in 1913.

In 1901 Sears and Rosenwald bought out Nussbaum. Business flourished. When they needed to expand to bigger headquarters, they took the advice of Rosenwald's friend and banker, Henry Goldman of Goldman, Sachs, and were the first merchandising company to go public. The stock offering was a great success and each partner received $4.5 million for his divested holdings. Rosenwald had become expert in customer relations, and kept the accounting, which Sears had previously treated with great carelessness, in order.

Sears kept up his energetic marketing, he initiated buying clubs and offered free items to those who agreed to distribute catalogues to friends and neighbors. He continued to write his flamboyant ad copy. Furniture might be carefully rendered and advertised at an inconceivably low price with the word "miniature" written in tiny type. This became a source of irritation and worry to Rosenwald. He wanted the firm's reputation to be unassailable but misleading ads would always be an obstacle to this. With the passage of the Pure Food and Drug Act in 1906, Rosenwald became more opposed to Sear's ads.

Perhaps one reason the brilliant ad man was able to devise a seemingly endless number of "creative promises" was that he never really believed that mail order had a future. In 1908, Sears sold his stock to Goldman, Sachs for $10 million, and Rosenwald became president of the company. Under his leadership, and later that of his son, the future indeed was fruitful for Sears, Roebuck. When the proliferation of cars reduced the need for mail order, Sears opened retail outlets across the country.

The profit-sharing and pension plans that Rosenwald initiated at Sears were called the most comprehensive to date. During the Great Depression of 1921, Rosenwald borrowed $7 million to guarantee 300 stock market accounts held by Sears employees.

His goal as a philanthropist was to give one-third of his income to social, educational, and Jewish causes, but he is best remembered for his support of American Negro education, to which he gave a major portion of his funds. His friendship with Booker T. Washington was one of the influences that made him want to help right this most egregious of national neglects. The Southern schools for black children were a sorry excuse for education. Only 20 percent of the black children even attended school, and then only four months a year, and only through the eighth grade. Their teachers were themselves badly educated. Rosenwald believed that the participation of the beneficiaries in furthering their own ends was essential to make philanthropy work. Accordingly, he outlined a plan to build one-room schoolhouses. Residents in the area, both black and white, would be required to contribute toward the project. He made sure the schools were incorporated into the local school system, and he contributed to the cost of building more than 300 schools. By 1935, 650,000 black children were attending these schools.

When he established the Julius Rosenwald Fund in 1917, he structured it differently than his philanthropic peers did theirs. He was against leaving gifts in perpetuity; he wanted his fund spent within 25 years of his death. To him it was common sense that the trustees should be able to dispense funds as they were needed, rather than being obliged to store them up for the future. He persuaded Andrew Carnegie to change the stipulations of a gift to the Tuskegee Institute which directed that the Institute use only the interest income of the gift. Rosenwald's way with philanthropy began to influence others. He felt money should be spent to benefit contemporaries, "them and their children; no more."

Like Jacob Schiff and Joseph Fels, Julius Rosenwald's philanthropy was not used as a monument to himself. "Permanent endowment," he said, "tends to lessen the amount available for immediate needs; and our immediate needs are too plain and too urgent to allow us to do the work of future generations."

CHAPTER EIGHT

LEFT
Adam Gimbel (1817–1896) arrived in America from Germany in 1835. He founded a dry goods store in Vincennes, Indiana in 1842; his sons and grandsons built the store into a chain of large department stores.

ABOVE

Emma Lazarus (1849–1887) was a poet and spokeswoman for American Judaism. Her sonnet "The New Colossus" is engraved on the pedestal of the Statue of Liberty.

THE RUSSIAN EXPERIENCE

CHAPTER NINE

It was the plight of the Jews under Tsarist rule to endure long periods of crushing brutality alternated with short periods of liberalization. But whether the climate was brutal or liberal, the purpose was always the same: to convert them to Christianity.

With the annexation by Catherine II of parts of Poland, eighteenth-century Russia inherited a Jewish population of over one million – enough to fan the flames of traditional Tsarist prejudice. Catherine, ten years before annexation, had issued her famous manifesto *Krome Zhydov*, granting to all foreigners – except Jews – the right to live and travel in Russia.

By 1791 a ukase legalized the confinement of Jews to the Pale of Settlement, territories that had been carved out of the former Polish provinces. There the Jews were kept apart, and developed a tightly knit society. Religion and everyday life became inseparable. Their spirituality lifted them out of the dreariness of their surroundings. Their piety, which had rules and regulations for every phase of daily existence, kept the influences of the outside world at bay. And their reverence for learning, which accorded more respect to the scholar than to the man of wealth, kept them a non-materialistic society.

When the seemingly liberal Tsar Alexander I (1801–1825) briefly gazed westward to a more enlightened Europe, Jews rejoiced at the possibility of better treatment. Many restrictions were relaxed. But eventually, proselytizing the Jews became this Tsar's aim too. He sought ways to entice them. Those who converted would get crown lands and other privileges. The response was negligible; the Jews were again placed under severe restrictions.

The despotic Nicholas I (1825–1855) was bent on Russification of all under his domain. Military discipline was his model for shaping up the minorities in Russia's vast lands. From Protestants, Roman Catholics, and Jews he wanted conformity with the rest of the country in language, dress – and, of course, religion. He offered the Jews equal rights (not to mention three years of exemption from taxes) if they would convert. If not, economic ruin. When this failed, Nicholas's government formulated schemes to push Jews into conversion that were so inhumane that they should have been sure to succeed. But first, he took the seemingly sensible step of abolishing the *kahals*, the Jewish system of self-government. The kahals had lost the people's respect. They had shifted the burden of taxes onto the poor; they had set Jews against each other by sending out men, called *klappers*, to pluck boys from the shtetls so they could meet the cruelly high percentage of Jewish conscripts demanded by the army. Once the kahals were abolished, however, Nicholas did not replace them with government services. The Jews were not full citizens, and they would not get the services of citizens.

Very quickly the Jewish genius for self-help came to the fore. *Hevras*, or voluntary associations, were formed to take care of every imaginable exigency. There was a hevra for burials, for the care of the elderly, for orphans, for the separate occupations so that carpenters or cobblers or masons could provide for their families in times of trouble. Hevras ran courts and arbitrated disputes. Instead of being disrupted, as Nicholas had hoped, their communal ties were strengthened.

Military conscription was one of Nicholas's cruelest innovations. The rule was that boys from 12 to 25 would have to serve for 25 years. Jews could no longer be exempted by paying for a stand-in. Jewish men fled and were hunted down. And then came the capstone: Jewish boys under 12 were seized and sent to live with peasant families in distant provinces, where they were baptized.

The policy lasted for 30 years, but Jewish life continued to be cohesive. Finally there was Nicholas's plan to secularize Jewish education *within* a Jewish school system. It was a set-up that would enable him to control the faculty of the school, eventually eliminating Hebrew studies and replacing them with instruction in the catechism. His plan dovetailed perfectly with the new Jewish movement of *haskalah*, or enlightenment, that had young Jewish intellectuals working to bring the philosophy and culture of the West into the shtetl. They were eager for the students of the Hebrew schools and rabbinical colleges to get secular instruction in other languages, in the sciences, and in the trades. They were

CHAPTER NINE

CENTER
Immigrants to America often entered the country in New York City. This group in 1912 has been processed at Ellis Island in New York Harbor and is awaiting the ferry to Manhattan and a new life.

ecstatic that this would be underwritten by the government. Nicholas offered to build schools throughout the Pale and to exempt from military service those who attended.

But the majority of Jews had the wisdom to sense a trap. Even before the Tsar's agenda leaked out, they knew that without equal rights – with no freedom to leave the Pale, live where they pleased, enter the professions, start certain businesses – secular education would be the tool of their undoing. Once having undertaken it, and having sensed the possibilities in the outside world, their children would have nowhere to go; they would convert or die inside. The game was always treacherous, always the same in different disguise: no equal rights without conversion. The Jews did not flock to Nicholas's schools.

The assassination of Tsar Alexander II in 1881 was the beginning of the end for the Jewish communities. Worn out from centuries of despotism, rage was welling up in the general population. In the coming years 3,000 bureaucrats would be assassinated. Then, as a way of diverting the widespread wrath the new Tsar Alexander III used the diversionary tactic of blaming the Jews for the country's ills – the sure-fire way to redirect the rage of his people. He adopted his tutor's thinking on the subject of the Jews:. "Force one-third to emigrate, another third to embrace Christiantiy, and the remainder to die of starvation."

Under Nicholas II there followed a series of pogroms in Russia and Russian territories. The most publicized, Kishinev in 1903, was followed by a succession of massacres in that year and the years following. Forty-seven were killed at Kishinev; many were wounded, hundreds of homes were burned. The pogrom caused a world outcry, but the Tsar's ears were closed. The medieval blood libels of ritual murder were revived as an excuse; the police watched from the sidelines. Jewish revolutionaries fighting along with their Christian counterparts had the dispiriting experience of watching them do nothing to curtail the anti-Jewish violence. Millions of Jews fled Eastern Europe and Russia. Between 1881 and 1920 two million came to settle in the United States.

RING AROUND THE STATUE

As the nineteenth century drew to a close it began to feel to many an old line American as if the ground of America were shifting right beneath his feet. Steamship companies made more profit from the immigrants, the majority of whom were cramped into steerage, than from the upper classes in the stateroom. At the same time evidence of the follies and foibles of snobbery and cultivated self images were everywhere. Old New York society refused to let the new millionaires buy boxes at the Academy of Music, not even at the proffered $30,000 for a box. The new millionaires could think of no better recourse than to build the Metropolitan Opera House at Broadway and 39th Street. At the opening, as one press report had it, "The Goulds and Vanderbilts and people of that ilk perfumed the air with the odor of crisp greenbacks." There the Jewish elite could, perhaps, rent, but not own, a box. The German Jews had all but forgotten that their congregation Emanu-El was started in a tenement on the Lower East Side in 1845. The German-Jewish press was quick to differentiate between the "enlightened" Germans and the new Russian immigrants, who were described in one paper as "a piece of Oriental antiquity in the midst of an ever-Progressive Occidental Civilization." These negative connotations would come full circle when poor Sephardim from the Balkans and Syria – some 10,000 between 1908 and 1914 – arrived in the U.S. Some of the old-line American Sephardim resented that the newcomers used the appellation Sephardic to describe themselves. They pressured the HIAS to call the section dealing with the newcomers' problems the committee on *Oriental*, not Sephardic, Jews. The newcomers resented it mightily and the usage was eventually stopped.

Meanwhile *Liberty*, the statue that French sculptor Frederic Auguste Bartholdi created to celebrate French-American friendship, was warehoused until the Americans could supply their share of the funds. The French had raised $400,000 for the statue – fund-raising had been slow, but a national lottery finally brought in the needed amount – and it was up to the U.S. to raise $250,000 for the pedestal and base. A lavish dinner given by the American committee yielded little. A literary auction, to which Bret Harte, Walt Whitman, Mark Twain and others contributed their original manuscripts, was held. Other writers were asked to donate original pieces on the statue, also to be auctioned for

fund raising. The poet Emma Lazarus, daughter of an old-line New York Sephardic family contributed her poem, *The New Colossus*.

Like the German Jews, her family honored Judaism, but rejected Jewish Zionist aspirations. Like the German Jews, too, they accepted the false construct of the dual-loyalty problem. Emma alone became an ardent Zionist. The Russian pogroms of 1881 affected her deeply. She felt a kinship with the Russian Jews whom she visited on Ward's Island; she was aroused by George Eliot's most singular and emphatic writing on Jews, and the Zionism that she urged in her novel *Daniel Deronda*.

Emma's poem *The New Colossus* brought $1,500 at the auction, but it was not until 1903, 16 years after her death, that the famous poem was inscribed on the pedestal of the statue. An appeal for funds in Joseph Pulitzer's *New York World* brought in, from New York's daily wage earners, the many small contributions that made up the final $100,000. *Liberty* was dedicated on October 28, 1886. From then on, as they rounded the bend into the New World, the immigrants would fix their sights on her. Few were aware of the shifting sands of New York social life. Nor, when they thought about America, did they visualize the help wanted ads that specified Christians only. America, they knew, was a place where things happened fast, where there is mobility, where the European past could be laid to rest and new selves created.

The land of possibilities assumed a central place within the imaginations of immigrants to America. Stories of plenty came to the Old Country back from loved ones who had left the shtetls and cities of Russia to make the arduous journey across the Atlantic. Children played at emigrating; for many of them it would soon be a reality.

Passing medical muster at Ellis Island and other entrance points in East Coast cities was essential for admission to the United States. The terror of rejection was a collective nightmare for all immigrants; for the Jews, more of whom came over in families, it was intensified. Other immigrants had the option of trying to make a better living in America and then, perhaps, of going back to their native villages to live out a mellow old age.

For Russian Jews, there was no going back. America was their frontier. If the strengths of the Sephardic settlers back in 1654 were not readily apparent to the Dutch, the untrained American eye could rarely spot the strengths beneath the uprooted, seemingly chaotic East European personalities. Their manners were direct; their language, Yiddish, was earthy and informal. They had vivid imaginations and an energetic zeal in conversation. The profit motive was often less strong in them than their idealism. It could be seen in their newspapers, as journalist Hutchins Hapgood noted: "Yiddish newspapers have, as compared with their contemporaries in the English language, the strong interest of great freedom of expression. They are controlled rather by passion than by capital."

Those who were skilled went into trades: ironworkers, tinsmiths, masons, plumbers, electricians, printers, cigar-makers. Of those who arrived between 1899 and 1914, 66 percent of the employed had industrial skills, a much larger proportion than the other immigrant groups. It was most common for them to earn their daily wage, singly and in families, in the making of clothes.

Immigrants and poor they may have been, but they were bold enough to want their children to become professionals – and to that end, as much as the day-to-day sweat for survival, they toiled. That did not stop them making observations that could pierce to the heart some of the self-serving pieties in American life. Unlike the German-Jews with their concern about rationalism, modernity, and fitting into the environment, the Russians had a tough, unapologetic love for, and allegiance to, their particular Jewish cultural heritage. It made many wary of becoming part of an homogenized American image. They were not interested in the world of appearances, as their simple, sometimes unesthetic synagogues showed; beauty was devotion, a good deed, a moral force. Many were decidedly not religious. They lived out a host of beliefs fostered in the climate of Russian despotism and political turmoil: socialism, Zionism, Yiddishism. In the crowded shtetls and Jewish quarters of East European cities, privacy was a rare luxury. Theirs was a communal society. Life revolved around ritual. Religious and dietary laws governed life; shtetls had communal bakeries and ovens for preparing Sabbath meals. They had communal *cheders*, schools for the study of Torah.

What they brought with them was not readily apparent. They brought tenacity developed over years of hardship. They brought their cultural and religious

CHAPTER NINE

RIGHT
The humanitarian work of Henrietta Szold (1860–1945) cannot be overstated. Always active in Zionist affairs, in 1912 she founded Hadassah, the Women's Zionist Organization of America. Hadassah quickly grew to have branches in every state in America. Its members work to provide health and educational services in Israel. With the rise of Nazism, the ever-energetic Szold founded Youth Aliyah, an organization responsible for saving thousands of young European Jews.

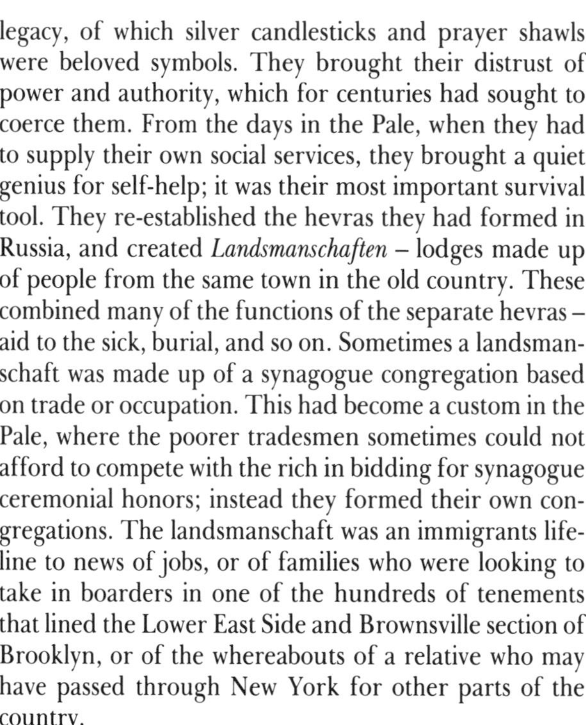

legacy, of which silver candlesticks and prayer shawls were beloved symbols. They brought their distrust of power and authority, which for centuries had sought to coerce them. From the days in the Pale, when they had to supply their own social services, they brought a quiet genius for self-help; it was their most important survival tool. They re-established the hevras they had formed in Russia, and created *Landsmanschaften* – lodges made up of people from the same town in the old country. These combined many of the functions of the separate hevras – aid to the sick, burial, and so on. Sometimes a landsmanschaft was made up of a synagogue congregation based on trade or occupation. This had become a custom in the Pale, where the poorer tradesmen sometimes could not afford to compete with the rich in bidding for synagogue ceremonial honors; instead they formed their own congregations. The landsmanschaft was an immigrants lifeline to news of jobs, or of families who were looking to take in boarders in one of the hundreds of tenements that lined the Lower East Side and Brownsville section of Brooklyn, or of the whereabouts of a relative who may have passed through New York for other parts of the country.

Landsmanschaften made sure to have doctors on retainer to treat their members.

Almost one million East European Jews belonged to a landsmanschaft at one time or another during their adjustment to America. Every town and shtetl in all of the East European territories was represented. After their massive dislocations the East Europeans were recreating in the U.S. their sense of place, and their sense of place consisted of the ways in which they regulated their community life. The landsmanschaft was a way station on the road to the larger society, particularly for those who were forced to flee their countries or were ill-prepared to emigrate. The landsmanschaften were traditional organizations and sometimes kept up hindering social forms – for instance, according places of honor to incompetent members because their fathers had held such places in the old country. But other landsmanschaften evolved into important organizations that went far beyond local concern.

One such landsmanschaft became the Hebrew Immigrant Aid Society (HIAS), and achieved international renown. HIAS emerged in 1882 out of a landsmanschaft's efforts to provide burial services for Jews who died on Ellis Island. Soon the members were helping all Jews through the island's red tape. HIAS representatives looked into the conditions of the shipping lines, made sure signs were posted in Hebrew, ran an employment office, helped to educate newcomers for naturalization. To counter rumors and misinformation and the tall tales of con artists, they sent bulletins to Russia that gave precise information on the requirements and procedures for entering the U.S. Along with

the German-Jewish organizations, HIAS became important in the fight against immigration restriction.

One who was prescient about the Russians was Henrietta Szold, the founder of Hadassah, the Women's Zionist Organization of America. "To say what the Russian Jew is and can be in America is to prophesy the course of the Twentieth Century . . . " Comparing them with the Sephardic and German Jews she wrote that "Eschewing the foolish pride of both," they will incorporate the experiences and virtues of the former immigrations and "use the institutions created by them as the stock upon which to engraft their intenser fervor, their broader Jewish scholarship, a more enlightened conception of Jewish ideals, and a more inclusive interest in Jewish world questions."

The Baltimore-born Szold, daughter of a renowned Conservative rabbi, Benjamin Szold, started out teaching in a fashionable girl's school. It wasn't long before she started to teach immigrants at night school. When the Jewish Publication Society was formed in 1888 she worked as an editor; among the books she readied for publication was the five-volume *History of the Jews* by the famous historian Heinrich Graetz. She was already a Zionist when she visited Palestine in 1909. But once there, Zionism became her life: "If not Zionism, then nothing." She saw what the settlers were accomplishing and the disease and hardships that had yet to be addressed, and she resolved to get American and European Jews to support the Zionist effort. In 1912 she transformed the Hadassah Study Circle, a U.S. group to which she had belonged since 1909 into a national women's fund-raising organization for Palestine. Its first achievement was the development of a program to send nurses to Palestine. During World War I she was responsible for organizing the American Zionist Medical Unit for Palestine – this at the behest of Louis Brandeis, who was head of the Provincial Zionist Committee. After 1919 she became a part of the Jewish community in Palestine, and in 1927 was elected to a three-member Palestine Executive Committee of the World Zionist Organization. In this capacity she often found herself negotiating with the Palestinian administration and taking a leadership role for policy decisions within the community, no easy task in light of the prevailing attitudes toward women, especially in that part of the world. Eventually she was in charge of the social worker training program for the entire country. During World War II she developed the Youth Aliyah movement for refugee children from German-controlled countries.

Another who saw the promise of the Russian immigrants was Lillian Wald. Like Henrietta Szold she started out teaching in a private girl's school. She made her first foray to the Lower East Side to look after the mother of one of the pupils in the home-nursing class she was conducting. The woman, who had just given birth, was lying ill, with no one to care for her and her vermin-bitten children. She called the experience a "baptism of fire", and was convinced that if people knew what she had witnessed, "such horrors would cease to exist." After a sleepless night she "rejoiced that I had had a training in the care of the sick that in itself would give me an organic relationship to the neighborhood in which this awakening had come . . ." She became the conscience, and the voice, and the deliverer, of the neighborhood.

CHAPTER NINE

LEFT
Lillian D. Wald, the dynamic founder of the Visiting Nurse Service, also founded the Henry Street Settlement and pioneered the first public school nursing system.

BELOW LEFT
The Henry Street Settlement in New York City's Lower East Side was founded by Lillian Wald (1867–1940) in 1893. From its founding until today, the settlement has provided health care and educational services to its community.

She made her home on the Lower East Side and began to ease the distress of the ill, most of whom preferred to stay at home rather than face the terrors of a hospital. With the financial help of Jacob Schiff, who wished to remain anonymous, she started the Visiting Nurse Service. Her nurses and trainees became everyday figures as they stepped from rooftop to rooftop to avoid hundreds of tenement stairs on their rounds to see patients. She got the city to undertake a program of public nursing, and before long convinced the Board of Education to put nurses into the schools, the first such program in the country. When she needed larger quarters for her nurses she rented a building on Henry Street and began the community center that would grow into the famous Henry Street Settlement, providing shelter, food, education, and recreation among its many services. Her influence could be felt in anything that had to do with the welfare of her community. When strikes hit the needle trades, she extended her support and practical advice to the hard-pressed strikers, and tried to rally legislators to the cause. Wrote crusading journalist Jacob Riis, "she arbitrates in a strike and men listen."

At her urging a young Herbert Lehman, future governor of New York, organized teenage clubs at the Henry Street Settlement. In 1910 he worked with her on legislation for a child labor bureau. She inspired her young social workers, many of them from well-off Jewish and Christian families, and she accomplished what she had set out to when she had her revelation. She trained the rich to see.

Crowning the Lower East Side social projects was the Educational Alliance, founded in 1893 largely through

CHAPTER NINE

RIGHT
The Visiting Nurse Service, also founded by Lillian Wald, was originally headquartered in the house on Henry Street. Here an elderly Russian couple receive a visit around 1920.

BELOW RIGHT
Governor Herbert Lehman (1878–1963) addresses a group of visiting nurses in honor of Lillian Wald's birthday in 1939. Lehman, a partner in the investment banking firm Lehman Brothers, was governor of New York from 1932 to 1942. From 1943 to 1946 he was the first director-general of the United Nations Relief and Rehabilitation Agency. He served as Senator from New York from 1949 to 1957. Lehman was a strong supporter of civil rights, an active member of the American Jewish Committee, and a Zionist.

the auspices of Isidor Straus and Jacob Schiff. At the five-story building on Jefferson Street – still Alliance headquarters today – children were drilled in English, taught patriotic songs, learned manners and comportment, all in an attempt to forge them into instant Americans. But soon the students began to protest – nothing of their culture was being emphasized. It was becoming clear that the donors wanted to transform them. They heard the patronizing and bigoted comments from the uptowners who came to organize and classify and make them over. "In the philanthropic institutions of our aristocratic German Jews," went a commentary in the *Yiddish Gazetten* of April, 1894, "you see beautiful offices, desks, all decorated, but strict and angry faces. Every poor man is questioned like a criminal."

In 1900 some of the young Russian Jews started their own center, the Educational League, where they held a ball parodying the German attitudes. The League lacked enough disciplined organization to endure, but a point had been made. German obliviousness lessened. They realized they could not rush acculturation. Yiddish, the language they had once derided, was offered along with other language classes at the Alliance. It was, in fact, from about 1900 to 1940 in America, that Yiddish poetry and prose began to find a new voice and to flower. From the sweatshop school of poets – most notably the poetry of Morris Rosenfeld, who wrote in a Yiddish that expressed the immediacy of his sweatshop experience – to novelists and journalists, Yiddish survived attacks by immigrant socialists and acculturated American Jews and began to take on new strength.

At the Alliance one could study philosophy with some of the brightest teachers in the city. Or one could take art classes along with students Ben Shahn, Leonard Baskin, Louise Nevelson, Louis Schanker, Barnett Newman, Mark Rothko, Jacob Epstein, Chaim Gross, Isaac Soyer, and Jo Davidson – just some of the burgeoning talent that was released with the coming out of Russia.

Paul Abelson, an inspiring teacher and the first Russian-Jewish immigrant to earn a doctorate at Teacher's College, taught English and civics at the Alliance. It was his curriculum that the New York Board of Education adopted for its adult evening classes. At the Alliance, too, the respected philosopher Morris Raphael Cohen taught classes in social education and lectured on the Book of Job.

Morris Raphael Cohen was born in Russia. His father ran a soda stand in New York City, but the only possessions he wanted, indeed, spent his life acquiring, were "the fruits of reason." He went to City College of New York and to graduate school at Harvard, where he studied with William James and other eminent philosophers. Despite offers from top universities he went back to his alma mater, City College, to teach. It was there he felt he was needed and there that he helped to build the outstanding reputation of this tuition-free urban college, which, by the early 1920s had a majority of Jewish students. He was one of America's best philosophers, but his legacy was not a system of thought – indeed, he abjured systems. It was his adaptation of the Socratic method for which he became known. His legacy can be measured by the many students who have carried his spirit throughout their lives. For Morris Cohen

CHAPTER NINE

LEFT, BELOW LEFT AND CENTER Making a living on the Lower East Side, around 1910 – pushcarts and the garment industry were principle means of entry into the entrepreneurial American economy for many thousands of newly arrived Jews. The Lower East Side teemed with life. People worked in the sweatshops, prayed in the storefront synagogues, lived in the crowded tenements, and sent their children to the excellent – and free – public schools and universities of New York City.

brought to his young students a world that would otherwise have been denied them. George Felsher, who was a Cohen student in the early 1930s describes the phenomenon:

"Question us he did. He showed no mercy as he led an overreaching student step by step into a maze of absurdities. There was no smugness in his demolition of an argument. He was only pleased – as he expected you to be pleased – that the truth had become evident. I even remember a few of the questions he raised. 'Which is more important – the reproductive or the life-maintaining function of the individual?' 'Do rituals become a part of an established religion or do they lead to the rise of the religion?' Again and again the verdict would be necessary, but not sufficient. Truths adduced might not be enough to give logical inevitability to an argument.

"In general terms if you had brains and money you went to Columbia. If you had some money and some brains, you went to New York University. If you had brains but no money, you went to City College. Aggressively. Almost arrogant about your intelligence, but suffering and rebellious because of your low caste status. To youngsters like us, Morris Raphael Cohen was almost an icon. We could bask in the reflected glory of this much-honored man. We could imaginatively, and temporarily, be equals of those who studied in ivy-covered halls. His influence didn't end in the classroom either. In the various alcoves that lined the college cafeteria some would be playing chess, or bridge, and a little group of Cohen-ites would be seeking for the truth in a proposition. 'A teacher affects eternity. One never knows where his influence will end.' Henry Adams said that and it surely applies to Morris Raphael Cohen. Fifty-five years have gone by. I remember the man and his Voltaire-like face. And I honor the man, or try to, in the way I think.'"

East Side Island

From the early years of New Amsterdam, the downtown streets of the settlement provided thoroughfare for all manner of people, objects of trade, and animals. The first marketplace was the Strand, located along the shore, with a field further in, where farmers and traders assembled their livestock, produce, and wares for the weekly market day. That day brought crowds, litter , and noise; residents in nearby precincts complained. By the early twentieth century 500,000 East European Jews were living in one-half square mile of New York's Lower East Side. Market day was every day except Saturday. It was an economy living off of itself. The pushcart peddler was ubiquitous on the crowded streets. Not only was everything for sale, but in the minutest quantities. One candle, a piece of dried fruit, the wing of a chicken, down through further diminutions: an egg; if not the whole egg, the yolk; if not the yolk, just the white.

On Thursdays the housewives bought food for the Sabbath meal. Kosher food cost more, but this was an area where they would not economize. Above the voices at the fruit and vegetable stands, or coming from the butcher shops, or bargaining at curbside, could be heard the fishmonger, bringer of elegant Sabbath fare, intoning, "Fish, fish, living, floundering, jumping, dancing, fish!"

CHAPTER NINE

RIGHT
Religious life on the Lower East Side tended to center around small synagogues, whose members usually all came from the same area of Eastern Europe. Here a group prays on the walkway of the Brooklyn Bridge, around 1909.

FAR RIGHT
Leaving a synagogue on Rivington Street on the Lower East Side, after Rosh Ha-Shanah services, around 1911.

BELOW RIGHT
The majority of the Eastern European Jews who came to America landed in the major cities of the Eastern seaboard – Boston, New York, Philadelphia, Baltimore – and tended to stay there. But some went on from the cities to rural areas, a movement that was encouraged by some to counteract Gentile complaints about Jews flooding the cities. Here the Jewish Farmers of America hold an exhibit on a rooftop of the Lower East Side in 1909.

A family of five living in a crowded three-room tenement apartment might take in two boarders, who slept in makeshift beds on the floor. The economy of East Side living depended on such arrangements. Sleeping in shifts was common, privacy unheard of. The frustration of living conditions was alleviated by a new kind of hope – the American one of making it financially into a world of comfort.

But uncertainty was everyone's constant companion. The other was toil. The humblest needle worker or pushcart peddler – who may well have been a scholar in the old country – had one day a week when he could transcend his lot. He was transformed by the ritual of the Sabbath dinner into a man of substance, who presided over family and invited guests, and assumed a place within the religious and cultural order of things.

There were certain paradoxes of poverty on the Lower East Side. One was the thousands of housekeepers employed by the tenement dwellers to clean and cook. If the woman of the house was a working mother, and she often was, the economics of the situation called for no less. She might earn $9 a week working in a garment factory, while the cost of a housekeeper's services was $12 a month.

There were 500 Jewish bakeries throughout New York by the twentieth century. Among the foods that Jews made popular in the rest of the country – bagels, bialys, lox, sour pickles – was soda water. Called "the worker's champagne," it was widely imbibed by this generally non–alcohol–drinking population; when the price of sugar rose, seltzer became king.

Trying to work their way into this society were the Christian missionaries who opened headquarters on the Lower East Side. They proselytized at meetings and on street corners and generally enraged the neighborhood. Their insensitivity to Jewish religious feeling, loyalty, and history was incomprehensible to the immigrants. But the rich Protestant families who supported these efforts were not concerned with the objections of immigrants, whose religion they considered not valid enough to earn them a place in heaven.

After a while the immigrants got used to their presence and developed a condescending tolerance that allowed the missionaries to carry on without physical harm to their persons. Conversions after all, were few and far between.

Though there were agencies to guide the immigrants to less populated towns and cities in the U.S. – the Industrial Removal Office, which was created in 1900, directed some 60,000 Jewish immigrants to points outside New York City – the vast majority insisted on settling in Gotham. There were hundreds, however, who made their way on foot to the small towns of lower New York State, or to villages on eastern Long Island, Riverhead and Sag Harbor among them. They were an interesting vanguard. They grew small vegetable gardens, fished in nearby ponds, and raised a few animals to help them eat when their meager incomes could not provide enough money. Though they kept kosher themselves, some fished for scallops – selling them but never tasting them. Some became rich trapping fur. In one of the publications of the Riverhead Historical Society, a Sag Harbor native, Harry Spodick, recounts that gentiles were reluctant to sell land to Jews. They finally bought some for a synagogue when a friendly gentile acted as a third party. Eventually they purchased more land from a farmer for a cemetery. "My father put up his gold watch as a deposit. Then the Hungarian and Russian Jews in town couldn't get along . . . There was so much discussion that they bought their own cemetery right alongside of the Russian Jews and put up a fence . . . The fighting is past but the fence is still there . . ."

JEWISH CELEBRITIES

ABOVE
One of the world's best- known musicians is Leonard Bernstein. Equally famed as a conductor and composer, Bernstein's works include the KADDISH *and* JEREMIAH *symphonies.*

ABOVE
The works of composer Aaron Copland include APPALACHIAN SPRING *and* RODEO.

ABOVE
Violinist Isaac Stern is known the world over for his virtuosity. He has appeared often with the Israel Philharmonic Orchestra.

LEFT
Author Bret Harte's depictions of the rugged life of miners in the West won him broad popularity. This portrait was painted by John Petite in 1884.

ABOVE
David Sarnoff, born in Russia, arrived in America as a boy in 1900. He began his career as a messenger and was later a telegraph operator; he received the first news of the sinking of the TITANIC. Sarnoff went on to a brilliant career as a pioneer in the radio and television business, becoming head of RCA and NBC.

ABOVE

Actor and director Woody Allen was born Allen Stewart Konigsberg in Brooklyn in 1935. His comic films, often with underlying serious themes, include TAKE THE MONEY AND RUN *(1969),* ANNIE HALL *(1977), which won an Academy Award,* MANHATTAN *(1979), and* ZELIG *(1984).*

ABOVE
Betty Joan Perske, better known as Lauren Bacall, starred with Humphrey Bogart in the film TO HAVE AND HAVE NOT, *among others.*

ABOVE
Well known for his starring roles in many films, Issur Danielovitch is famed the world over as Kirk Douglas.

ABOVE
Shown here in a scene from the film PRIVATE BENJAMIN *(1983), actress Goldie Hawn has made many appearances on television and in the movies.*

ABOVE

Superstar Bette Midler first burst upon the entertainment scene as a singer, and has since gone on to a career as a performer on Broadway and in the movies, including THE ROSE, DOWN AND OUT IN BEVERLY HILLS, *and* RUTHLESS PEOPLE.

ABOVE

Crusty comedian George Burns (born Nathan Birnbaum in 1896) appeared with his partner Gracie Allen (1906–1964) on radio and television for decades. He won an Oscar in 1975 for his performance in THE SUNSHINE BOYS.

ABOVE
Blue-eyed actor Paul Newman has starred in COOL HAND LUKE, THE STING, BUTCH CASSIDY AND THE SUNDANCE KID, THE HUSTLER, *and many other fine films.*

ABOVE

The film THE BOSTON STRANGLER *brought Tony Curtis (born Bernie Schwartz) to national acclaim. More recently he has appeared in* MAFIA PRINCESS, *playing a mobster.*

ABOVE
Barbara Streisand and Mandy Patinkin part forever in a scene from the film YENTL. *Streisand starred in and directed this 1983 film, based on the story by I. B. Singer.*

ABOVE
Born in Russia around 1886 as Asa Yoelson, Al Jolson became famous as an entertainer. His film THE JAZZ SINGER (1927) was the first major movie to use sound. Jolson died in 1950.

ABOVE

A Jewish family does garment piecework at home, making garters in a tenement kitchen in 1912.

FROM PIECE WORK TO PEACE WORK

CHAPTER TEN

BELOW LEFT
Women sweatshop workers assemble dolls on a long wooden table at the Shrenhat Toy Company, Philadelphia, in 1912.

In mid-nineteenth-century New York a system of contracting in the clothing industry was already in place. English, German, and Irish immigrants worked at home assembling garments from the cut goods supplied by a contractor. When better-equipped factories became the hub of production, the contracting system, it seemed, was losing economic viability. Instead the large pools of unskilled immigrant labor saw the role of the contractor expand within a new system that compounded the workers' problems.

By 1900 the U.S. garment industry was growing at twice the rate of most other industries. German Jews owned a majority of the factories for which directly, or through contracting, the East European immigrant toiled. The contractor was often himself a recent toiler who had managed often by working day and night, to accumulate the $500 or so needed to run a sweating operation out of a tenement or rented loft space. He was often a relative or a landsman of the people he recruited. In fact, it was so customary for a contractor to hire people from his old shtetl in the Pale that shtetls became known by the kind of garments their emigrants turned out. The landsman in turn would feel extremely loyal to the contractor, who took care to employ him. This at first impeded many of the Jewish immigrants from perceiving the state of exploitation in which they were living. Whole families, plus boarders, would do piece work for a contractor in a system filled with hundreds and hundreds of little outlets of production like his. But in this familial setting a worker did not have to toil on the Sabbath, nor confront the outside world until he was more knowledgable about life in America.

In his manufacturing space the contractor assembled his operators, basters, finishers, buttonhole makers, and other workers. To keep costs down, workers were no longer paid by the piece or the hour; pay was based on the work quotas that the team or group were able to meet. In one of his early pieces for the *New York Commercial Advertiser*, journalist Abraham Cahan wrote of a young task worker trying to describe to an outsider the system under which he worked: "... the day is measured not by the number of hours, but by the number of coats. This quota rises and falls like stock on Wall Street. Just at present our 'day' is made up of twenty-two coats. This takes a little less than two solar days . . ."

This minute division of labor did provide work for the unskilled and newly arrived. The conditions, of course, were inhuman: dirty, crowded, airless. Wages could be irregular; a contractor could fold up overnight.

How could the workers organize in such a system? The contracting system made strikes seem a futile business. Workers never saw, let alone negotiated with, the clothing kings. The business was seasonal; a worker could be unemployed for months on end. The contractors, or "sweaters," signed agreements during the busy season but rarely honored them. When the slack season came the union men were laid off and those less skilled worked for less money. Just the existence of the sweating operations kept the factory workers from making too many demands on their employers. Then there was the landsman network; the gratitude of a greenhorn to a landsman contractor was another obstacle to unionization.

The competition between contractors kept down the cost of production for the manufacturers. But as newer, better machinery began to be installed in the factories, manufacturers saw that they could keep costs down by

CHAPTER TEN

RIGHT
The government response to strikes and Socialism was severe. Here the Second Battalion of the IX Coast Artillery Corps demonstrates the hollow square formation to be used in the event of a street riot. This picture was taken in New York City in 1918.

CENTER
Union members carrying placards in Yiddish march in a Socialist demonstration in New York City on May Day, 1911.

using it more. As the factories began to employ more workers directly, labor had its first real chance to begin organizing effectively. With what seemed like a flash flood of change, strikes began to besiege the Lower East Side. The squalid conditions in which they worked made them angry, the more so because this was happening to them in America. Life was still far better for them here than in the Pale, but they expected more of America. They wanted justice, not economic exploitation.

The young women who worked in the rapidly growing shirtwaist, or blouse, industry, for instance, were being exploited both as workers and as women. Male employees of the factories began to employ the young girls as assistants, called "learners," or temporaries, as a way of getting around the labor laws. They worked for meager pay and could not be promoted. In shirtwaist factories women were subject to a host of taxes that seemed more horrendous for their pettiness than the arbitrary tolls exacted by lords in the Middle Ages. They were taxed for the chairs they used. They had to pay for supplies such as needles – not even at cost, but at a profit of 20 per cent. They were fined dearly if they were late by a minute or two.

Local 25 of the International Ladies Garment Workers Union (ILGWU), founded in 1900, was still a financially foundering proposition in 1909, but the time seemed right for a general strike throughout the shirtwaist industry. No real groundwork had been done, but on November 22, the local called a general meeting at Cooper Union, and were astounded when thousands showed up. Among the speakers was Mary Dreier, president of the New York Women's Trade Union League. Just a month before, the Woman Suffrage Party had been formed to win the vote for women in New York State; the feminists supported the women workers. The social reformers who lent their efforts to helping the Jewish labor movement win its cause were there. These gentile and Jewish settlement-house workers and reformers wielded influence in the larger community, especially as they moved out to jobs as foundation directors and politicos. Samuel Gompers, the greatest force in American trade unionism, spoke. Meyer London, the independent-minded socialist, who as the first Socialist elected to Congress would go on to win three congressional elections, and thus spur the Irish politicians of Tammany Hall to a greater concern for its Jewish constituents, was there. But with no clear plan from the union leadership, the speakers could not be conclusive about what actions to take. Without warning, a mere teenager named Clara Lemlich went to the podium. In an impassioned, four-sentence Yiddish speech that ended, "I offer a resolution that a general strike be declared – now!" She sent the crowd into roars of approval. They all took the Jewish oath, "If I turn traitor to the cause I now pledge, may this land wither from the arm I now raise." Twenty thousand shirtwaist makers went out on strike. During the next two months incredible sights were seen on the streets outside the factories being struck. Led by Clara Lemlich, the striking girls sang their native Russian and Italian songs until hired thugs charged them, beating and knocking quite a few down, (Lemlich included) so they could get scab workers into the factory. There was pandemonium until

employees threatened to produce ugly consequences. With one side excoriated by outsiders as exploiters and the other, especially the socialist unionists, seen as menacing anarchists, nothing good could come of it.

A successful Boston lawyer, Louis Dembitz Brandeis, known as the "people's lawyer," was called in to arbitrate. He had gained his reputation by defending the residents of Boston against the unethical practices of utility companies and other monopolies. He was keenly aware of the outdated laws – and judges – who took no measure of the emerging industrial society. In a defense of the Oregon 10-hour law for working women, he had brought medical and health data to bear on his arguments, demonstrating the effects of overwork on the women. In so doing he forced the courts to take into

CHAPTER TEN

BELOW
Justice Louis Dembitz Brendeis was born in Kentucky in 1856. Brandeis's distinguished legal career was closely involved with the public interest. His labor mediation work in the New York garment industry from 1910 to 1916 was crucial for obtaining better working conditions and labor peace. Brandeis was not an observant Jew, but his work with Jewish labor leaders led him to active Zionism. Brandeis was appointed to the Supreme Court by President Wilson in 1916 and served with distinction until his retirement in 1936. He died in 1941. Brandeis University in Massachusetts is named in his honor.

the police came and arrested – the girls!

On the streets of the Lower East Side, Mrs. Oliver Belmont's cars were driven by Wellesley girls, who had contributed $1,000 to the strike fund, and who marched with the strikers along with picketers sent by the Women's Trade Union League. Ann Morgan, sister of J.P., put up bail money as the girls were arrested – 732 in the first month.

The girls themselves, young shirtwaist workers, were brave and resolute and endured insult and injury. They were thrown into jail with prostitutes who were hostile to them; in this still Victorian climate they knew that the law required that their arrest records be listed on their marriage licenses. They had the courage not to be thwarted by blights on their reputations. The example of these young women roused labor and infused the community with a feeling of pride. Their gains were not conclusive, but they had provided the momentum. Within five months some 60,000 clockmakers went out in a strike called The Great Revolt.

As this strike dragged on – the sticking point was the union's demand for a closed shop – the uptown Jewish community became more and more uneasy. The spectacle of Jewish employers pitted against Jewish

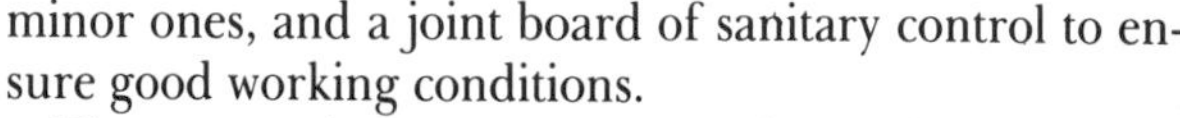

CHAPTER TEN

BELOW
Socialist Morris Hillquit was born in Riga in 1869; he came to America in 1887. He became a lawyer and defended many socialists and trade unionists who were bought to trial. He died in 1933.

account the extent to which industrialization had changed the nature of the workplace.

In dealing with the cloakmaker's strike and their closed shop demand, he came up with the solution of "the preferential union shop." Union men would get preference in the hiring process so long as they "are equal in efficiency to non-union applicants." The union was still reluctant to accept anything less than a closed shop. Louis Marshall and Jacob Schiff lent their efforts to help gain settlement. They took pains to emphasize the importance of arbitration in the Jewish tradition. When agreement was finally reached Marshall called its structure a "Protocol of Peace." On the immediate issues, wages were increased, work-week hours were decreased, the hated fines were abolished, and so was subcontracting. But the protocol of peace contained within it machinery to protect long-term needs as well: peacemaking devices included a permanent board of arbitration for major issues, a committee of grievances for minor ones, and a joint board of sanitary control to ensure good working conditions.

These negotiations were a turning point in labor-management relations, and a turning point for Louis Brandeis as well. He came away from them with an admiration for the way each side – though riddled with tension and grievances – treated the other with respect. He was impressed by the way each side admonished the other to respect Jewish ethics. It was an impression that lingered.

There were many rocky years ahead, but a major contribution of the Jewish community to American labor had been made: to insist on the premise that both labor and capital are responsible for the wellbeing of an industry.

But the struggle was just beginning. The tragic Triangle Shirtwaist Company fire on March 11, 1911 killed 146 people – most of whom were young Jewish and Italian women – covered the Lower East Side in grief. The words of Rose Schneiderman, the dynamic leader of the Hat and Capmaker's Union, were etched into the memories of the Lower East Side workers: "Every year thousands of us are maimed. The life of men and women is so cheap and poverty is so sacred! . . . It is up to the working people to save themselves."

A Factory Investigation Commission was appointed by the New York State legislature to look into violations of fire and health codes. Frances Perkins, a former social worker who would become Franklin Roosevelt's Secretary of Labor, future New York Senator Robert Wager, and Alfred E. Smith, New York's future governor and later a presidential candidate, were commission members. As Perkins wrote of her two colleagues, "They got a firsthand look . . . and from that look they never recovered." They spent their careers fighting for and obtaining, social legislation that would protect Americans from abusive industrial conditions. "We made sure," Perkins recalled, "that Robert Wagner personally crawled through the tiny hole in the wall that gave egress to a steep iron ladder covered with ice and ending twelve feet from the ground, which was euphemistically labeled 'Fire Escape' in many factories." On the basis of the commission's recommendations, the legislature passed tough laws for factory construction, workmen's compensation for accidents, child labor, shorter working hours for women. This was but a preamble to the social concern that would become a major focus of national New Deal legislation.

It was the pragmatists among the Jewish union leaders who – fitting best into the American political mode – were responsible for steering a course that enabled their unions to succeed both at the bargaining table and in creating a better life. The early trade union battles were a hands-on education for the immigrants into the working of American politics – a less idealized democracy

CHAPTER TEN

LEFT
While president of the Amalgamated Clothing Worker's Union from 1915 to 1946, Sidney Hillman (1887–1946) was a leading advocate of constructive cooperation between labor and management.

FAR LEFT
Samuel Gompers was born in London in 1850. He came to America in 1863, was active in the cigarmaker's union, and became a leader in the struggle for workers' rights. Gompers was elected the first president of the American Federation of Labor in 1886, holding that office until his death in 1924.

than many had envisioned when they were across the seas, but one in which their efforts would have a place. It took great strength for labor leaders to rise through the in-fighting among the various socialist factions within the unions. Whether or not they agreed with his politics, Samuel Gompers was their inspiration, their best example of successful pragmatism. He was American labor's most important leader. It was his influence and success that helped the Jewish trade union leaders limit their aims to the practical rather than the ideological realm. Gompers was born in England of Dutch-Jewish parents, came to New York at 13, and worked as a cigar maker. He helped establish the cigar maker's union, and from this experience he derived his trade union methods. In 1886 he became the first president of the American Federation of Labor and was re-elected every year but one until 1924, the year in which he died. He managed to fight off the socialists and other idealogues by setting his sights on one goal at a time. He won the eight-hour day, and the five-, instead of six–, day work week. He believed that "the question of how [mankind] are going to get their rights can only be solved by the organized labor movement, not by revolution, but by evolution. The true object of the labor movement is the seeking of a rational method by which these wrongs can be righted." He did not believe that American trade unionism could benefit from socialism or any other European ideology.

The ILGWU's famous president, David Dubinsky, was a Bundist (Socialist) in Tsarist Russia, with the consequence that he was sent to prison in Siberia. His focus in the ILGWU was on negotiation. Strikes were a last resort. Through his time-study plans he showed employers how they could increase wages and not lose profit. Sidney Hillman, a former rabbinical student, became the first president of the Amalgamated Clothing Workers. Like Dubinsky, he was a "business unionist." The Amalgamated offered its members insurance and pension funds. Both it and the ILGWU became so financially solid that they provided loans to the manufacturers.

The Jewish union leaders as well as the Jewish unions brought a new dimension to American unionism. They took into consideration the quality of life of their members – the members insisted on it. The unions complied by building housing cooperatives, providing education, social insurance, medical care, and cultural experiences. It was the principle of sedakah, the social well-being and balance of the community, at work once again.

Another who succeeded because his aims were pragmatic was the socialist editor Abraham Cahan. He became a radical as a youth in Tsarist Russia. In America he was founder of the *Jewish Daily Forward*. At its inception in 1897, he became the editor. He wanted this Yiddish daily to be a paper with broad appeal, but his plans were stifled by the various radical factions, who insisted on printing their polemics, charges, and countercharges in the paper. He left and went to work for the *Commercial Advertiser*, edited by Lincoln Steffens. There, writing in English, he not only gained experience in American journalism, but realized that with his portraits of life on the Lower East Side he had become an interpreter for the rest of New York of this new and controversial group. The people who seemed so mysterious were rendered into flesh and blood with all their worries and strengths. He returned to edit the *Forward* in 1902 when he was promised full editorial control. He turned it into a paper that addressed along

CHAPTER TEN

RIGHT
Abraham Cahan (1860–1951) emigrated to New York from Lithuania in 1882. He was a fiery speaker for Marxist socialism and organized the first Jewish tailors' union. As the founder and long-time editor of the JEWISH DAILY FORWARD, *Cahan had great influence with Yiddish-speaking American Jews and with the labor movement in general. He is also the author of a classic novel of American immigrant literature,* THE RISE OF DEVID LEVINSKY.

with socialist issues – the reader's most practical concerns. In the famous Bintel Brief (Bundle of Letters) column were printed questions from readers that described their everyday woes, and sought the editor's response with earnestness. The *Forward*'s job, in Cahan's view, was to Americanize the Russians, but not to deprive them of their culture. Despite a socialist bias against religion, at the *Forward* all Jewish holidays and festivals were duly noted, and the concerns of day-to-day Jewish living were addressed. The *Forward* became the leading Yiddish daily in the world, with a circulation of over 200,000.

By the 1920s Cahan, despite his Socialist leanings, was forced to recognize the cruelties of the Bolshevik regime when he gained first-hand information while traveling through Soviet Russia. His paper, now critical of the Communists unearthed and printed the facts about Soviet labor camps, one of the first to do so in the U.S. For Cahan, socialism and democracy went hand in hand. By the 1930s the *Forward* became a paper of Jewish liberal-labor persuasion. As the Jewish trade unions became more pragmatic and mainstream, so too the *Forward*, whose existence was very much tied up with trade unionism, made its own adjustment to America.

For the social workers and educators and young union organizers, the teeming Lower East Side was a school. With its visionaries, its socialism, its European-style coffee shops rife with intellectual debate on the state of the world, they realized, amidst the squalor and noise, that they were inhabiting a progressive world. They formed their value system from the practical Judaism and social Christianity of the Jewish and Protestant social services agencies (some of which eventually merged) in which they were trained. There, too, they became familiar with labor problems, since some of the settlements were involved in strike arbitration. Harry Hopkins, who would become a powerful Roosevelt brain truster first as head of federal unemployment relief and later as head of the WPA (Works Progress Administration), started out as social worker at the Lower East Side's Christadora House and worked for the Board of Child Welfare.

It was through Eleanore Roosevelt that the social workers and union organizers got to know Franklin Delano Roosevelt. He had contracted polio in the midst of a promising career in Democratic politics. Just a year before, in 1920, he had run for vice president on a ticket with James M. Cox. During his recuperation period his wife wanted him to keep abreast of the changes, needs, and social movements of the nation by meeting with people who were actively involved in grappling with its problems.

Among the people she brought home were two members of the Women's Trade Union League. The eloquent Rose Schneiderman, who voiced the feelings of the stricken Lower East Side after the Triangle Factory fire, learned her trade union theory in classes offered by the garment unions. She worked tirelessly during the garment strikes, and later helped to start health and recreation centers for workers. The English-Irish Maude Schwartz brought to America her experience in British trade unionism. Both women were knowledgeable analysts of the labor scene. They gave Roosevelt the background, drawing pictures of the exploitation out of which the trade union movement had sprung. They explained which occupations caused which diseases. He heard refutations of the easy and cruel theory that higher pay for workers caused immorality. He also heard about hired thugs, and about the improvements in certain industries. According to Frances Perkins, had he talked to union men, who were able in bargaining but who lacked the descriptive ability and theoretical thinking of these women, he might not have taken in as well as he did all they had to impart.

The New Deal ethos built itself up in part on the dissents of Justice Louis Brandeis, which helped make new social legislation possible. The work of New York Governor Al Smith, whose chief assistant, Belle Moskowitz, formed a first-rate Reconstruction Commission, was also very significant. Like the Factory Investigation Commission, it brought the people concerned and the experts in with the legislature to effect changes.

A 35-year-old statement by Samuel Gompers favoring work relief programs in times of crisis was a precedent

used to formulate the Civil Works Administration. In trying to establish minimum wages and limitations on working hours, Frances Perkins used Justice Felix Frankfurter's interpretation that the federal government could mandate the working conditions for the manufacture of goods bought by the government. Frankfurther helped shape much New Deal legislation. He brought in many of his former students to staff agencies that he had a hand in helping to establish. Henry Morgenthau, Jr., was Secretary of the Treasury; his was the task of overhauling the banking system. David K. Niles served under both Roosevelt and Harry Truman. Under Roosevelt he worked for Harry Hopkins at the WPA, and then was labor advisor for the War Production Board. He was President Truman's liaison with the Jewish community, and so could report to him in detail the extent of American Jewish commitment to Zionism (which had grown enormously after the German genocide of European Jewry) when Truman had to decide whether or not to recognize the state of Israel. All these men shared the ideological premises of New Deal philosophy. That poverty is preventable, indeed, unacceptable, was a given. The Jewish principle of social justice was well represented in their efforts to combat it.

Within a generation the Russian Jews had produced American children who were moving into the mainstream and had begun to distinguish themselves in scholarship, the arts, and the sciences. By 1930, the Jewish garment unions were no longer predominantly Jewish. In the end it took them a shorter time to become acculturated Americans than it had the German Jews, who proudly held onto the language and customs of a Germany they considered to be culturally and scientifically advanced. In the main, the great German successes were in merchandising. It was left to the irrepressible Russians to produce the intellectuals, artists, and comedians. And, as Jews have always had to do, the Russians went into marginal or new business ventures for which they sensed a market. The motion picture business was a product of Russian Jewish ingenuity. From the small nickelodeons lodged in saloons that projected the earliest moving pictures, the pioneers went into movie distribution. These were businesses that commercial banks would not finance. What seemed flimsy and fly-by-night was not just a popular fad, the pioneers sensed, it was a medium with which America would fall in love. The distributors built lavish theaters. Then, because more films were needed, than were being produced, the distributors, who were now also movie house owners, became producers.

The corporate world was closed to the Russians, but the entrepreneurial spirit was theirs. Many went into real estate – starting small, buying a tenement or brownstone, for a down payment living in it and serving as

LEFT

Justice Felix Frankfurter (1882–1965) was a close associate of Justice Louis D. Brandeis. He was a founder of the American Civil Liberties Union. He was appointed to the Supreme Court by President Franklin Roosevelt in 1939; he served until 1962. Frankfurter was also an active Zionist who worked closely with Chaim Weizmann.

CHAPTER TEN

BELOW RIGHT
The Leo Frank case of 1913 was a blatant example of anti-Semitic violence. After Frank was lynched in Georgia, the B'nai Brith accelerated plans to form the Anti-Defamation League.

janitor, collecting rents, and buying another. And of course there was the fashion industry.

The vicissitudes of anti-Semitism in Russia had made the Russians ashamed of their urban existence. Some sought their freedom in back-to-the-land movements in the U.S. and Palestine. It occurred to very few, including patronizing advice-givers, that their entrepreneurial skills and experience were just what the service economy of the United States of the future would require.

THE LEO FRANK CASE

In 1913, Louis Marshall got the New York State Legislature to enact legislation that made it a misdemeanor for hotels to advertise discriminatory policies. In 1913 as well, an incident that would be remembered by Jews for years to come occurred: the Leo Frank case. Leo Frank was the manager and part-owner of a pencil factory in Atlanta, Georgia. A 14-year-old girl named Mary Phagan, who worked in the factory, was found dead in its basement. Leo Frank was arrested. He was a Jew who had grown up in New York and graduated from Cornell University. From the start there was no reason to believe that the janitor, who testified against him, was lying, and was himself the murderer. He offered conflicting versions of events, and had a criminal record. The trial was a farce. The defense could not be heard above the booing, and cries of "Hang the Jew" were uttered with some regularity. The janitor, Jim Conley, testified that notes found beside Mary Phagan's body, which described the murderer as "a long, slim, Negro" (as was Conley), were dictated to him by Frank. The prosecutor depicted Frank as a rich Northerner whose family held large amounts of Wall Street securities. The family was actually of fairly modest means. Frank was convicted. When enough people became outraged enough to demand a new trial for him Tom Watson, a former Georgia political boss, and the publisher of two papers (in which he maligned equally Catholic, blacks, and Jews) launched a hate campaign in his publications. He also led a boycott against Jewish businesses. At his urging, too, a vigilante group calling itself the Knights of Mary Phagan was formed. Southern Jews were slow to come to Frank's aid. Not until the anti-Semitism had spread, and they saw lawyers across the country demanding a new trial, did they rally to him. As Southerners, they were in the habit of keeping genteel silences. Frank petitioned for a new trial 13 times. Louis Marshall presented his appeal to the Supreme Court and lost. Finally, the governor of Georgia, Frank Slaton, to whom Frank's innocence was obvious, commuted the sentence to life in prison, and risked an encounter with 5,000 armed people who marched on his mansion and were fought off by the horse guard.

The Knights of Mary Phagan went into action. On August 17, 1915 they stormed the prison where Frank was incarcerated, and lynched him. After this initiation rite the Knights renamed themselves the Reincarnated Invisible Empire of the Knights of the Ku Klux Klan; this Klan attracted a membership of 4.5 million and persisted in anti-Jewish, anti-black and anti-Catholic harrassment. Many Jews decided to leave Georgia.

It was the first time in the United States that a whole Jewish community was actually in danger of violence from bigots.

As a result of the case the Anti-Defamation League of B'nai Brith, which was already in the planning stages, was established ahead of schedule as a full-fledged organization.

On March 8, 1982, 83-year-old Alonzo Mann revealed the secret he had been carrying since age 13. In a sworn affidavit he said he had seen Jim Conley, the janitor, carrying Mary Phagan's body – she was still alive, but Conley had threatened to kill him if he told. The young boy's mother counseled him never to speak about what he had seen. "At last" the 83-year-old man said "I am able to get this off my heart."

The case that shook the Jewish community's belief in the American rule of law, and that was a point of sorrow for Jews who knew Frank was an innocent sacrifice to anti-Semitism, came to a close without much notice 70 years later.

CLOSED AMERICA

In the years after World War I, isolationism seemed to predominate in America. A fear of Reds, after the Bolshevik victory in Russia, of all radicalism, or thought

CHAPTER TEN

LEFT
The hate-mongering articles published by Henry Ford in his DEARBORN INDEPENDENT *newspaper in the 1920s was finally stopped by a lawsuit and the threat of a boycott of Ford automobiles.*

processes that could be defined as such, brought with it xenophobia. Raids in which Woodrow Wilson's Attorney General A. Mitchell Palmer went in search of alien radicals by unlawfully descending on the homes of foreigners and rounding them up for interrogation, and the Sacco and Vanzetti case, came out of these times. In dissent from other members of the Supreme Court Justices Oliver Wendell Holmes and Louis D. Brandeis had to hold the fort for free speech. In 1921, the immigration restrictionists began to close in. The new immigration law limited each country's quota to 3 percent of the number of its countrymen living in the U.S. in the year 1910. This effectively limited entry of the countrymen of the most recent immigrants – Southern and East Europeans – the Italians and the Jews. In 1924 the quotas were reduced to 2 percent and the base year was pushed back to 1890. Nordic and Anglo-Saxon immigrants thus became most favored nations. In the words of the venerable historian Jacob Rader Marcus, "Jewish immigration sprung westward for almost three centuries until it was brought to a halt by the Johnson-Lodge Bill of 1924."

Anti-Semitism was having its day in postwar America. Henry Ford published articles in his *Dearborn Independent* accusing Jews of everything from secretly ruling New York to corrupting American baseball and music. He published the scurrilous *Protocols of the Elders of Zion*, a hate-mongering collection of apocrypha originally used by Tsarist police to malign the Jews. Ford refused to stop his publications, at least until he was threatened with a boycott of his cars, and a lawsuit. It was Louis Marshall who, as part of the settlement of the lawsuit, got Ford to write a retraction and an apology to the Jewish community.

Al Smith's campaign for president in 1928 was the first in which more Jews voted Democratic than Republican. It was a sign that liberalism and a concern for social issues were now more a part of the Democratic than the Republican fabric. Alfred E. Smith was immensely popular with the Jewish community, but the

CHAPTER TEN

RIGHT
Four times Governor of New York, Alfred Emanuel Smith (1873–1944) was born on the Lower East Side of New York City. A popular, crusading reformer, Smith ran on the Democratic ticket in 1928 as the first Roman Catholic candidate for president. He lost to Herbert Hoover. Smith was enormously popular with the Jewish community.

country was not yet ready for a Catholic president; people still allowed themselves to believe that his election would be giving the country over to Popish control. Years later Smith remarked, "The time just hasn't come when a man can say his beads in the White House."

During Franklin Roosevelt's third term, when it looked as though he would not choose to run again, Democratic headquarters reviewed possible candidates. The two governors most widely known outside of their states were Herbert Lehman of New York and Henry Horner of Illinois. Both were Jewish, and so it was an automatic given that they couldn't be seriously considered. The country was not yet ready for a Jewish president.

In 1929 Louis Marshall died. His funeral service was the first held in the new Temple Emanu-El; its first Russian-Jewish head rabbi officiated. The brilliant constitutional lawyer and president of the American Jewish Committee did things quietly, but always managed to be there as arbitrator and defender of a host of civil rights issues. It was he who argued against the Russian treaty, got legislation outlawing exclusionary ads, fought for black rights, demanded Henry Ford's retraction, and at the Versailles Peace Conference, drafted the resolution for Jewish minority rights in East Europe – rights which were extended to all minorities. This was a championing of the individual's right over the state's in a part of the world where such thinking had little precedent.

When Franklin Roosevelt first assumed the presidency, the country was laid flat by the Great Depression. New Deal programs provided jobs, social security, unemployment insurance, machinery for collective bargaining, and the minimum wage. A conservation program saved the land of the Dust Bowl. Mortgages were financed so people could buy homes and plan a future. Though there were nine million unemployed, things had greatly improved.

Some anti-Roosevelt factions, made up of segments of big business, conservatives, and rugged individualists outraged by what they considered to be government incursion into the private sector, expressed their hostility in an anti-Semitic form that had them calling the New Deal the "Jew Deal". Weren't several of Roosevelt's top aides and a host of New Deal lawyers Jewish? Roosevelt himself became Mr. Rosenfelt.

A more serious threat – because it came from an

emerging political base – was the anti-Semitic frame of reference of the Detroit Catholic priest, Father Coughlin. In his radio broadcasts he railed against capitalism, international bankers, and Jews (who were, during this time, often depicted as rabid capitalists except in those moments when they were rabid Communists). Coughlin received 80,000 letters a week from his listeners.

As the Nazis secured power in Germany, they exported their propaganda to the U.S. Nazi Germany supplied money, and most important, organizational leadership to the German American Bund. The Bund held rallies and disseminated anti-Semitic propaganda. At Madison Square Garden they managed to fill 19,000 seats. The Nazis poured money into nativist groups as well. The Bund members could be seen on the streets of New York and other large cities handing out leaflets. More than one fight broke out when incensed citizens, often Jewish, could no longer refrain from direct response.

A boycott of German goods was urged by Jewish groups. When Hitler was elected chancellor, Dr. Stephen Wise, President of the World Jewish Congress, and the Zionist Organization of America, called a protest meeting at Madison Square Garden. The German embassy tried to bargain with him; they promised to lighten their persecutions if he would cancel the meeting. He went ahead. The great sin would have been to barter with the Nazi beast.

And then came the war. The president mobilized industry, calling on top business and labor leaders to work in concert. There was a labor shortage and the beginnings of prosperity. With Germany now the enemy, nativist anti-Semitism went into remission. American war propaganda, and newspaper reports of Nazi cruelties, showed the Nazis as evil, and evil as well was the anti-Semitism *they* preached. Later, when reports of the death camps got back, the consequence of the easy – some might have thought harmless – impulse to use the Jews as the focus for discontent silenced many.

While the American population at large sensed the un-American and subversive character of anti-Semitism, certain powerful agencies of the government were indulging their anti-Jewish bias. The State Department gained a reputation for non cooperation with American Jewish efforts to rescue European Jews. Letters addressed to Stephen Wise, care of the American Embassy in Switzerland, which testified to the slaughter of Jews in concentration camps, were held back from him by the department. Only later, with the intervention of Undersecretary Sumner Welles, did he get his mail – and make it public.

When Secretary of the Treasury Henry Morgenthau, Jr., received word that it would be possible to ransom 70,000 Hungarian and Polish Jews he, with Roosevelt's go-ahead, approved the funds. The State Department sat on the matter for months and the opportunity was lost. Efforts by Jewish groups to get immigration authorities to admit more refugees were met with the accusation from State Department officials that Jews were trying to pressure them.

By August 1942 journalists had gotten word from the American Jewish Congress of Hitler's plan to wipe out European Jewry. A mass rally was called in New York to ask the Allies to negotiate with Germany for the rescue of the Jews. But while the genocidal Nazi campaign may have begun to strike some as a unique evil, in a theater of war where hundreds of thousands of soldiers were dying in combat, and civilians of all persuasions were being murdered for their political opposition and resistance, it was hard to insist on the uniqueness of Nazi intentions toward the Jews.

Yet there were those in the administration who knew. By 1939 Roosevelt knew there were six main concentration camps, and an organized plan for rounding up the Jews. He was American Jewry's most beloved president. They saw him put into practice on the national level many of the social safeguards against poverty and exploitation that they had evolved out of their religious culture and the exigencies of history. He had asked Stephen Wise to trust him in his efforts to help the European Jews. But hindsight tells us that even as he professed to be doing everything in his power to rescue them, his policy was to steer clear of such action. Immigration quotas remained fixed. Winning the war was the only goal.

The anti-Semitic Assistant Secretary of State, Breckenridge Long, held sway in a State Department that was responsible for administering the national-origins quota system. He was in charge of refugee policy and went out of his way to make sure that even fewer refugees than the law allowed gained entry into the U.S. The State Department actively opposed the Wagner-Rogers Bill of 1929 which would have admitted 20,000 Jewish refugee children into the U.S. over a period of two years. Anti-Semitic demagogues, plus the fear of many Americans, in the period before the U.S. entered the war, that refugees would vie with them for scarce jobs; and the strong objections from organizations such as the Daughters of the American Revolution and the American Legion were all factors in the defeat of the bill. Roosevelt, who remained silent while the bill was hotly debated, may well have decided that the immigration issue was too much of a liability for him – and since he already had the Jewish vote, he need make few concessions on the issue.

On May 27, 1939, the S.S. *St. Louis*, with 936 refugees on board, was denied access to any port in the U.S. and had to return its passengers to a perilous future in Europe.

ABOVE
After the horrors of the Holocaust became known to the world, the American Jewish community became outspoken on behalf of a Jewish homeland in Israel. This massive Zionist rally took place in Madison Square Garden in 1948.

AFTER THE HOLOCAUST

CHAPTER ELEVEN

A world of closed borders heaped its bitterest fruits on the Jewish populations. If immigration was of greivous concern to the American Jews, it was the paramount issue for the Jews in Palestine. It made them resolve, as soon as World War II was over, to become a sovereign state. British actions had eliminated any other option, including a more gradual working toward statehood. In a series of White Papers issued over the years, the British had eaten away at the Balfour Declaration – with its promise of support of the Jewish national home – by limiting immigration. The last paper, issued in 1939, limited it to no more than 75,000 over a five-year period, after which all immigration was to stop. In addition, Jews were no longer able to purchase land in Palestine. Thus, the very basis for the Jewish national home was being undone. Clearly, Britain was treating Palestine as if it were a colonial possession rather than a mandated territory held in trust. A total of 52 League of Nations members, and the non-League United States, had signed and ratified a mandate into which the Balfour Declaration was incorporated; this gave the Declaration the weight of a treaty. Furthermore, the U.S. and Great Britain signed a separate treaty, in December 1924, which secured the rights of U.S. nationals in Palestine and obliged Britain to consult with the U.S. government over any basic changes in its policies toward the territory. Britain never troubled to fulfill this obligation, nor did the U.S. complain. The administration let the final betrayal of the Declaration, the 1939 White Paper, go by without protest. American Zionists, however, were not so quiet. Six hundred met in New York to urge that the Jewish Agency be allowed to control immigration into Palestine, and that a Jewish commonwealth be established.

The Middle East was a crucial military zone in World War II, and Britain continued to do everything in its power to win the Arabs to the Allied cause. There was, too, the consideration of Arab oil. Even after the war ended, and the Arabs had made clear their hostility to the British by fighting for the Axis powers, the new Labor government backed the Arabs; it was intent on maintaining its presence in Palestine, where its military and naval installations were a check against Soviet expansion.

Fast on the heels of the 1939 White Paper was World War II. For the Jews of Palestine, outrage at the British had to be suppressed in order to fight the Nazis. A Nazi defeat was crucial. A Nazi victory would be death. Thousands of Jews enlisted to fight with the British. The Palestine community supplied not only troops, but crucial war provisions and food that came from the flowering of the desert that their years of hard work and farming and experiments with new techniques had brought about. The Jews expected that their loyalty would soften the British position on immigration, but the British were unyielding. During the war the Jewish settlers watched with fury as Jewish refugee boats were turned back over a damning horizon. After the war, in 1946 and 1947, they watched again as refugee ships with displaced persons aboard were, likewise, refused entry. The Mossad, the European arm of the Haganah, undertook an ingenious program of illegal immigration, smuggling in as many people as possible while playing cat-and-mouse with the British Mediterranean fleet. Five thousand of 25,000 made it into the country.

World opinion was sympathetic to the efforts of refugees to get into Palestine. The press gave it wide coverage. Especially stirring was the saga of the ship *Exodus*, which struggled with the British who boarded it as it entered the waters of Palestine, and fended them off for some hours until the ship was fired upon. Three were killed, 100 wounded; the ship made headlines. Coverage of this resolute group continued as it was returned to France and the passengers refused to disembark. French dockworkers went out on a sympathy strike.

If the British counted on continued tacit U.S. support, presuming that it was in the American economic interests to approve British policy backing the Arabs – oil companies, Protestant missionaries in the Middle East, and State Department officials were urging such – Harry Truman was another matter. He wavered back and forth between the State Department position and his

own sympathy for the Zionist cause. Finally, he decided to follow his own instincts in the light of what he considered to be State Department shortsightedness. He made it known that as a party to the Balfour Declaration the U.S. had a responsibility to the Jews of Palestine.

Britain, frustrated at the loss of world opinion, decided to refer the whole matter to the United Nations. U.N. proposals called for an end to the British mandate, and the partition of Palestine into two sovereign states, one Arab, one Jewish. The General Assembly voted in favour of partition on November 29, 1947.

Britain hastily pulled out of Palestine, making sure there was no orderly transference of civil administration, and leaving the Jewish settlers without services. It was counting on an Arab victory in the war that the Arabs had long been threatening. On May 14, 1948, as Egypt made ready to attack, Prime Minister David Ben-Gurion and his cabinet proclaimed the Republic of Israel. Ten minutes later, in an announcement that took the United States delegation to the U.N. unawares, President Truman extended de facto U.S. recognition to the State of Israel. That done, other countries soon followed.

The Israelis had the further ordeal of the Arab wars ahead of them – they were ridiculously outnumbered and still hampered by a U.S. arms embargo on the Middle East – but now, after two thousand years, they would be defending a commonwealth recognized as theirs, and nurtured from the wellsprings of their ancient soil.

For the Jews the world over, Zionist or not, the Holocaust made the state of Israel imperative. Out of the ashes a spirit, a reality that was wholly Jewish must be born. What Austrian author Stefan Zweig said of the need for Jews to unite to provide aid to Jewish refugees of World War I, was the expression of a practical truth, which, like the existence of Israel, precludes argument: "Later, at some future date, we shall again gladly and passionately discuss whether Jews should be Zionists, revisionists, territorialists, or assimilationists; we shall discuss the hair-splitting point of whether we are a nation, a religion, a people, or a race. All of these time-consuming theoretical discussions can wait. Now there is but one thing for us to do – to give help."

And that is what American Jewry did. As much American in its generosity as Jewish in its concern for other Jews, the American Jewish community raised $317.5 million throughout the year of the 1967 war, and a total of $670 million for the 1973 Yom Kippur War. For the 1948 war it raised over $150 million, considered an exceptional amount in those days.

After World War II the melting-pot ideal – and pressures – began to give way to the more inclusive concept of "cultural pluralism" espoused by Horace Kallen, a disciple of William James. He argued that in a real democracy where individuals can express their individuality, groups should be able to retain their "cultural diversities."

Morris Raphael Cohen brought similar thoughts to bear on the role of Jews in America as he looked into the question of why Jewish scientists proliferated in America. "The Greeks, when they made their great contribution to science, were a commercial people traveling from one country to another and thus liberating their minds from complete subservience to customary or inherited views. So it has been with the Jews who since the end of the eighteenth century have been a people on the move. Breaking away from old routines, the Jews have been spiritual explorers ready to appraise and enter new realms of thought . . . Jews such as Einstein, Levi-Civita, Minkowsky, Michelson . . . Such being the fact I have not been able to embrace the assimilationist idea that Jews should give up as quickly as possible all those characteristics which distinguish them from their non-Jewish neighbors . . . Why should we object to the concentration of Scottish immigrants in the engineering profession? . . . We can be better Americans if, instead of being blind imitators, we approach American civilization critically and try to contribute something distinctive to the general fund of its spiritual goods."

Dr. Joseph Goldberger, saved the health of countless impoverished Southerners when he discovered in 1914 that vitamin deficiency causes pellagra. Jewish-American Nobelists include Albert Michelson, who paved the way for the theory of relativity when he measured the exact speed of light; Julius Axelrod, who researched enzyme and hormone metabolism; Rosalyn Yallow, who measured body changes from the normal state to diseased; Selman Waksman, who discovered antibiotics; and the two scientists who found two different but effective polio vaccines: Jonas Salk and Albert Sabin, but a few of the outstanding scientists in America. And, of course, the giant, Albert Einstein, who was admitted along with some of Germany's most talented Jewish men and women – Hannah Arendt, Kurt Weil, Emil Durkheim and others – in a special lifting of quota restrictions meant to ensure for the United States the benefits of their creativity.

After World War II a large influx of Hassidic Jews put down roots in America. They have recreated here the religion-centered life of the lost communities of East Europe. Of their followers they ask the kind of deep commitment that is necessary when religious devotion is a way of life. Their influence began to grow even as that of modern Orthodoxy, at least between the two wars, was seen to be declining. Because Orthodox worship is the established rule of the state of Israel, the prestige of the Hassidim has been enhanced. When Israeli politicians visit the U.S. they pay their respects to the Lubavitcher Rabbi in Brooklyn, where other Hassidic sects

CHAPTER ELEVEN

also live: the Bobovers have settled in Borough Park, the Satmars moved from Williamsburg to Monroe, New York, and the Lubavitchers are in Crown Heights, Brooklyn. One of their key activities is as missionaries to the non observant.

Recently the modern Orthodox movement, perhaps taking its cue from the Hassidim and the general renewed interest in religion in present-day America has become reinvigorated. If counted along with the Hassidim, the Orthodox are part of the fastest-growing denomination in American Judaism. A sense of purpose and religious mission is part of the pull of Orthodoxy, and for this reason many affluent professionals have become drawn to it. Nonetheless there are difficulties. Orthodox women have left because women are not permitted to become rabbis and cannot participate in a *minyan*. While the Conservative and Reform movements ordain women rabbis and allow them full participation, and while some Reform congregations recognize as Jewish those of patrilinear Jewish descent, the Orthodox position remains fixed. Conservative Judaism has spawned the Reconstructionist movement, which concerns itself with the history, language, music, art, and culture of what it calls the "evolving religious civilization of the Jewish people."

World War II, not democratic idealism or the "American way," opened many opportunities to Jews and other Americans. During the war the huge demand for manpower brought more acceptance and more mobility to everyone. During this time, too, gifted scientists were on top of the needed list. Corporate research laboratories began to change their closed policies. Barred by law firms, many Jewish lawyers worked for the New Deal administration. Soon corporations saw they needed those lawyers who could negotiate with trade unions, and knew labor and tax law and later, mergers and acquisitions. Merit triumphed not in and of itself but because those most able were needed quickly to fulfil unanticipated functions. Old-line law firms often lacked within their staffs expertise in the newer fields. Out of necessity Jews have, over the centuries, learned to spot new economic and political trends, sense the winds of change for good or ill, and then ride them. In corporations, taking important foreign office jobs – frontier jobs, really – enabled many to get a foothold into top management.

In his book *A Certain People* author Charles Silberman contrasts the careers of Gerard Swope, president of General Electric from 1922 to 1940 (and brother of journalist Bayard Swope) with that of Irving Schapiro, chairman of E.I. Du Pont. Swope's Jewish background was not emphasized. Irving Schapiro's appointment seemed impossible for a Jew to attain, especially one whose Jewishness was very much a part of his identity. Schapiro, who in the 1940s rejected friendly advice that he change his name in order to get a job after law school in one of the firms in Minneapolis, was very clear about being himself.

He worked in Washington during and after World War II, as did many a Jewish lawyer. He was at the Office of Price Administration and later, the Criminal Division of the Justice Department. By the 1950s a former boss at Justice offered him a job at Du Pont on the legal staff. In 1973 he became chairman and chief executive officer of Du Pont.

In the Old Country, the Jews organized their own communities, with little assistance – or interest – from the authorities. The tradition of self-help and public service was brought to America, where it gave rise to many important public figures in politics, philanthropy, the law, and other areas.

The first Jew to serve in the United States Senate was David Yulee (1810–1886). He represented Florida in 1845–51 and 1855–61. During the Civil War Yulee was a member of the Confederate Congress.

Justice Benjamin Cardozo (1870–1938) succeeded Oliver Wendell Holmes on the Supreme Court in 1932. A liberal jurist, he was noted for his humane approach to the law. Justice Abe Fortas was appointed to the Supreme Court in 1966; he stepped down in 1969 and returned to the practice of law. Fortas died in 1984.

Arthur Garfield Hays (1881–1954) was highly successful as a corporate lawyer, but he is best remembered as a fighter for civil rights and as a defense attorney in the Scopes trial and the Sacco and Vanzetti case. He was general counsel to the American Civil Liberties Union from 1912 to 1954.

David Eli Lilienthal served as a director of the Tennessee Valley Authority from 1933 to 1946 and as chairman of the Atomic Energy Commission from 1946 to 1950.

Jacob K. Javits, Congressman and Senator from New York, was born in 1904. Throughout his long political career he was active in the liberal wing of the Republican party; he died, after a long illness, in 1986.

In his long political career Abraham Ribicoff served as a Congressman, as Governor of Connecticut, as Secretary of Health, Education and Welfare, and as Senator from Connecticut.

Active Jewish politicians today include Mayor Ed Koch of New York, Mayor Dianne Feinstein of San Francisco, Senator Howard Metzenbaum of Ohio, Congressman Stephen Solarz of New York, Senator Frank Lautenberg of New Jersey, and Senator Carl Levin of Michigan. Other prominent government advisors include Henry Kissinger, pollster Loi Harris and Robert Strauss.

The first nuclear submarine, launched in 1954, was the godchild of the late Admiral Hyman G. Rickover. Born in Russia in 1900, Rickover finally retired from active duty in 1981.

ABOVE
Even Albert Einstein enjoyed Yiddish theater. Here he poses with actor Maurice Schwartz, who is portraying the Rabbi of Neshev in the play YOSHE KALB.

AMERICAN JEWS, THE ARTS, & SCIENCE

CHAPTER TWELVE

BELOW
Jacob Adler was the patriarch of a theatrical family. His wife Sarah was a leading lady in Adler's troupe; his son Luther was an actor and a founding member of the Group Theater (closely associated with the works of Clifford Odets, among others); his granddaughter Stella was a member of the Group Theater and a well-known acting teacher.

By forcing the Jews of Europe into ghettos and distant villages, the authorities hoped to destroy their culture by isolating it. The opposite happened. These Jews developed a vibrant tradition of music, theater, literature, and comedy – traditions they brought with them to the New World. And in America, where talent, not religion, was the measure of success, these traditions flourished in a much wider world.

THE YIDDISH THEATER

Among the emigrants from Eastern Europe were members of Yiddish theater companies. So great was the demand that the United States soon became the world center for the Yiddish theater. Jacob P. Adler, Boris Thomashefsky, Molly Picon, and Jacob Gordin – great performers by any standard – were soon well-known names capable of packing the house.

Jacob A. Adler (1855–1926) began his career as an actor in Russia. When the Russian government banned all Yiddish theater in the early 1880s, Adler went first to London and then to America in 1888. He quickly became a leading figure on the Yiddish stage as the leading man in syrupy romances. Later, he collaborated with the Yiddish playwright and actor Jacob Gordin to produce plays with a more serious content. Boris Thomashefsky had arrived in America from the Ukraine in 1881. A theatrical jack-of-all-trades, he wrote, adapted, produced, and starred in dozens of successful plays in the Yiddish theaters of New York City; he died in 1939. The Yiddish Art Theater, the highwater point of Yiddish theater in America, was organized by Maurice Schwartz in 1921. This popular company performed a wide variety of plays, both original and in translation, as well as musicals.

There was also an idiom all its own: the Yiddish-American movie. These were generally tearjerkers in which loss – and being lost – played big symbolic parts, creating a catharsis for all the real loss many members of the audience had been forced to experience: the homeland, parents, family, and friends all left behind. In these movies folk customs – such as spitting against the evil eye – have their rightful place. In a Yiddish version of *The Jazz Singer*, the singer does not go out into the wide world and marry a gentile woman. The plot is changed to effect a happier, Old World conclusion: the hero leaves his American girlfriend, goes back to the Old Country, and marries the girl next door.

THE MOVIES

The importance of American Jews in the motion picture industry, starting from the very beginning, is almost unbelievable. In 1912, a fellow named Jesse Lasky, the brother-in-law of a man named Sam Goldwyn (originally Goldfish), scouted Los Angeles with a card-playing playwright friend of Goldwyn's named Cecil B. De Mille. They were looking for a place to make a movie called *Squaw Man*. Goldwyn had invested in the venture, although none of the partners had any movie experience.

RIGHT
The spectacular films of Cecil B. De Mille include THE TEN COMMANDMENTS, REAP THE WILD WIND, *and* THE GREATEST SHOW ON EARTH.

CENTER
The great Samuel Goldwyn – the man who invented Hollywood – in 1959. He formed Goldwyn Pictures in 1916, then merged with L.B. Mayer to form Metro-Goldwyn-Mayer in 1924.

Lasky rented a barn from a realtor named Jacob Stern and hired Dustin Farnum as the star. De Mille directed. Thus America's first full-length feature film was made in a distant place called Hollywood.

Goldwyn and Lasky were pioneers in Hollywood. Other Jews who became powerful producers and directors there include Adolph Zukor, Lewis Selznick, David O. Selznick, Carl Laemmle, Irving Thalberg, Ernst Lubitsch, Joseph L. Mankiewicz, the Warner brothers, William Wyler, Lee Strasberg, and William Fox. Among the many present-day directors and producers who are Jews, perhaps the most outstanding are Woody Allen, Mel Brooks, and Steven Spielberg.

That distinctly American art form, the movie cartoon, owes a great deal to Max Fleischer, who developed and improved many of the techniques used to make cartoons.

Many Jewish writers worked in the movie business, making their mark there as well as in the world of letters or as dramatists. The list is extensive, and includes: S.N. Behman, Moss Hart, Ben Hect, Lilian Hellman, Garson Kanin, George S. Kaufmann, Clifford Odets, Elmer Rice, Irwin Shaw, and Budd Schulberg.

An important figure in American theatrical history is David Belasco (1853–1931). As an actor-manager and dramatist in New York from 1882 onward, Belasco was

CHAPTER TWELVE

LEFT
Theatrical producer David Belasco was best known for his innovative and spectacular stage settings.

FAR LEFT
Lillian Hellman, author of the plays THE CHILDREN'S HOUR (1934), THE LITTLE FOXES (1939), and WATCH ON THE RHINE (1941), is also noted for her autobiographical writings, including AN UNFINISHED WOMAN, PENTIMENTO, and SCOUNDREL TIME.

BELOW LEFT
The plays of Elmer Rice are still relevant today. THE ADDING MACHINE was first produced in 1923. STREET SCENE won a Pulitzer Prize in 1929 and was made into an opera by Kurt Weill in 1947.

LEFT
The works of playwright Clifford Odets contain strong elements of social protest. He is best known for the plays AWAKE AND SING (1935), WAITING FOR LEFTY (1935), and GOLDEN BOY (1937).

BELOW LEFT
Born Melvin Kaminsky in New York City in 1927, Mel Brooks is one of today's foremost comic directors, writers, and actors. Among his best-known films are THE PRODUCERS and BLAZING SADDLES.

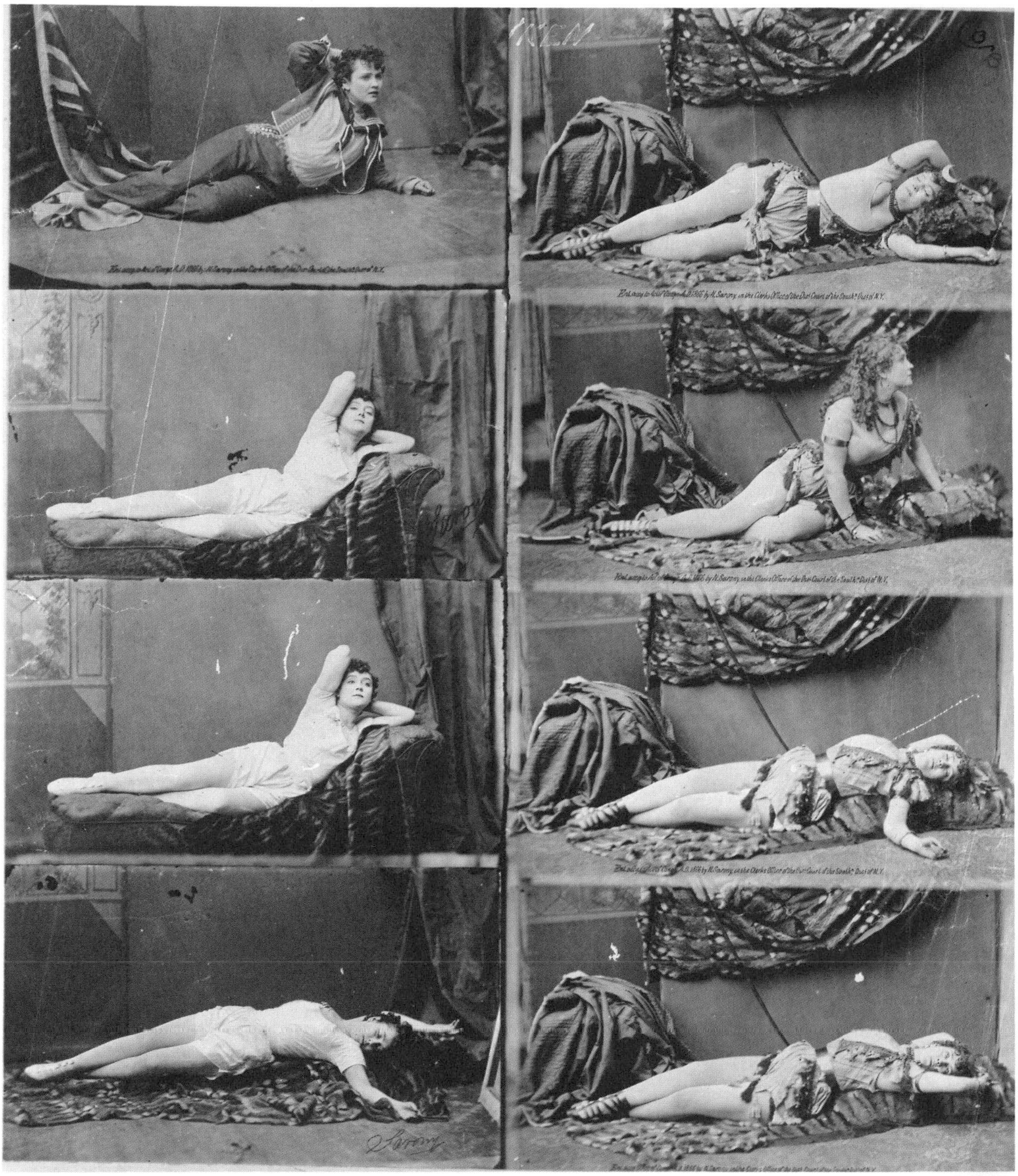

RIGHT
Actress Adah Isaacs Menken (1835–1868) in a variety of poses considered highly suggestive for their time. Menken was a stage sensation in New York, London, and Paris. She also wrote serious poetry with a Jewish theme.

one of the foremost producers of his era. He was particularly noted for his ability to discover and train stars. Another impresario, Sol Hurok, was born in Russia in 1890 and came to the United States in 1905. He brought many of the world's leading artists to America, and also presented many American performers abroad.

Show business is a traditional American way up from the minority ghetto – whether the ghetto be an Irish, Jewish, Italian, or black one. The list of Jewish screen stars is lengthy and include many names from the golden age of the movies. Theda Bara, Jack Benny, Fannie Brice, George Burns, Eddie Cantor, Kirk Douglas, John Garfield, Paulette Goddard, Judy Holliday, Al Jolson, Danny Kaye, Jerry Lewis, the Marx Brothers, Paul Muni, Luise Rainer, Edward G. Robinson, the Three Stooges, and Conrad Veidt are all examples. Among the many well-known Jewish actors performing today are Ed Asner, Richard Benjamin, Neil Diamond, Goldie Hawn, Dustin Hoffman, Barbara Streisand, and Eli Wallach.

CHAPTER TWELVE

LEFT
Douglas Fairbanks was born in Denver in 1883, the son of a Jewish father. His real name was Douglas Ullman. He starred in swashbuckling movies such as THE MARK OF ZORRO *and* THE THIEF OF BAGDAD. *He died in 1939.*

FAR LEFT
Eddie Cantor was born Edward Israel Isskowitz in 1892. He won fame on the stage, on radio, in the movies, and on television. Cantor was also president of the Jewish Theatrical Guild, the Screen Actors' Guild, and the American Federation of Radio Artists. He died in 1964. He is shown here in a scene from the movie ALI BABA GOES TO TOWN *(1937).*

CENTER
The great magician Harry Houdini was Jewish. So is Tony Curtis, shown here playing Houdini in a film of the magician's life.

FAR LEFT
The original vamp of the silent screen – Theda Bara – in a scene from CLEOPATRA.

LEFT
The late Danny Kaye was beloved by millions for his comic roles and active fundraising for charity.

RIGHT
Comedian Phil Silvers played Sgt. Bilko in the long-running television series of the same name.

BELOW RIGHT
Although he was famed for playing tough guys in such films as LITTLE CAESAR (1930), Edward G. Robinson was a cultivated man who was an avid book collector. He was born in Rumania in 1893 and came to America in 1903. He died in 1973.

ABOVE CENTER
The Marx Brothers—Groucho (Julius, center), Harpo (Arthur, right), and Chico (Leonard, left)—brought their own particular brand of zany comedy first to vaudeville and then to Hollywood. Their films include HORSE FEATHERS (1932), DUCK SOUP (1933), and A NIGHT AT THE OPERA (1935).

CHAPTER TWELVE

LEFT
Joel Grey has sung and danced his way to stardom in films such as CABARET and on Broadway.

BELOW LEFT
The popular musical-comedy entertainer Sophie Tucker (1889–1966) made the song "A Yiddishe Mamme" famous.

BELOW
Entertainer George Jessel showed his versatility by appearing on the vaudeville stage, on radio, on television, and in the movies.

CENTER BELOW
One of today's best actors is Dustin Hoffman, shown here playing the lead in Arthur Miller's DEATH OF A SALESMAN.

RIGHT
Actor John Garfield starred in PRIDE OF THE MARINES, *produced by the Warner Brothers during World War II.*

BELOW RIGHT
Actor Muni Weissenfreund was a star of the Yiddish stage. As Paul Muni, he was one of Hollywood's greatest character actors. He is shown here in a scene from THE LAST ANGRY MAN *(1959).*

BELOW FAR RIGHT
Actors Jack Klugman (right) and Tony Randall (left) argued their way into nationwide popularity on the television series THE ODD COUPLE.

CENTER
Actor Michael Landon is known across America for his roles in the the television series BONANZA *and* LITTLE HOUSE ON THE PRAIRIE, *among others. He is shown here (second from right) with his* BONANZA *co-stars, including Canadian Jewish actor Lorne Green (second from left).*

CHAPTER TWELVE

LEFT
Walter Matthau has appeared in dozens of movies, including THE BAD NEWS BEARS, THE ODD COUPLE, CHARADER, *and* THE SUNSHINE BOYS.

BELOW LEFT
Actor George Segal has starred in A TOUCH OF CLASS *with Glenda Jackson and in many other films. He is shown here in a scene from* NO WAY TO TREAT A LADY.

BELOW
Rod Steiger has played many starring roles in Hollywood and on Broadway. He is particularly noted for his work in the film IN THE HEAT OF THE NIGHT *with Sidney Poitier.*

RIGHT
The early television comedy and variety show of Sid Caesar was immensely popular.

CENTER RIGHT
Actress Fanny Brice was a stage star who successfully made the transition to movies.

BELOW RIGHT
Milton Berle and Gracie Fields whoop it up for the audience. Berle, better known as Uncle Miltie, was a pioneer in television entertainment.

BELOW FAR RIGHT
Actress Shelly Winters appeared in a number of films, including THE DIARY OF ANNE FRANK.

FROM THE BORSCHT BELT TO BROADWAY

One way to deal with the difficulties of life as a Jew is to joke about it. As thousands of Jews from East Europe poured into America, they brought their own brand of wry humor with them. And in turn, some very funny people became comedic stars.

The Borscht Belt is a term coined in the 1920s for the resort area of the southern Catskill mountains in New York State. Starting at the turn of the century and lasting until today, this region has attracted vacationing Jews to hundreds of hotels, bungalow colonies, and boarding houses. Out of this attraction grew such famed hotels as Grossinger's, The Concord, Kutsher's, and others. Starting in the 1920s, the Borscht Belt became the training ground for a new generation of talent, particularly comics. Among the many performers who went on to wider fame are Sid Caesar, Elia Kazan, Dore Schary, Shelley Winters, Milton Berle, Phil Silvers, Eddie Cantor, Eddie Fisher, Jerry Lewis, and many others. The tradition of Jewish humor lives on today in the work of performers known all over the world, such as David Brenner, Woody Allen, Mel Brooks, Jackie Mason, and others.

CHAPTER TWELVE

LEFT
Actor Zero Mostel won the hearts of all Americans—not just Jews—for his remarkable performance as Tevye the Milkman in the hit musical FIDDLER ON THE ROOF. Here he is shown in a studio recording the role.

CENTER LEFT
Jerry Lewis is known for his many comic roles in the movies. He is also known for his active fund-raising efforts on behalf of the Muscular Dystrophy foundation.

BELOW
Comedian Jack Benny and his violin. Born Benjamin Kubelsky in Illinois in 1894, Benny became famous through his radio and television shows, which featured jokes about his violin-playing and his famed miserliness. Benny died in 1974.

THE MUSICAL WORLD

One of the best-loved American composers is Aaron Copland. Although Copland stressed the American part of his heritage in such works as the ballets *Appalachian Spring* and *Rodeo*, he also was aware of his Jewish roots. This is best expressed in his chamber work *Vitebsk*, based on a Jewish melody.

Composer Ernest Bloch (1880–1959) was born in Switzerland and settled in America in 1917. A consciously Jewish composer, Bloch's works include symphonic poems, chamber music, two operas, several concertos and symphonies, and the piece for which he is best known, the *Shelomoh* rhapsody for cello and orchestra.

Atonal composer Arnold Schoenberg (1874–1951) fled the Nazis and came to the United States in 1933. Here he returned to Judaism and composed, among many other works, the opera *Moses and Aaron* and the works *Kol Nidre* and *A Survivor from Warsaw*.

Another refugee from Nazism was composer Kurt

BELOW
Jazz pianist Dave Brubeck, shown here at a benefit concert in 1969, is one of the giants of the jazz world.

BELOW RIGHT
Conductor Arthur Fiedler became the director of the Boston Pops Orchestra in 1930 and led it until his death in 1979.

RIGHT
Pianist and caustic wit Oscar Levant was a leading interpreter of the work of George Gershwin.

FAR RIGHT
Philanthropist Adolph Lewisohn (1849–1938) made his fortune in mining. He devoted his money to cultural causes, including free concerts in Lewisohn Stadium, which he donated to the college of the City of New York.

Weill (1900–1950), who came from Berlin in 1935. While in Berlin he wrote, in collaboration with Bertolt Brecht, *The Threepenny Opera*. In America he wrote the film scores to *Lady in the Dark* and *Lost in the Stars*, among others.

The music of George Gershwin (1898–1937) is known around the world. George and his brother Ira were born and raised on the Lower East Side. In his symphonic music George incorporated jazz and blues melodies and rhythms. The best examples are *Rhapsody in Blue* and *An American in Paris*. Gershwin wrote musical comedies, film scores, and an opera based on the life of black Americans, *Porgy and Bess*. Many of the lyrics were written by Ira. The pianist Oscar Levant was noted for his interpretations of Gershwin's music.

One of the best-known musicians in the world is Leonard Bernstein. Born in 1918, Bernstein became assistant conductor of the New York Philharmonic Orchestra in 1943; he became the permanent conductor in 1957 and today is conductor emeritus. In addition to

BELOW LEFT
Singers Alma Gluck (in furs) and Louise Homer listen to a gramophone in 1913. Gluck was born Reba Fiersohn in Rumania in 1884. She became a star soprano at the Metropolitan Opera and married violinist Efrem Zimbalist.

FAR LEFT
Pianist Emauel Ax is one of the rising new generation of talented young musicians.

BELOW FAR LEFT
Tenor Jan Peerce made his operatic debut at the Metropolitan Opera House in 1941. He was also famed for his interpretations of Jewish cantorial music.

BELOW
Russian-born pianist Sergei Edelmann is one of many talented musicians to leave the Soviet Union for America.

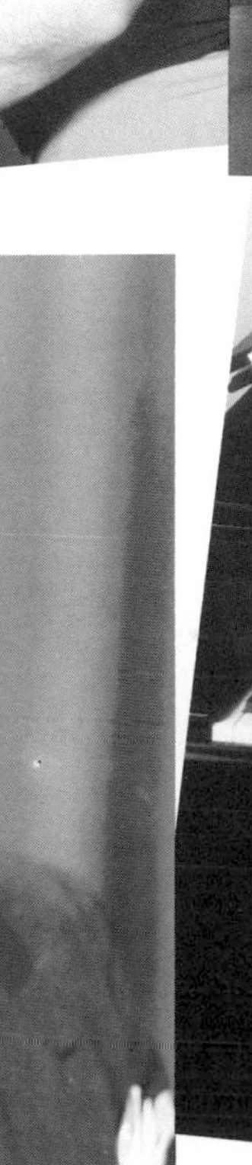

RIGHT
The late pianist Artur Rubinstein was born in Poland in 1887. He was an internationally acclaimed virtuoso from an early age, noted for his performances of Chopin. He died in 1982.

FAR RIGHT
Conductor Leonard Slatkin has led orchestras throughout the world.

BELOW RIGHT
The members of the famed Guarneri Quartet (left to right): Michael Tree (viola), John Dalley (violin), David Soyer (cello), and Arnold Steinhardt (violin).

FAR RIGHT
Conductor James Levine is best known as artistic director of the Metropolitan Opera.

BELOW RIGHT
Clarinetist Richard Stolzman is known for his sparkling stage presence and virtuoso performances.

FAR RIGHT
Pianist Vladimar Horowitz made his Russian debut in 1921; he first appeared in America in 1928 and later became a citizen. He is noted for his fine technique and his interpretations of Chopin, Liszt, and Rachmaninoff.

his talents as a conductor and pianist, Bernstein is equally well known for his compositions. These include the *Jeremiah* and *Kaddish* symphonies, the ballet *Fancy Free*, and the scores to the hit musical shows *On the Town*, *West Side Story*, and *Candide*.

Walter Damrosch (1862–1950) conducted the New York Symphony Society Orchestra from 1903 to 1927. Damrosch was active in bringing music to those who could not afford expensive concert tickets. Many a young Jewish child heard his or her first concert at an outdoor or free performance conducted by Damrosch. The outdoor concert bandshell at Lincoln Center in New York is named for him. Another famed Jewish conductor is Erich Leinsdorf. Born in Vienna in 1912, Leinsdorf came to the Metropolitan Opera House in 1937. In 1943 he became conductor of the Cleveland Orchestra; in 1947 he became conductor of the Rochester Philharmonic Orchestra; and in 1961 he became conductor of the Boston Symphony. Conductor Eugene Ormandy was born in Hungary and settled in the United States in 1920. From 1936 until his recent death he was conductor of the Philadelphia Orchestra.

Librettist Oscar H. Hammerstein II (1895–1960) collaborated with composer Jerome Kern to create the musical *Show Boat* in 1927. He also worked closely with Richard Rodgers on the musicals *Oklahoma!* (1943), *Carousel* (1945), and *The King and I* (1951).

The list of well-known Jewish musicians is a long one, dating back to the turn of the century and earlier. Many came to America from Eastern Europe in the period from 1900 to 1920, others fled Nazism in the 1930s; many today were born in America. To mention just a few: virtuoso harmonica player Larry Adler, pianist Emanuel Ax, violinist Mischa Elman (born in Russia in 1891, moved to America in 1923), Benny Goodman (band leader and jazz, swing, and classical clarinetist), violinist Jascha Heifetz, pianist Vladimir Horowitz, violinist and conductor Yehudi Menuhin, violinist Nathan Milstein, cellist Gregor Piatigorsky, pianist Artur Rubinstein, pianist Artur Schnabel, pianist Rudolf Serkin, violinist Isaac Stern, and opera stars Beverley Sills, Richard Tucker, Roberta Peters and Jan Peerce.

LEFT
Bandleader and clarinetist Benny Goodman was called "The King of Swing." He formed a big band in 1934 and went on to achieve fame and popularity on the radio, in movies, and on records.

BELOW RIGHT
Arthur Hays Sulzberger (1891–1968) joined the NEW YORK TIMES in 1918, following his father-in-law Adolph Ochs as publisher. His son, Arthur Ochs Sulzberger, became publisher in 1963.

JOURNALISM

Perhaps in response to the freedom of America after the repression of Europe, many Jews were attracted by the open press. The nation's newspaper of record, the *New York Times*, has been published by the family of Adolph Ochs (1858–1935) since 1896. A successful newspaper publisher in Chattanooga, Ochs took over the *Times* when it was on the verge of bankruptcy and built it into one of the world's greatest papers. His daughter married Arthur Hays Sulzberger, who became publisher of the paper in 1935. Julius Ochs Adler (1892–1955), another member of the family, was associated with the paper all his working life.

The Pulitzer prizes, awarded annually for outstanding accomplishment in journalism, are named for Joseph Pulitzer (1847–1911). Only half Jewish, Pulitzer came to America from Hungary in 1864. He published the *New York World* from 1883 to 1911; he founded the Columbia School of Journalism in 1903.

Ernest Gruening, governor of Alaska from 1939 to 1953, and later United States Senator from that state, was also a newspaperman, having served as editor of *The Nation* and the New York *Tribune*.

The influential writings of Walter Lippmann have had an important role in foreign affairs. Lippman edited the liberal *New York World* until 1931. His political columns in the *New York Herald Tribune* were widely syndicated.

The columns of witty journalist Franklin P. Adams (1881–1960), better known by the initials F.P.A., were also widely syndicated. The theater criticism of another witty writer, George Jean Nathan (1882–1958), was widely read and greatly respected. Nathan joined with H. L. Mencken to found and edit the *American Mercury* in 1924.

THE YIDDISH WRITERS

The career of Abraham Cahan, founder of the *Jewish Daily Forward*, has been discussed earlier. The *Forward* quickly became the center of a thriving Yiddish press in America, one that today, sadly, is just a remnant. Louis Bandes (1866–1927) was the founder of the first Yiddish Marxist weekly, and later helped found the *Forward*. The prolific author Joseph Opatoshu published hundreds of short stories in the American Yiddish press. He also wrote a number of novels. Sholem Asch (1880–1957) was born in Poland and arrived in America in 1910. He became famous as a novelist and playwright. His controversial later works, including *The Nazarene*, attempted to show the common roots of Judaism and Christianity. Asch settled in Israel in 1955. The poetry and short stories of Isaac L. Peretz (1852–1915) are outstanding examples of Yiddish writing. Peretz vividly captured the language and emotions of the common man. Although Peretz lived in East Europe, his works were widely published in the American Yiddish press. Best known of all the Yiddish writers is Sholem Aleichem, the pseudonym of Shalom Rabinovich (1859–1916). Rabinovich lived in East Europe but visited America twice, in 1906 and 1914. His humorous and poignant tales of Tevye the Milkman appeared in the Yiddish papers and later as books. The stories are the basis for the musical *Fiddler on the Roof*. Many short stories by Nobel Prize-winning author Isaac Bashevis Singer first appeared in the *Forward*. Singer was born in Poland and emigrated in 1935. Many of his novels, including *The Family Moskat* and *The Magician of Lublin*, achieved wide popularity in translation. The poetry and novels of Chaim Grade (1910–1984) have also achieved wide acceptance in translation.

CHAPTER TWELVE

LEFT
The beloved stories of Yiddish author Sholem Aleichem were the basis of the musical FIDDLER ON THE ROOF.

FAR LEFT
Yiddish novelist Sholem Asch dealt with American Jewish life in his novel EAST RIVER.

BELOW FAR LEFT
The works of Yiddish author I. L. Peretz, particularly his HASSIDIC TALES, *appeared serially in the American Yiddish press.*

BELOW LEFT
The Nobel Prize for literature was awarded to Yiddish author Isaac Bashevis Singer in 1978.

RIGHT
Author Norman Mailer is celebrated for his controversial novels, including THE NAKED AND THE DEAD *and* THE DEER PARK.

FAR RIGHT
Historian Salo Wittmayer Baron taught at Columbia University, where he held the first professorship of Jewish history at an American university.

BELOW RIGHT
Author Philip Roth raised a storm of controversy with his novel PORTNOY'S COMPLAINT *(1969).*

BELOW FAR RIGHT
The late Bernard Malamud is best known for his novels THE ASSISTANT *(1957), the Pulitzer Prize-winning* THE FIXER *(1966), and* DUBIN'S LIVES *(1979).*

THE LITERARY WORLD

Many American Jews have achieved a lasting place in American letters as historians, critics, and authors. Salo W. Baron, professor of Jewish history at Columbia University from 1930 to 1963 is famed for his monumental, multivolume study, *A Social and Religious History of the Jews*. Another professor, Sidney Hook, achieved fame through his studies of philosophy and Marxism.

Philip Roth, E. L. Doctorour, Allen Ginsberg, Tillie Olsen, Joseph Heller, Bernard Malamud, Howard Fast, Erica Jong, Cynthia Ozick, Dorothy Parker, S. J. Perelman, Norman Mailer, Chaim Potok, Susan Sontag, Irwin Shaw, Irving Stone, Lionel Trilling, Diana Trilling, Leon Uris, Herman Wouk, Mark Helprin, Irving Howe, and Leo Rosten are just some of the many who have published successful books. Novelist Saul Bellow received the Nobel Prize for Literature in 1976.

ARTISTS

Compared to other areas, Jewish artists are a little late to appear on the American scene. In the nineteenth century, the only artists of note were Solomon Nunes Carvalho, Henry Mosler, and sculptor Moses Ezekial. In the twentieth century, the number grows rapidly to include Ben Shahn, the brothers Raphael, Isaac, and Moses Soyer, Max Weber, Leonard Baskin, sculptor Jo Davidson, Louise Nevelson, Maurice Sendak, George Segal, Mark Rothko, Saul Steinberg, and photographers Alfred Stieglitz, Richard Avedon, Irving Penn, and Curnell Capa.

American Jews have also been important patrons of the arts. Philanthropist Benjamin Altman left his personal art collection to the Metropolitan Museum in 1913; it was the largest single bequest ever received by the museum. More recently, the famed Hirshhorn collection of modern art has been moved into a spectacular new building and become part of the Smithsonian Institution in Washington, D.C.

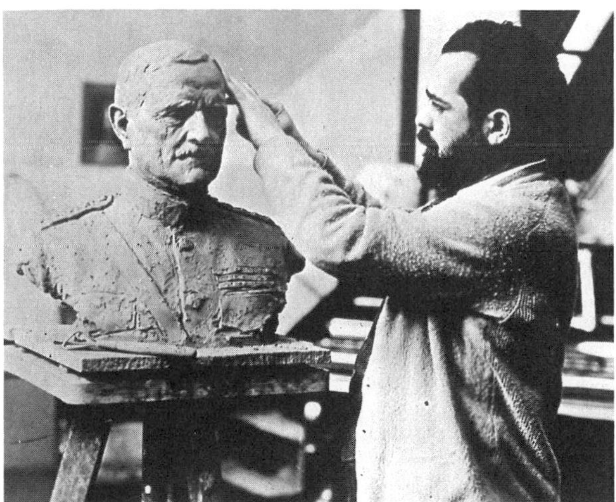

CHAPTER TWELVE

LEFT
Sculptor Sir Jacob Epstein was born in new York in 1880 and settled in England in 1904. His monumental work, controversial at first, became widely accepted during his lifetime. He died in 1959.

FAR LEFT
Sculptor Jo Davidson (1883–1952) was noted for his busts of famous people.

BELOW FAR LEFT
Artist Ben Shahn was born in Russia in 1898 and arrived in the U.S. in 1906. He is best known for his graphic work, including an illustrated Passover haggadah.

LEFT
When painter Max Weber (1881–1961) held a one-man exhibit of his work in 1911, it was widely attacked for being too modern. Weber's work eventually received great recognition; his paintings now hang in museums around the world.

BELOW
Albert Einstein (seated, center) was an active Zionist. Here he attends a benefit dinner in the late 1920s with: Felix M. Warburg (seated at left), Mrs. Einstein (seated at right), and (standing left to right) Robert Szold (president, Zionist Organization of America), Morris Rothenberg (chairman, American Palestine Campaign), Rabbi Stephen Wise, and Jefferson Seligman.

THE SCIENCES

The number of American Jews prominent in science and medicine has always been disproportionately large. Whatever the reasons, the story begins early in American history.

THE PHYSICISTS

The later work of twentieth-century physicists was based on the work of Albert Abraham Michelson (1852–1931). After a short career as a naval officer, Michelson became a professor at the University of Chicago in 1892. His work measuring the speed of light was crucial for laying the experimental base for Einstein's special theory of relativity. He won the Nobel Prize for physics in 1907.

The outstanding mind of the twentieth century belonged to physicist Albert Einstein. Born in Germany in 1879, Einstein began to develop his theory of relativity in 1905; he published his findings in 1913–16, and received the Nobel Prize in 1921. Einstein became director of the Kaiser Wilhelm Institute of Physics in Berlin. In 1933 he fled the Nazis and settled in America, becoming a citizen in 1940. He was a professor of theoretical physics at the Institute for Advanced Studies at Princeton University until his death in 1955. Although not particularly observant, Einstein was aware of his Jewish heritage and was an active Zionist. He was also a trustee of the Hebrew University.

J. Robert Oppenheimer is often called the father of the atom bomb. Born in New York in 1904, Oppenheimer directed the research and construction effort during World War II that led to the atom bomb. From 1947 through 1966 he was director of the Institute for Advanced Studies. He served as chairman of the advisory committee of the Atomic Energy Commission until 1954, when, amid great controversy, he was suspended over allegations of left-wing involvement.

The development of the hydrogen bomb owes a great deal to the work of Edward Teller, who emigrated to America from Budapest in 1934. Teller also served on the advisory board of the Atomic Energy Commission.

Many American Jewish physicists have received the ultimate honor of the Nobel Prize. Otto Stern, a refugee

LEFT
The experiments of Albert Michelson determined, among other things, the speed of light, providing the groundwork for the later work of Albert Einstein.

BELOW
Nobel Prize-winning physicist I. I. Rabi was closely involved with the development of radar and the atomic bomb.

BELOW RIGHT
A live-virus vaccine for polio was developed by Dr. Albert Sabin (left) after Salk developed his killed-virus vaccine. Both types are widely used today.

FAR RIGHT
Dr. Abraham Jacobi was a leader in the provision of health care to the poor, especially children. Jacobi Hospital in the Bronx is named for him.

BELOW FAR RIGHT
The discoverer of the antibiotic streptomycin, Dr. Selman Waksman, won the Nobel Prize for medicine in 1952.

from Nazi Germany, won the Nobel Prize in 1943 for his work on the detection of protons. Isidor Isaac Rabi won in 1944 for his work in nuclear physics, magnetism, and quantum mechanics. In 1952 the prize went to Felix Bloch for his work in measuring nuclear magnetic fields. For developing the bubble chamber for photographing atomic phenomena, Donald A. Glaser received the Nobel Prize in 1960. Robert Hofstader, a professor of physics at Stanford University, received the Nobel Prize in 1961 for his work on the peaceful uses of atomic energy. In 1965 the Nobel Prize went to Julian Schwinger and Richard Feynman for their work on elementary particles.

THE DOCTORS

Pediatrician Abraham Jacobi (1830–1919) was imprisoned for revolutionary activities in Germany from 1851–53. He then came to New York, where he taught medicine from 1860 to 1892. He founded the first free clinic for children in America. The first school of public health at Harvard University was founded in 1909 by Milton J. Rosenau (1869–1946). His contributions to hygiene, sanitation, and preventive medicine were numerous.

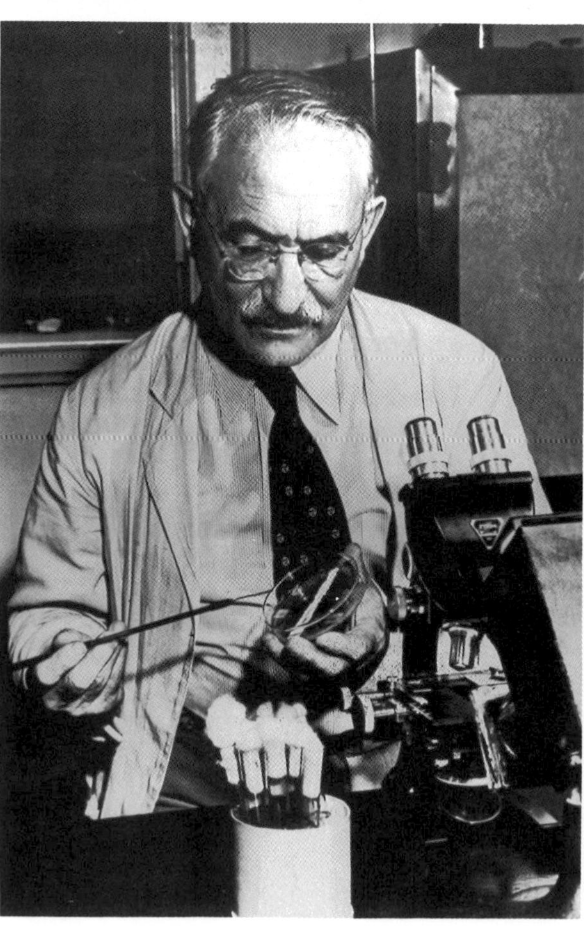

Dr. Joseph Goldberger (1874–1929) was the discoverer of Vitamin B_2. He showed that the disease pellagra is caused by dietary deficiency.

Important work on the development of the wonder drugs known as antibiotics was done by Selman Waksman. In 1944 Waksman isolated streptomycin; he was awarded a Nobel Prize in 1952.

The terrifying scourge of polio was finally conquered by Jonas Salk. His vaccine, developed in the late 1950s, has saved millions from the disease. Another polio vaccine using live virus was developed by Albert Sabin, an emigrant from Poland, in 1959.

More recent winners of the Nobel Prize for medicine include Rosalyn Yalow, Julius Axelrod, Michael Stuart Brown, and Joseph L. Goldstein.

LEFT
The dreaded scourge of polio was brought to an end by the vaccine developed by Dr. Jonas E. Salk.

BELOW FAR LEFT
A founder of the American Medical Association was Dr. Isaac Hays (1796–1879).

BELOW LEFT
Dr. Joseph Goldberger was for many years the head of the United States Public Health Service. He discovered the cause and cure of pellagra.

ABOVE

Soviet dissident Natan (formerly Anatoly) Shcharansky (center) was freed and allowed to go to Israel in large part because of the storm of international protest his continued imprisonment aroused. Here he is shown at a Solidarity Sunday rally in New York City in 1986 with Benjamin Netanyahu (left; first Israeli ambassador to the UN) and Alan Pesky (right; chairman of the Coalition to Free Soviet Jews).

THE JEWISH COMMUNITY TODAY

CHAPTER THIRTEEN

The American Jewish community today is well over five million strong. Of these, nearly two-thirds live in the North Central states. Nearly two million live in the New York metropolitan region. Indeed, over ten percent of New York State's total population of nearly 18 million is Jewish. In larger terms, the world Jewish population is about 13 million, of whom over three million live in Israel and nearly three million live in Europe; about 1,650,000 Jews live in the Soviet Union.

In recent years the Jewish baby boomers of the 1950s have grown older, achieved success, and started families. Many have felt a need to return to active Judaism, leading to an unexpected – but very welcome – new vibrancy among many synagogues.

Nationwide, Jews continue their active role in charitable organizations of various sorts. Nearly two thousand different organizations provide religious, educational, cultural, community, social welfare, and Zionist services. Their activities are reported in nearly two hundred Jewish periodicals published across the country. Nearly $600 million is pledged each year to the United Jewish Appeal alone.

THE NEWEST ARRIVALS

The outspoken protest of American Jews has helped force the authorities to allow some Jews to leave the Soviet Union. The numbers vary each year according to the political situation. In the 1980s emigration has been relatively restricted. Continued pressure by American Jews and by outraged members of the world community has resulted in the release of some celebrated individuals, such as Anatoly Shcharansky and pianist Vladimir Feltsman, but free emigration from the Soviet Union remains an unlikely goal. Until then, American Jews will continue to show their support for their persecuted brethren by writing to American and Soviet officials, and by gathering for mass rallies such as Solidarity Sunday.

Jews leaving the Soviet Union often go to Israel, but more often come to America.

Svetlana (now called Lana) came to New York ten years ago with her husband and 12-year-old daughter. For most Soviet Jews, Vienna is their first introduction to the West. Lana remembers, "We felt like monkeys that had just jumped down from the trees. On the streets I saw I could buy bananas – not just one for my daughter, but many for all of us."

Lana, a math teacher, and her husband, an engineer, were given $300 to take out of the Soviet Union with them. Of one thing she was sure. She wanted to settle in America, in New York, and this despite the rumors, rampant among the Russian immigrants in Vienna, that you could not walk on the streets of that city without taking your life in your hands.

After Vienna, the family was sent to Italy where they had to await further processing until they could go to America.

"We took a picture of our car on the highway with signposts pointing to Milan one way, Venice another, Perugia another. We sent that photo to our friends back in Russia, and needed to write no words. It showed we had choices. The photo was circulated to everyone we knew."

The first two days in New York were spent at the apartment of a cousin in Queens, who'd only arrived a few months before. Margot wanted desperately to see Manhattan. Next day she was on the subway with her family to look at the beautiful city.

That week they found a small apartment. Support from the Hebrew Immigrant Aid Society enabled them to go to English and job-training schools for several months, attending with immigrants from all over the world.

For a while Lana worked as a bookkeeper; her husband was having a hard time getting placed as an engineer. HIAS told him his skills were too valuable to be wasted. They gave him plenty of time and finally helped him land an engineering job.

Margot left the bookkeeping, which only paid minimum wage, and went into the travel business. Within one year of moving to the U.S. she had enrolled her daughter in private school, her first priority. Had she

RIGHT
The vocal support of the American Jewish community for Jews in the Soviet Union has played a role in forcing the authorities to allow some to leave.

stayed in the Soviet Union there was no way her daughter could have gotten a first-rate education. For them, as Jews, the opportunities had diminished with each generation. Lana's mother is a pediatrician, with a fine medical education. But Lana and her Jewish friends were not allowed into the better schools. Her daughter, too, would have been stymied. She explains, "In Soviet life everything depends on the times. Whether you are young in a period of [Jewish] repression or a period of ease will determine if you get a good education, a good job. In the Soviet Union, it is the point in time which will determine what, in fact, is your country."

Another recent arrival is Marina. She was trained as a cosmetician in Russia. She remembers the resplendent light of Vienna playing over the variety of goods that could be bought at the stalls on just one street. "Sometimes," she says, "Jews in the Soviet Union bribe officials to get 'Russian' put on their papers. This way they and

CHAPTER THIRTEEN

their children can live better, get good educations. But most of us did not want to do that. The funny thing is, if we had, we never would have gotten out.

"A few years back, when the officials were letting out more Jews, non-Jews were trying to get Jewish papers. It's a funny thing!"

As the newest Russian Jews settle into Brooklyn's Brighton Beach (now called Little Odessa), in Queen's Forest Hills, in Manhattan's Washington Heights – some 50,000 in New York City and environs – some are re-discovering the synagogues. Others are beginning to visit other parts of the country. They are working hard in small businesses and the service industries, learning to adjust to a competitive economic system. For them, for all of us, life in America is a constant re adjustment to reality from the push/pull of the American dream and the untoward events – natural disasters, depressions, pockets of bigotry – that interrupt that dream.

INDEX

A

B

C

D

E

F

M

N

O

P

Q

R